RISK REGULATION AT RISK

I0032663

Risk Regulation at Risk

Restoring a Pragmatic Approach

SIDNEY A. SHAPIRO

ROBERT L. GLICKSMAN

STANFORD LAW AND POLITICS

An imprint of Stanford University Press • Stanford, California

Stanford University Press
Stanford, California
© 2003 by the Board of Trustees of the
Leland Stanford Junior University
Printed in the United States of America

Library of Congress Cataloging-in-Publication Data

Shapiro, Sidney A.
  Risk Regulation at Risk : Restoring a Pragmatic Approach / Sidney A.
Shapiro and Robert L. Glicksman.
      p. cm.
  Includes bibliographical references and index.
  ISBN 0-8047-4593-5 (cloth : alk. paper) —
  ISBN 0-8047-5102-1 (pbk. : alk. paper)
      1. Environmental law—United States.   2. Environmental risk
assessment—United States.   3. Technology—Risk assessment—United States.
4. Risk assessment—United States.   I. Glicksman, Robert L.   II. Title.

KF3775 .S53   2003
344.73'046—dc21   2002009778

This book is printed on acid-free, archival-quality paper

Original printing 2003

Last figure below indicates year of this printing:

12   11   10   09   08   07   06   05

Designed and typeset at Stanford University Press in 10/13 Minion

To Senator Edmund S. Muskie

Contents

Preface

The landmark legislation that Congress enacted during the 1960s and 1970s to protect the environment and individual health and safety has come increasingly under attack in the last two decades. Collectively, this legislation is known as "risk regulation" because it addresses the risk of harm that technology creates for individuals and the environment. Employing a utilitarian philosophy and analytical tools such as cost-benefit analysis, the critics claim that risk regulation is excessive and irrational, wasting millions of dollars that could be put to more productive uses. Supporters of risk regulation deny these claims, and they argue that cost-benefit analysis is inappropriate for evaluating risk regulation. The supporters, however, do not employ a systematic theme similar to the critics' use of utilitarianism. Unlike the critics, who are all singing the same tune, the supporters of risk regulation have appeared to be singing different tunes.

Risk regulation appears to lack a common theme for several reasons. As this book explains, Congress clearly rejected utilitarian premises as the basis for the risk reduction legislation, but it did not specify another unified set of premises as the basis for the legislation. The legislation also appears to be disjointed because it employs a number of different regulatory standards, rather than basing regulation on a common cost-benefit standard. It is also difficult to see a universal basis for risk regulation because of its complexity. The relevant statutes take up hundreds of pages in the U.S. Code.

As academics who have written about risk regulation for the past twenty years, and who have participated in the debate over the wisdom of current risk regulation, we were challenged by the apparent lack of a unifying scheme or set of ideas that may explain risk regulation. There are environmental philosophies that support important aspects of risk regulation, but risk regulation protects consumers and workers in contexts that do not relate to environmental protection. Moreover, important risk regulation statutes, such as the Clean Air Act, seek to protect both the environment and the public health. Environmental philosophies can explain this health protection as an effort to return the environment to its prior, cleaner status (or to prevent its deterioration), but people also directly value the act's public health goals.

This book responds to the vacuum we perceive: is there a common basis or set of ideas that can explain, clarify, and provide a basis for analyzing risk regulation? Our original intuition was that Congress designed risk legislation to be a lawyer's system of decision-making. That is, it employs methods of analysis that are familiar to lawyers (and perhaps for that reason are unpleasing to economic analysts). In turn, we were led to an emerging literature that explores the affinity between the American philosophical tradition of pragmatism and the role of judicial review in our legal system.[1] Proponents of pragmatism contend that it offers a useful methodology for addressing how judicial review should function. One of the principal proponents of using pragmatism to guide judicial review, Professor Daniel Farber, has suggested that pragmatism might play a similar role in the context of environmental policy.[2] Professor Farber's suggestion led us more broadly to consider whether pragmatism furnishes the missing basis for risk regulation. We concluded that it does.

Our claim is that the structure of risk regulation is consistent with pragmatic principles, and that pragmatism is an appropriate baseline from which to design and implement risk regulation. In response to the critics' reliance on utilitarian principles, we contend that pragmatism offers a better way of conceiving and implementing risk regulation than the economic paradigm favored by its critics.

Although Professor Farber pointed the way, his book offers only a brief justification for applying pragmatism to environmental law. Moreover, whereas Professor Farber considers environmental policy, we address the body of risk reduction regulation enacted primarily in the 1960s and 1970s, which, besides environmental law, also includes other safety and health regimes, such as those administered by the Occupational Safety and Health Administration, the National Highway Traffic Administration, and the Food and Drug Administration. As we explain in Chapter 1, all of this legislation shares a common denominator. These laws are designed to reduce human and environmental injury before it occurs. We are therefore interested in justifying this essential trait and in explaining how it relates to other important social values, particularly avoiding adverse economic impacts attributable to reducing these risks.

We extend the use of pragmatism in analyzing risk regulation in two other ways. In Chapter 3 we map a structure of risk regulation that has not been previously recognized. Our map allows us to identify the key common features of risk reduction legislation. Our argument that risk regulation statutes are consistent with pragmatic principles is based on the key common features of risk regulation identified in this map. Finally, we break new ground by applying pragmatic principles to relevant important issues of risk policy: the role of regulatory impact studies (Chapter 7), the debate over alternative regulatory methods (Chapter 8), the importance of incremental adjustments to regulatory policy (Chapter 8), and the comparative suitability of alternative forms of regulatory oversight (Chapter 9).

The possibility that pragmatism might play this role would come as no surprise to the founders of the American philosophical tradition of pragmatism. As originally conceived by, among others, Charles Sanders Peirce, Williams James, and John Dewey, pragmatism was the dominant mode of social analysis in the early decades of the twentieth century. Pragmatism, according to Charles Anderson, "shaped the distinctly American disciplines of political science and institutional economics," "greatly influenced our theories of philosophy, education, and law," and "formed part of the intellectual background for Progressive Reform and the New Deal."[3] Although pragmatism fell into a relative decline for a time after these events, there recently has been renewed interest in pragmatism in philosophy and other disciplines—including law, as mentioned earlier.[4]

We employ pragmatism in this book not only to support risk regulation against arguments by its critics but also to agree with some of these criticisms and level criticisms of our own. Thus, while pragmatism offers a methodology or set of ideas to support risk regulation as it was originally conceived, it also offers a perspective from which risk regulation can be held up to critical appraisal. In the end, we reject the picture painted by the critics of widely excessive and irrational regulation, but we do not entirely exonerate risk regulation either. Our pragmatic perspective leads us to a number of ideas about how risk regulation might be usefully reformed, although these are often different reforms than those favored by critics who are influenced by utilitarianism.

The journey that produced this book was enabled by the support of two universities and the comments and criticisms of a large number of people. Sidney Shapiro is indebted to the School of Policy and Environmental Affairs (SPEA) at the University of Indiana, which hosted him during a sabbatical, during which this book was conceived and started. Both of us wish to acknowledge research support from the University of Kansas School of Law. Sidney Shapiro benefited from faculty workshops sponsored by SPEA and by the University of Indiana Law School. Both of us benefited by presenting chapters of this book at faculty workshops at the Chicago-Kent Law School and at the Environmental Studies Center and the Hall Center at the University of Kansas. Robert Glicksman thanks the participants of a faculty workshop at Washington University Law School in St. Louis. We are also indebted to those who read drafts of various chapters of the book. At the risk of missing someone, we would like to thank Professors John Applegate, Daniel Farber, Dietrich Earnhardt, Rob Fischman, Lisa Heinzerling, Rosemary O'Leary, Craig Oren, J. B. Ruhl, and Dan Tarlock.

RISK REGULATION AT RISK

1

Pragmatism and Risk Regulation

The 1950s were a time of unprecedented prosperity in the United States. Housing starts skyrocketed and highway construction reached into virtually every corner of the nation. This frenetic development helped produce a booming economy, but modern technology also extracted a considerable toll on humans and the environment. Congress responded to the growing public awareness of these events with an outpouring of legislation whose scope was unprecedented, even by the standards of the New Deal. Congress enacted comprehensive changes to air, water, and pesticide regulation; created new agencies to regulate dangerous automobiles, consumer products, and workplaces; and gave existing agencies, such as the Food and Drug Administration (FDA), new authority to regulate. According to various (conflicting) estimates, Congress during this period passed sixty-two consumer protection laws and seven occupational safety and health laws, twenty-five consumer, environmental, or social regulatory laws, and forty-two laws to regulate business.[1]

Until Congress acted, the federal government had little involvement in solving the various problems that were targeted by the new legislation. Instead, the country had relied primarily on the tort system, administered by the state courts, to address personal and environmental injuries. The tort system promotes safety by requiring a person who has injured someone else to pay compensation if the defendant has violated applicable tort rules that define when compensation is due. Risk regulation, by comparison, seeks to reduce personal and environmental injuries before they occur by addressing the potential causes of such injuries—that is, the "risk" of such injuries. Because risk regulation operates before injuries occur, it does not require that people die or be injured, or that the environment be harmed, before it goes into effect. By design, risk regulation is preventative in character.

Since the 1970s, risk regulation has come increasingly under vigorous attack. Criticisms have arisen in academia, particularly among economists who analyze government regulation, and they have been popularized by well-financed conservative think tanks in Washington.[2] The mantra of these criticisms is that risk regulation is "irrational." Risk regulation is irrational, they maintain, because regulators too often address problems that pose minimal risks to the public or the environment and ignore other more pressing problems. Risk regulation is also irrational because regulators too often impose solutions whose economic benefits to the public are millions (or even billions) of dollars less than the economic costs of the regulation. To address the problems they perceive, the critics would subject risk regulation to a cost-benefit test and other decision-making methodologies that generate, in their view, more rational regulation.

The goal of this book is to examine closely the nature of risk regulation and its results. Our argument is that risk regulation is "pragmatic," and that the results of that regulation likewise have been pragmatic. When we say that risk regulation is pragmatic, we mean it is consistent with the tradition of American philosophical pragmatism that dates back to John Dewey. We are not making a historical claim: we do not assert that the members of Congress consciously sculpted the legislation in light of pragmatic precepts. We do claim, however, that the structure of the legislation is consistent with pragmatic principles and that pragmatism is an appropriate baseline from which to design and implement risk regulation.

We reject the unrelenting attack on risk regulation by its critics. Risk regulation is not perfect, some of the criticism of risk regulation is justified, and we will endorse a number of reforms. The basic structure of risk regulation, as it currently exists, however, better accommodates the difficult policy issues—particularly the difficult value conflicts—that must be resolved for regulation to occur than the structure favored by the critics. Moreover, according to the existing evidence, risk regulation accommodates these trade-offs without producing the type of extreme consequences that the critics claim. Our ultimate conclusion is that pragmatism offers a better way of conceiving and implementing risk regulation than the economic paradigm favored by the critics. Our analysis of pragmatism and risk regulation begins with a description of the origins of risk regulation and the nature of the criticisms that have been made regarding it.

The Origins

Popular consciousness began to focus on the risks associated with modern technology after scientists discovered the presence of strontium 90 in milk, apparently as a result of the radioactive fallout from the testing of atomic weapons. In the early 1960s, Rachel Carson's book *Silent Spring* called attention to the environmental destruction caused by the widespread use of pesticides, while Barry Commoner's book *The Closing Circle* warned that, unchecked, the use of "counter-ecological technologies" could result in environmental ruin. These academic warnings were confirmed by events such as the routine smog alerts in Los Angeles in the 1960s and the Santa Barbara oil spill in 1969. At about the same time, the public learned that modern medicines could injure, as well as heal, after it was revealed that Frances Kelsey, an employee of the FDA, almost single-handedly kept thalidomide from being sold in the United States. Dr. Kelsey acted before it became widely known that the use of the drug in Great Britain had resulted in serious birth defects among children whose mothers had taken it while pregnant.[3] The issue of automobile safety came to the public's attention after General Motors admitted in a congressional hearing that it had hired private investigators to follow Ralph Nader in order to discredit his book *Unsafe at Any Speed*.[4] Frequent mining catastrophes, such as the death of eighty-eight miners in Farmington, West Virginia, and the discovery of new occupational diseases, such as "brown lung," focused the public on occupational safety and health risks.[5]

By the late 1960s, Congress had determined that the tort system, augmented by minimal federal regulation, was incapable of providing an effective response to the increasing threats to the public health and safety and the environment attributable to new technologies and development. The legislation that resulted included several statutes that constitute the heart of risk regulation. Congress adopted the National Environmental Policy Act (NEPA) in 1969, the Clean Air Act (CAA) and the Occupational Safety and Health Act in 1970, and the Federal Water Pollution Control Act amendments two years later. In the next decade, Congress added the Consumer Product Safety Act; Federal Insecticide, Fungicide, and Rodenticide Act; Safe Drinking Water Act; Toxic Substances Control Act; Comprehensive Environmental Response, Compensation, and Liability Act; and the Solid Waste Disposal Act.

Risk Regulation

The environmental and consumer movements that were instrumental in obtaining risk regulation were premised on the belief that the operation of private markets must be consistent with the social values that citizens establish through democratic deliberation and lawmaking. The supporters of these movements also believed that public participation in regulatory decision-making was necessary to ensure that laws—and the social values they embody—were faithfully implemented after their enactment. This section indicates how these beliefs led to two fundamental shifts in the nature of the regulation of technological risks.

Social Values and Private Markets

In the 1950s, Louis Hartz wrote his famous book, *The Liberal Tradition in America*, which perceived wide public support for the political values associated with John Locke—especially atomistic individualism, capitalism, and limited government. Thus, in the Lockean tradition, government is only a corrective instrument at the margins of economic markets, and the nature of the federal government in the 1950s reflected that axiom. There was only very limited federal regulation of the type of hazards addressed by current risk regulation. Instead, to the extent that such risks were addressed, it was by state tort law, which, as we explain below, is based upon traditional liberal principles.

With the 1960s, in Samuel Huntington's words, came a "spirit of protest, the spirit of equality, the impulse to expose and correct inequities that were abroad in the land." The "themes of the 1960s," Huntington continues, "were those of Jacksonian Democracy and the muckraking Progressives; they embodied ideas and beliefs which were deep in the American tradition but which usually do not command the passionate intensity of the commitment that they did in the 1960s."[6] Michael McCann calls the 1960s reformers "public interest liberals" because, while they agreed with many of the concepts of traditional liberalism, they also looked to government regulation to right the wrongs of the time—to regulate in the "public interest."[7]

Thus, the supporters of risk regulation believed that a society uses its political system to establish collective social values that define how citizens will interact. Once those values are defined, citizens accept the operation of the market system only to the extent that it does not conflict with collective social values. As Richard Andrews explains, "In this conceptual framework, government is . . . [a] central area in which members of society choose and legitimize . . . their collective values. The principal purposes of legislative action are to weigh and affirm social values and to define and enforce the rights and duties of members of society, through representative democracy."[8] For supporters of risk regulation, the protection of individuals and the environment from the harm posed by technology is a preeminent social principle. Risk regulation implements these collective values.

The importance of protecting human life and the environment led the 1960s reformers to reject tort law as the basis of government regulation of technological risks. In a tort system, persons who have been injured by corporate behavior have the burden of initiating expensive legal action to prove that their injury was caused by the defendant's actions. Moreover, someone who anticipates a potential injury usually cannot obtain protection against that risk. Although injunctive relief is theoretically available in actions such as private nuisance to avoid harms alleged to be the imminent result of technological development, the courts are reluctant to enjoin such "anticipatory nuisances" on the basis of the plaintiff's speculation.

In light of its evidentiary burdens, tort law starts with the baseline assumption that individuals and corporations that operate in private markets should be free from government regulation until and unless a plaintiff can compile convincing proof that their conduct has caused an injury to a person or that person's property. This baseline comports with traditional liberalism and its emphasis on limited government, private autonomy, and the protection of private markets.

The impotence of tort law was vividly demonstrated in the 1960s by the various prominent accidents and environmental injuries that occurred. Tort

law failed in part because of what Talbot Page has called "ignorance of mechanism."[9] The tort system will not compensate an individual unless that person has convincing evidence that the defendant caused the plaintiff's injury.
If, however, the injury is allegedly caused by exposure to chemicals or other
by-products of technological activity, few plaintiffs will be able to meet their
burden of proof because the mechanisms of cancer are still not very well understood. Scientists and policy-makers understood even less about how the
disease is caused and develops in the 1970s, when most risk-reduction statutes
were adopted. The "ignorance of mechanism" is exacerbated by the long latency period that typically elapses between exposure to the disease and its
manifestation. By the time the disease appears it is often impossible to isolate
its cause or causes; the long latency period means that years if not decades'
worth of exposure have already occurred by then. Plaintiffs who sue over environmental injuries face an even more difficult task. Scientific understanding of the manner in which the by-products of technological development
adversely affect the ecosystems into which they are discharged is, if anything,
even more inadequate than our understanding of cancer mechanisms.[10]

Risk regulation was a paradigm shift from the common law because Congress authorized regulators to act on the basis of anticipated harm, which
permitted regulators to reduce personal and environmental risks despite an
"ignorance of mechanism." As John Applegate has pointed out, risk regulation therefore changed the baseline of government regulation in fundamental
ways: "Regulation based on risk permits regulatory action based on *ex ante*
collective danger rather than *ex post* individual injury, and also operates pre-
ventively to avert injury to the public as a whole."[11]

The *Ethyl Corporation* case,[12] decided in 1976, illustrates this new political
orientation. In that case, the Court of Appeals for the District of Columbia
Circuit considered the authority of the Environmental Protection Agency
(EPA) under the 1970 Clean Air Act. That act gave EPA the power to regulate
gasoline additives whose emission products "will endanger the public health
or welfare."[13] The court determined that EPA could act "before the threatened
harm occurs" and that "no actual injury need ever occur." This interpretation
was justified because "the very existence of such precautionary legislation
would seem to *demand* that regulatory action precede, and, optimally, prevent the perceived threat." In addition, the court refused to insist upon

"rigorous step-by-step proof of cause and effect" as a prerequisite to regulation, given the precautionary thrust of the legislation and the uncertainty surrounding the effects of exposure to potentially toxic fuel additives. Instead, EPA was authorized to "apply [its] expertise to draw conclusions from suspected, but not completely substantiated, relationships between facts, from trends among facts, from theoretical projections from imperfect data, from probative preliminary data not yet certifiable as 'fact,' and the like." In other words, EPA could justify regulations using factual determinations, policy choices, and "predictions dealing with matters on the frontiers of scientific knowledge."

Public Participation

The 1960s produced another type of reform that constituted a second paradigm shift. Studies by Nader's Raiders documenting the existence of the failure to regulate corporate abuses convinced the consumer and environmental movements that agencies routinely ignored and subverted "the rule of law itself—whether it be antitrust law, environmental regulations, freedom-of-information procedures, or OSHA standards."[14] In light of agency capture, public interest liberals were "acutely aware that what had been won in Congress could easily be lost in the halls of administrative agencies."[15] Administrative procedure had failed to prevent "capture," because the courts, in determining who had the right to appeal an administrative decision, focused exclusively on legitimating the regulation of private property. Because there was no similar appeal right for statutory beneficiaries, judicial review biased the regulatory system in favor of those who were regulated. Business interests adversely affected by agency decisions could sue, but when agency decisions worked against the interests of those who would benefit from regulation, they could not sue. The courts responded by authorizing lawsuits by statutory beneficiaries—persons who were supposed to receive protection from a risk-regulation statute. The courts also adopted other legal doctrines that strengthened the ability of statutory beneficiaries, or the public interest groups that represent them, to hold agencies accountable.[16]

Congress was also convinced that the procedural playing field was uneven. It passed open government laws, such as the Freedom of Information Act and the Federal Advisory Committee Act, which made it more difficult for agencies to adopt industry-friendly policies behind closed doors that would then be difficult to dislodge. In 1969, Congress also passed the NEPA, which required agencies to analyze and disclose to the public the potential environmental impacts of agency actions. The courts soon determined that agency compliance with these requirements was subject to judicial review. NEPA, like the open government laws, made it easier for environmentalists and other public interest groups to monitor agencies, such as the Department of Agriculture, that were perceived by them to be excessively friendly to corporate and business interests. Congress also passed legislation to permit persons who sued the government to collect legal fees, which reduced the transaction costs of collective action by statutory beneficiaries.

The Critics

Since the 1970s there have been noticeable, and in some cases dramatic, reductions in human and environmental risks posed by modern technology. Among other things, the air and water are cleaner, toxic emissions have been reduced, and workplaces and automobiles are safer.[17] Yet there has been a steady drum beat of criticism of risk regulation. As noted earlier, the critics contend that existing approaches have produced "irrational" regulation. They attribute this result to the two achievements of the 1960s reformers: the tilt toward preventative regulation and increased public participation in regulatory decision-making.

Irrational Preferences

The critics of risk regulation contend that risk regulation ends up being irrational because of the interaction of the two important features of risk regulation. Existing statutes require agencies to regulate technological risks before the dangers they pose are well understood. Nevertheless, agencies seek maximum levels of protection in response to the irrational risk preferences of public interest groups and citizens at large.[18]

The critics offer several explanations why the public favors what they regard as "irrational" regulation. One explanation, which originated in the 1970s, claims that public interest activists and like-minded agency officials are motivated by their hostility to corporations, private markets, and economic growth. The claim is that they do not, on balance, like free, commercial society. According to Paul Weaver, these activists therefore have "little or no concern for the cost and consequences of [their] pursuit."[19] Irving Kristol has ominously warned that if public interest activists do "not acquire the necessary economic education [about the virtues of free enterprise], the dangerous result will be the destruction of freedom."[20]

Because of this bias, public interest activists are said to ignore scientific evidence that undermines their arguments for regulation. Edith Efron, for example, claims that, during her journalistic study of the proponents of risk regulation, she "bumped into evidence of such hostility to the objective disciplines of science, evidence of so aggressive a rejection of facts and logic, that I could scarcely credit my senses."[21] In *Risk and Culture*, Mary Douglas and Aaron Wildavsky reach a similar conclusion based on a sociological investigation. Environmentalism is popular, according to these authors, because it supports a certain kind of "social criticism." They claim, for example, that asbestos poisoning has received more attention than skin cancer because it "justifies a particular anti-industrial criticism," whereas "there is no obvious way in which the incidence of skin cancer caused by leisure-time sunburn can be mobilized for criticism of industry."[22]

Other critics attribute the irrationality of risk regulation to its susceptibility to group politics,[23] which produces governmental policies that benefit the interest group or groups that lobby for the policies, but not the public as a whole. Cass Sunstein, for example, attributes what he regards as the "draconian" provision for regulating toxic substances in the Occupational Safety and Health Administration's (OSHA's) mandate "in part" to the "lobbying efforts of [labor] unions."[24]

Another explanation has received considerable attention because of the prominence of its author. Justice Stephen Breyer argues that risk regulation is subject to a "vicious circle" that starts with pervasive public misconceptions of risks that result from the inevitable limits of public attention and selective media coverage.[25] According to this explanation, Congress responds to these erroneous public perceptions by going the "last mile" and ordering regulatory agencies to eliminate all vestiges of risk, even when experts agree that

they are not particularly dangerous. Relatedly, to gain public confidence, an
agency is forced to "prove that it has erred on the side of safety" and to adopt
"the public's risk agenda of the moment." Thus the political system prevents
more rational regulation because it ties regulators' hands with detailed legislation based on unreasonable health fears, rather than trusting agency experts
to choose appropriate levels of risk regulation.

Others, such as Cass Sunstein support this scenario by claiming that public
perception of risks is subject to cognitive biases and other psychological
processes that distort how individuals perceive risks.[26] Thus they contend that
the public evaluation of risk problems differs "radically" from the expert consensus of scientists in the field.

Rational Calculation

In light of these "irrational preferences," critics of risk regulation seek
to filter demands for regulation through decision-making tools, particularly
cost-benefit analysis, that promote more "rational" public policies. As Deborah Stone explains, "The rational model of decision making is reasoning by
calculation. It rests on estimating the consequences of actions, attaching values to the consequences, and calculating to figure out which actions yield the
best results."[27] The goal is not only "calculation" but also "comprehensive
analytical rationality." Tom McGarity explains:

> The term "comprehensive" suggests that this kind of thinking ideally explores all
> possible routes to the solution of a problem. The term "analytical" implies that it
> attempts to sort out, break down, and analyze (quantitatively, if possible) all of
> the relevant components of a problem and its possible solutions. The term
> "rationality" captures the pride that its proponents take in its objectivity and the
> dispassion with which it debates the pros and cons of alternative solutions without
> regard to whose ox is being gored.

"In practice," McGarity concludes, "comprehensive analytical rationality has
been dominated by the paradigms of neoclassical micro-economics."[28] Stone
likewise locates this "rationality project," as she characterizes what the critics
seek, at the "nexus of rational choice theory, microeconomic efficiency models, and cost-benefit analysis."[29]

Process Reforms

The critics of risk regulation have secured a number of administrative procedures that implement their rationality project, and they continue to seek the adoption of additional legislative and administrative changes. These reforms, consciously or not, are modeled on the previously mentioned NEPA. As noted, NEPA requires agencies to analyze and disclose to the public the potential environmental impacts of agency actions. Similarly, the White House and Congress have required agencies to study the potential economic and other impacts of proposed regulatory action and disclose those impacts to the public. Several presidents have issued Executive Orders that require agencies to assess comprehensively the potential consequences of risk regulation. Congress has augmented the Executive Orders with statutory requirements, including the Regulatory Flexibility Act[30] and the Unfunded Mandates Reform Act of 1995.[31] Moreover, Congress has attempted to enact a comprehensive set of amendments to the Administrative Procedure Act (APA) that would codify and extend the analysis requirements imposed by Executive Order each year since 1994. These requirements will be described more extensively in Chapter 7.

The Executive Orders have included a substantive requirement prohibiting agencies from promulgating any regulation whose costs are greater than its benefits, but the orders do not apply when this test is inconsistent with the statutory mandate the agency is implementing. As we will explain in greater detail in Chapter 3, almost all of the risk regulation statutes reject a cost-benefit test as the standard to determine the level of risk regulation. Thus, although agencies are required to calculate and publicize the anticipated costs and benefits of their actions, regulators are not legally bound to promulgate regulations that pass a cost-benefit test. Many critics of risk regulation therefore seek a legislative change that would prohibit enactment of any risk regulation that does not pass a cost-benefit test. In 1995, Congress considered such a change, known as the "supermandate," as part of the Contract with America, but it was dropped in order to gain more support for later versions of that legislation.[32]

Pragmatism and Risk Regulation

The critics object to the "irrational" way that risk regulation is implemented, which they attribute to the inability of citizens to assess risks objectively, the outcome of interest group politics, the hostility of public interest liberals to corporations and private markets, and a lack of concern about the economic efficiency of regulation. Consistent with those concerns, Congress and Presidents Reagan, Bush, and Clinton required agencies to engage in comprehensive regulatory analysis, including the calculation of anticipated costs and benefits, in order to mitigate these pathological tendencies.

This book contests the basic premises of the critics of risk regulation. Our analysis proceeds in five steps. Chapter 2 elaborates on the nature of philosophical pragmatism and its relationship to risk regulation. Chapter 3 describes the basic structure of risk regulation. Chapter 4 demonstrates how this structure is consistent with pragmatic principles. Chapter 5 rejects the premise that comprehensive analytical rationality will produce better public policies than decision-making methods that utilize pragmatic principles. Finally, Chapter 6 finds that the most persuasive evidence is that risk regulation does not produce the excessive costs claimed by its critics.

Although risk regulation is not nearly as defective as its critics claim, it is also not without its flaws. The final three chapters of the book describe the problems of risk regulation and analyze the remedies favored by its critics in light of pragmatic principles. Chapter 7 considers the role of regulatory analysis. Chapter 8 discusses the debate over methods of regulation. Finally, Chapter 9 discusses how to promote accountable risk regulation.

Conclusion

This chapter has painted a broad picture of the beliefs of the proponents and critics of risk regulation. These descriptions undoubtedly ignore many of the subtleties of the arguments about risk regulation made by academics, policy writers, and politicians. Thomas McGarity, for example, seeks to capture the multifaceted nature of the debate about risk regulation by dividing the supporters and critics into five groups.[33] Nevertheless, our description is sufficient to indicate the remarkable shift in regulatory policy accomplished by risk regulation and the main thrust of the criticisms since that time.

Although the debate over risk regulation is well-traveled territory, this book is among the first to consider the usefulness of pragmatism as the basis for risk policy, and it is the first to claim that the existing statutory structure of risk regulation reflects pragmatic principles. Our claim is that the design of risk regulation in this country reflects a pragmatic understanding of the relationship between technological risks, regulatory politics, scientific understanding, and social goals. Our further claim is that pragmatism offers a method of deciding risk issues that is preferable to the comprehensive analytical rationality favored by the critics of risk regulation.

2

Principles of Pragmatic Risk Regulation

This chapter provides the foundation for our claims that pragmatism generally explains, justifies, and provides a basis for critiquing risk regulation. We first identify several key themes of pragmatism, and we then extrapolate six principles of pragmatic risk regulation from those themes. Subsequent chapters analyze specific risk regulation policies and approaches from the perspective of pragmatism and either argue in favor of their retention or propose specific reforms.

Philosophical Pragmatism

Although there is no settled definition of pragmatism, it is possible to identify several key themes that have relevance for regulatory policy, particularly risk regulation. These themes support the characteristics of pragmatic risk regulation that we recommend later in the chapter.

Rejection of Foundationalism

First, and perhaps foremost, pragmatists are antiessentialists. Pragmatists believe that it is not possible to find universal, certain foundations for belief because "truth is provisional, grounded in history and experience, not fixed in the nature of things."[1] There are, as Richard Rorty states, "no essences anywhere in the area."[2] Pragmatists therefore reject a "picture of reasoning in which both the acceptable methods of reasoning and their permissible raw materials are specified in advance."[3] This means that no particular discipline or culture has a privileged view of knowledge or truth.[4] Pragmatists therefore find little value in pursuing metaphysical concepts such as "truth" or "reality."

When first adopted, this viewpoint constituted a major break with the then-dominant philosophical approaches. Until the pragmatists, philosophers envisioned a dualistic conception of human beings consisting of a "spiritual or immaterial mind somehow lodged in a material body."[5] In this account, "human knowledge of an objective, material and external world must somehow be built up from subjective and immaterial impressions and ideas occurring in an internal and intangible mental medium."[6] As Thomas Grey explains, the pragmatists' innovation was to reject mind-body dualism and treat inquiry or thought as a "mode of the human organism's activity, an adaptive product of biological and cultural evolution."[7]

Instrumentalism

The pragmatists' rejection of foundationalism leads to a second general theme of pragmatism. If there are no essential truths, how does the pragmatist determine the value of an idea or claim? In the words of William James, the "cash-value" of an idea is assessed "in terms of practical experience."[8] As James explained, "The true is the name for whatever proves itself to be good in the way of belief, and good, too, for definite and assignable reasons."[9] The value of an idea or belief therefore arises out of criticism of existing ideas and beliefs. A new idea is valuable when it serves the community better than an existing belief. In Louis Menand's useful phrase, a belief is true when "holding the belief leads us into more useful relations with the world."[10]

Inasmuch as the early pragmatists considered a belief to be true when it was more useful than a prior understanding in explaining or clarifying the world around us, they valued those ideas that had the capacity to solve social problems. Following Darwin, they understood the human capacity for inquiry as one that "evolve[s] as a problem-solving capacity, oriented towards survival."[11] The founders of pragmatism therefore regarded "thinking as an adaptive function of an organism, practical in the sense that it was *instrumental*."[12] As John Dewey observed, "If ideas . . . are instrumental to an active organization of [a] given environment, to a removal of some specific trouble or complexity . . . they are reliable, good[, and] true." By comparison, "[if] they fail to clear up confusion . . . they are false."[13]

Critical Community of Inquiry

The third theme of pragmatism relates to how pragmatists determine whether an idea leads to "more useful relations with the world." Ideas are "true" in this sense when they are accepted by a "critical community of inquiry." A critical community of inquiry is a group of persons, who, after study, debate, and deliberation, accept an idea or belief as superior to a prior understanding in explaining the world or resolving a problem. Richard Bernstein explains: "[It] is only by submitting our hypothesis to public critical discussion that we become aware of what is valid in our claims and what fails to withstand critical scrutiny. It is only by the serious encounter with what is other, different, and alien that we can hope to determine what is idiosyncratic, limited, and partial."[14]

The concept of critical community of inquiry encourages pragmatists to make critical judgments about the validity of analytical and empirical claims. This distinguishes philosophical pragmatism from "political" pragmatism.[15] It is common to describe policy-makers, particularly politicians, as "pragmatic," but this refers to their willingness to ignore important principles in order to reach a consensus or to solve a problem. By comparison, a critical community of inquiry is an attempt to vet the usefulness of policy ideas based on critical scrutiny and close analysis. The concept was derived from the pragmatists' understanding of the scientific method. Peirce, for example, understood the scientific method as "testing one's ideas in practice, and maintaining an attitude of fallibilism toward them."[16]

Dewey connected the scientific method, critical communities of inquiry, and democratic decision-making. According to Kloppenberg, "Dewey valued the scientific method because it embodied an ethical commitment to open-ended inquiry wherein human values shaped the selection of questions, the formulation of hypothesis, and the evaluation of results." He "conceived of the idea of a scientific community as a democratically organized, truth-seeking group of independent thinkers" who tested their results against "pragmatic standards."[17] Dewey regarded the state as analogous to a scientific society because citizens likewise were "engaged in an ongoing, experimental search for an increasingly durable conception of the public order."[18] Thus, for Dewey, citizens were the ultimate critical community of inquiry in a democracy. Regarding social problems, he sought "experimental inquiry combined with free and full discussion," which required "the maximum use of the capacities of citizens for proposing courses of action, for testing them, and for evaluating the results."[19]

Risk and Contingency

A fourth theme running through the pragmatic tradition concerns the relationship between risk and the contingent nature of the world around us. Richard Bernstein explains:

> [Another] theme running through the pragmatic tradition [is] the awareness and sensitivity to radical contingency and chance that mark the universe, our inquiries, our lives. Contingency and chance have always been problematic for philosophy. In the concern with universality and necessity, there has been a deep desire to master, contain, and repress contingency—to assign it to its "proper" restricted place. For the pragmatist, contingency and chance are not merely signs of human ignorance, they are inescapable and pervasive features of the universe.[20]

Bernstein continues:

> [The pragmatists'] insistence on the inescapability of chance and contingency—on what Dewey called "the precariousness of existence" where the "world is a scene of risk" and is "uncannily unstable"—conditioned their understanding of experience and philosophy itself. We can never hope to "master" unforeseen and unexpected contingencies. We live in an "open universe" that is always at once threatening and a source of tragedy and opportunity. This is why the pragmatists placed so much emphasis on how we are to respond to contingencies—on developing the complex of dispositions and critical habits that Dewey called "reflective intelligence."[21]

Pluralism

Finally, by rejecting foundationalism, pluralism has no choice but to consider any belief or thesis open to further interpretation and criticism. Pragmatism is therefore pluralistic in the sense that it is willing to consider a plurality of traditions, perspectives, and academic orientations. Thus pragmatism's mission, as Gene Shreve notes, is "to test, clarify, and mediate impulses generated elsewhere within a large community of ideas."[22]

Since pragmatism draws its understanding of the world from a plurality of traditions, perspectives, and academic orientations, it is not possible to create an all-comprehensive, internally consistent meta-account of pragmatic beliefs. The test of a pragmatic belief is not its coherence to some theoretical set of consistent beliefs, but its correspondence to the world in which we live. Despite its possible lack of internal coherence, pragmatic reasoning can offer a more persuasive account of the world in which we live. As Peirce explained, an argument built on a "chain" of reasoning is "no stronger than its weakest link." By comparison, a pragmatic argument is a "cable," and even though its "fibers may be ever so slender," the argument itself is "strong" if its fibers are "sufficiently numerous and intimately connected."[23] Daniel Farber and Suzanna Sherry use a different metaphor to make the same point. A pragmatic approach is more like a "web," because it draws on many sources, than a "tower, built on a single unified foundation."[24]

Summary

To summarize, the pragmatist rejects the concept that the rationality of a belief can be established by reference to a metaphysical concept. Instead, an idea is rational if holding it leads to more useful relations with the world. In public policy, an idea has this attribute when it solves some specific complexity or problem better than existing beliefs and understandings. The pragmatist determines "what works" through a critical community of inquiry in which existing ideas are subject to criticism and debate. This process mimics scientific inquiry in the sense that the citizens are engaged in an ongoing, experimental search for a durable conception of the public order. In this process, an idea is rational when it is accepted, at least for the present time, by the critical community as useful to public policy. The pragmatist recognizes, however, that determining the worth of an idea—its capacity to improve society—may be a complicated task in light of the inescapable role of contingency and chance in the universe. This is one reason that the pragmatist considers it essential to consider a plurality of traditions, perspectives, and academic orientations. As a result, pragmatic beliefs are often composed of disparate ideas in the sense that they arise from different sources. Because pragmatism draws from different traditions and disciplines, a pragmatic understanding has the potential to better explain some aspect of the world in which we live. The value of any such "cable" or "web" of ideas, however, is ultimately determined by whether it is persuasive to the relevant community of inquiry.

Ends and Means

Pragmatism is relevant to determining both what are appropriate goals for society and what is the most appropriate way to achieve those goals. Moreover, pragmatism is constantly willing to reconsider both ends and means. Dewey believed that "'inquiry' in the widest sense—that is, human dealings with problematical situations—involves incessant reconsideration of both means *and* ends."[25] Both means and ends are open to debate because pragmatism rejects foundationalism. In Dewey's view, "[It] is not the case that each person's goals are cast in concrete in the form of a 'rational preference function' somehow mysteriously imbedded in his or her individual mind, or that all we are allowed to do so as long as we are 'rational' is to look for more efficient means to these immutable but idiosyncratic goals or values."[26] Thus a particular "means" may be very effective at serving a particular "end," but pragmatism will consider arguments that the end itself is inappropriate. As Hilary Putnam explains, any "inquiry has both 'factual' presuppositions, including presuppositions as to the efficacy of various means to various ends, and 'value' presuppositions, and if resolving our problem is difficult then we may well want to reconsider both our 'factual' assumptions and our goals."[27]

The willingness of pragmatism to question society's goals leads skeptics to question whether pragmatism ultimately has any core values that permit the analyst to decide which social options are valuable. While pragmatism has no substantive content of its own, it avoids an analytical muddle by adopting and clarifying existing values relevant to the problem at hand. A pragmatist, as Frank Michelman indicates, "envisions political argument as a kind of ethical argument that is culturally and historically situated and conditioned but that also proceeds without foundations." Thus it is "animated and constrained by a consciousness of its situation within, and answerable to, a public normative culture and history—within and to, if you like, a normative practice."[28]

Although pragmatism is anchored by the normative culture and history of a society, the pragmatic method does not necessarily produce clear answers to pressing social problems. The difficulty is that our society adheres to a number of important social values, and some of these may be in conflict concerning a specific issue. Charles Anderson observes, for example, that despite the importance of liberal principles in American culture and history, it is possible to construct "very different" social goals starting from essentially the same liberal premises. According to pragmatism, Anderson continues, a person cannot demonstrate that any one of these goals is uniquely rational and beyond disinterested criticism or reasonable doubt. Thus the decision concerning which goal (or goals) to apply to particular kinds of cases and controversies inevitably requires "an act of judgment."[29] That is, the pragmatist must determine how best to reconcile a value conflict.

When a conflict between social values arises, the pragmatic approach seeks to reconcile collective judgment and social principles in the best manner possible, recognizing that particular problems may require difficult trade-offs. At the same time, the pragmatic method is always open to additional criticisms of the trade-off that has been made. In the end, however, society accepts such a criticism only if it serves the community better than the existing arrangement.

Pragmatic Risk Regulation

Our discussion of pragmatism so far has been at a general level. To be useful in workaday deliberations, however, pragmatism must generate, in Charles Anderson's words, "standards of pertinence and soundness."[30] In this section, we suggest a number of such characteristics drawn from the pragmatic themes discussed earlier. In subsequent chapters, we connect our support of risk regulation, as well as our criticisms of it, to these characteristics.

Widely Shared Social Values

In pragmatism, public policy should reflect widely shared values that arise from a society's political culture and history. Because pragmatism proceeds without foundations, it considers the extent to which different social values impact a given problem and what solutions they may require. There is no basis for ignoring a value that is an important part of a country's political culture. The test of the wisdom of a solution to a problem is the extent to which it accommodates social values that are implicated by the nature of the problem. When these values conflict, pragmatism attempts the difficult task of finding solutions that accommodate conflicting values to the greatest extent possible.

Risk regulation inevitably involves a trade-off between the protection of individuals and the environment, and the costs of providing such protection. In other words, there is a value conflict—how does one decide between protection and cost? One way of deciding how to make this trade-off is to use a cost-benefit decision-making standard. This method would protect individuals and the environment up to the point where the economic costs of doing so are greater than the economic benefits of such protection, as these are conventionally measured using economic measurement techniques. As Chapter 1 discussed, many critics of risk regulation seek adoption of this approach. Congress, however, has almost universally rejected the use of a cost-benefit standard to determine the trade-off between protection and the costs of protection. Instead, as Chapter 3 will demonstrate, Congress generally employs two alternative techniques: constrained balancing and open-ended balancing.

Our argument is that the employment of these alternative techniques by Congress is distinctly pragmatic. It is pragmatic because these alternative methods do a better job of reconciling the conflicting values at stake in risk regulation decisions. These alternatives are preferable to a cost-benefit standard because they better recognize the fundamental value of protecting human life, avoiding damage to individuals, and preserving and improving the environment in which we live. As Chapter 4 will develop, the goal of these alternatives is to maximize protection of individuals and the environment to the extent possible consistent with taking economic costs into account.

This goal—the maximum level of protection to the extent possible—is more consistent with widely held fundamental social values than an economic decision-making standard. Under a cost-benefit standard, harm to individuals or the environment does not warrant any special consideration beyond the economic value of preventing additional deaths or environmental damage revealed by market transactions. The objective of this economic approach is to achieve the "optimal" level of injury, death, and environmental degradation. In short, there is no recognition that for most people the protection of human life and the environment has a fundamental value that is unrelated to economic measurements. By comparison, existing laws recognize these important shared values. Rather than seeking the optimal level of fatalities, injury, or environmental damage, the current policy seeks the maximum level of protection consistent with taking economic costs into account. In short, existing policy seeks to do the "best we can" to protect individuals and the environment, rather than treating individuals and the environment as economic units whose protection is determined by utilitarian calculations.

Opponents of risk regulation raise the objection that risk policy has been unsuccessful because current policies have produced economic costs greatly in excess of their economic benefits. A pragmatic approach to risk regulation must take these allegations seriously because economic efficiency itself is an important social value. In Chapter 5 we examine these claims of excessive regulation and find them unpersuasive. For the reasons that we will discuss, the calculation of costs and the benefits of risk regulation can be extremely difficult, and reasonable estimates often vary widely. The critics choose valuations that support their criticisms, but other equally plausible evaluations indicate that risk regulation generally meets its objective of maximum protection consistent with taking costs into account.

Current laws seek to reconcile, as best we can, the cost of human and environmental protection with the recognition that protecting human life and the environment is invaluable. This approach is distinctly pragmatic because it honors the fundamental value of human and environmental protection without ignoring the costs that such protection entails. In other words, it attempts the difficult task of finding solutions that accommodate fundamental social values and the cost of protection to the greatest extent possible.

Bounded Rationality

In pragmatism, the value of a policy is dictated by its success under actual conditions rather than by its consistency with theoretical precepts. As noted earlier, pragmatists consider a belief to be true when "holding the belief leads us into more useful relations with the world."[31] A pragmatic approach to risk regulation therefore rejects as impractical the "comprehensive analytical rationality" sought by the critics of risk regulation. Instead, it starts from the central insight of the literature on organizational decision-making that "bounded rationality" inevitably applies in the contexts in which organizations actually operate.

The "behavioral" school of organizational decision-making, led by Herbert Simon and James March,[32] originated the idea that institutional decision-making is subject to "bounded rationality." Simon's essential insight was that decision-making in any institution is "bounded" by time, resources, and cognitive constraints that make it virtually impossible to verify that the solution chosen is optimal. In other words, an effort to find the "best" solution to a problem will be hindered by time and cost constraints that limit the search for alternative solutions and information for measuring which solution is better. In addition, individuals are subject to significant cognitive limitations that restrict their ability to make the judgments necessary to pick an optimal solution. As Charles Lindblom recognized years ago:

> For complex problems, [the effort to formalize rational policy formation] is of course impossible. Although such an approach can be described, it cannot be practiced except for relatively simple problems and even then only in some modified form. It assumes intellectual capacities and sources of information that men simply do not possess, and it is even more absurd as an approach to policy when the time and money that can be allocated to a policy problem is limited, as is always the case.[33]

The impossibility of engaging in comprehensive rationality forces individuals to engage in what Simon called "satisficing," which involves finding "a course of action that is satisfactory or good enough." To satisfice is to take into account "just a few of the factors of the situation regarded as most relevant and crucial." Thus, the best that organizations can do is to rely on habits, practices, and tests, such as "rules of thumb" or "heuristics," that take into account real-world limitations.[34] Although organizations do not employ comprehensive rationality, satisficing is rational because the organization is attempting to secure its goals in the face of the limits on human knowledge and reasoning. Thus "behavior in organizations is, if not wholly rational, at least in good part *intendedly* so."[35]

In light of bounded rationality, when the critics of risk regulation argue that risk reduction should be controlled by a cost-benefit standard, they cannot claim as an advantage that this methodology accomplishes comprehensive rationality or that it represents the "optimal" solution to balancing costs and benefits. As Charles Anderson recognizes, Simon and Lindblom "argued against the cognitive possibility of idealized utilitarianism, represented as the comprehensive cost-benefit analysis, as a workable conception of practical reason."[36]

Although cost-benefit analysis cannot accomplish comprehensive rationality, its supporters who recognize this limitation argue that it still should be used to decide regulatory issues, although its limitations must be taken into account. This presents a pragmatic issue. Under conditions of bounded rationality, is a cost-benefit standard more likely than current approaches to improve the policy process in terms of the aims that Congress has adopted for risk regulation? For the reasons we explain in Chapter 4, the reality of bounded rationality and other insights of the organizational literature support the current laws over reliance on a cost-benefit standard.

This is not to say that pragmatic administration would ignore what risk analysis, cost-benefit analysis, or other analytical techniques might teach us in a particular situation. Under pragmatism, current beliefs are always open to revision in light of new knowledge or arguments. As we explain in Chapter 7, however, a pragmatic approach would change how these sources of information inform risk regulation in recognition of their limitations in informing public policy analysis.

Incremental Decision-making

A characteristic idea of the pragmatic tradition is efficacy in practical application. Pragmatism seeks those solutions that work out most effectively. Building on this orientation, Charles Lindblom made his famous recommendation that "muddling" through is often the most rational way to proceed. In light of bounded rationality, he proposed that government rely on incremental steps that permit administrators to adjust decisions over time.[37] Lindblom's endorsement of incrementalism echoes Dewey's recommendation that government should try different policies in the spirit of establishing a hypothesis for approaching solutions to problems.[38]

Lindblom's recipe of "muddling through" does not want for critics who object to the lack of analytical rigor in an incremental process. In particular, critics contend that because strategies like satisficing and incrementalism fail to consider the "big picture," administrators too often fail to establish rational priorities, engage in unproductive or counterproductive strategies, and miss opportunities for more productive policies. These complaints, of course, are similar to the criticisms of risk regulation described in Chapter 1. For critics of risk regulation, the process is already too incremental. As we discuss in Chapter 8, agencies can do better than "muddling through" in terms of rationalizing their approach to risk protection.

Nevertheless, because pragmatism understands that efforts such as priority-setting are subject to bounded rationality, pragmatists accept that a degree of "muddling through" is inevitable. In particular, pragmatists understand that agencies are often unable to engage in the type of comprehensive decision-making that the critics of risk regulation favor. Following Lindblom, pragmatic risk regulation does not attempt to obtain regulatory perfection in its initial decisions, but it does adjust those decisions in light of new information and new developments. The incremental nature of decision-making flows directly from the limits imposed by bounded rationality on initial decision-making. Policy is experimental in the sense that regulators adjust decisions in light of experience and knowledge that was unavailable to them when the initial decision was made.

Although current risk regulation provides for an incremental system of regulation, it should do more to allow policy-makers to adjust policies, correct mistakes, and take into account new scientific and technological developments. At the present time, there is too much emphasis on trying to perfect regulatory decisions on the front end, at the time when agencies promulgate regulations that require risk reduction. The risk regulation process would be more incremental if regulators made adjustments on the back end, by adjusting the impact of regulations through time extensions, waivers, rule amendments, and other forms of *ex post* alterations. The regulatory process could also be made more incremental if agencies developed better procedures for review of existing regulations. In Chapter 8 we argue that these types of adjustments are more likely to fine-tune the process than greater reliance on cost-benefit analysis or other techniques of comprehensive rationality.

Theory versus Practice

The existing approaches to risk regulation are hardly perfect. Critics have succeeded in exposing some of the maladies of risk regulation for all to see, and from a distance their alternative approaches may look preferable. The enthusiasm for reform is augmented in some cases by an ideological attachment to the underlying theory of the reform. Economic analysts, for example, endorse a cost-benefit standard because it is consistent with their utilitarian outlook.[39] With its instrumental emphasis, however, pragmatism requires a close examination of both the existing approach and the approach that critics favor to replace it. Rather than relying on the theoretical advantages of changing an existing approach, pragmatism requires evidence of the superiority of that change.

Pragmatism embraces the potential for reform because it is also open to new evidence and argument about the desirability of existing arrangements. Nevertheless, on the basis of the existing evidence, we are not prepared to endorse wholesale reform of risk regulation. As we discuss in Chapter 8, the policy literature fails to show the clear superiority of many reforms popular with critics of risk regulation. A pragmatic approach is skeptical about wholesale reform for another reason. The regulation of human and environmental risk is extraordinarily diverse and complex. What works in one situation may be totally inappropriate in another. Thus reforms may hold great promise in one situation but not another.

Administrative Discretion and Flexibility

A pragmatic approach to risk regulation recognizes the necessity of administrative discretion and flexibility. Pragmatism does not leave bureaucracy unchecked, but it recognizes that, in comparison to other governmental decision-makers, administrators are in the best position to implement risk policies, because they are in the best position to exercise the judgment that risk regulation inevitably requires.

A pragmatic approach to risk regulation understands the reality that regulatory decisions normally involve choices by regulators that are policy, rather than scientific, issues. As discussed earlier, it is often impossible to determine which policy choice is optimal, because of limitations of knowledge, time, and understanding. For this reason, pragmatism favors incremental decision-making and experimentation. Even with these adjustments, regulatory decision-making inevitably requires individual judgment. As a matter of relative competence, regulators are in a better position to exercise the necessary judgment than other governmental decision-makers, including the President's staff and individual members of Congress. The reason is that regulators operate within a critical community of inquiry in an agency that is devoted to and specializes in the regulatory issues faced by the agency. This agency community is simply more acquainted with the day-to-day details and difficulties of regulatory decisions than the communities of inquiry that operate in the White House, Congress, and the federal judiciary, which are not specialized in the same way.[40]

No one can deny that regulators sometimes use their flexibility and discretion in ill-advised ways. Pragmatism therefore seeks to preserve administrative discretion and flexibility, while making regulators accountable to elected officials and the public. This is a difficult balancing act, because it requires oversight by elected officials and judges of agency decisions that is neither too intrusive nor too lenient. In Chapter 9 we consider efforts by critics of risk regulation to increase regulatory oversight by elected officials and the courts. Critics look to these overseers to correct the irrational risk policies that they believe agencies produce. In assessing these efforts, our guiding principle is that of relative competence. Agencies should have discretion and flexibility to make difficult policy decisions for which regulators are likely to have more experience and expertise.

Public Participation

Pragmatism believes that good public policy results from open debate, inquiry, implementation, and re-evaluation. As discussed earlier, Dewey regarded the state as analogous to an ideal scientific society in which citizens are engaged in an ongoing experimental search for "an increasingly durable conception of the public order."[41] Thus pragmatism favors administrative arrangements that promote public participation in risk decisions and disfavor arrangements that hinder it. In Chapter 9 we consider methods of political and judicial oversight and how they measure up against this characteristic.

As noted earlier, the promotion of public participation in risk regulation

was an important achievement of the consumer and environmental movements during the 1960s and 1970s. The critics of risk regulation have sought to
reduce citizen access in response to their perception that risk regulation is
overly sensitive to the irrational demands of the public for protection. A
pragmatic system of risk regulation is suspicious of such efforts. Dewey believed in the "capacity of human beings for intelligent judgment and action if
proper [that is, democratic] conditions are furnished." A key condition was
the ability of individuals to converse freely. Dewey predicted that "[a]nything
that blocks communication engenders 'antagonistic sections and factions'
and undermines democracy."[42]

To ensure that proper democratic conditions are met, pragmatism empha-
sizes the importance of transparency and openness in regulatory decision-
making. As noted earlier, the adoption of open government laws and practices was another of the achievements of the reformers during the 1960s and
1970s. This principle is relevant to several aspects of risk regulation. As we will
elaborate in Chapter 4, for example, reliance on cost-benefit analysis and
other utilitarian forms of calculation makes it more difficult for the public to
understand and contribute to regulatory decision-making because decisions
center on disputes over scientific and mathematic modeling and calculation.
The issue of openness and transparency also arises in Chapter 9, in which we
emphasize the importance of publicly accountable legislative and presidential
oversight of regulators.

Conclusion

The guiding idea of this book is that the American philosophical tradition of
pragmatism can explain, justify, and critique the basic policies and approaches to risk regulation adopted in legislation passed during the 1960s and
1970s. This tradition contains a number of themes that are relevant to risk
regulation. Pragmatists reject foundationalism, value ideas on the basis of
their practical effects, determine the practical effect of ideas by experimentation and re-evaluation, understand that effects are difficult to measure because events are subject to contingency and change, and are willing to use
different perspectives to understand the world in which we live. Drawing on
these themes, we argue that pragmatic risk regulation would have several

characteristics. A pragmatic approach to risk regulation attempts to accommodate widely held and conflicting social values implicated by risk reduction, and it acknowledges how "bounded rationality" confounds efforts to understand and reduce risks. Pragmatic risk regulation requires proof that reforms will work in actual practice, and it requires that regulators have sufficient discretion and flexibility to adopt appropriate policies. In developing those policies, regulators should use incremental approaches. Finally, a pragmatic approach to risk regulation seeks decision-making methods, particularly openness and transparency, that promote public participation in risk decisions.

Professor Daniel Farber's book *Eco-Pragmatism* has started an incipient debate about the usefulness of pragmatism as a guide to environmental policy.[43] Essentialists, as one could easily predict, are highly critical. Environmental foundationalists reject his willingness to accommodate concerns over costs,[44] while libertarians reject his willingness to accommodate an ecological perspective.[45] Others, while willing to endorse pragmatism, have reservations. Professor J. B. Ruhl faults pragmatism for a "lack of passion": "Maybe pragmatism does not lend itself to being passionate. Maybe passion is not a pragmatic virtue. But why is that—why is no one willing to [lie] down in the road in the name of being pragmatic?"[46]

We do not think that pragmatism's commitment to being open-minded requires one to abandon passionate beliefs. Pragmatism does not require a community to give up its strong commitment, even its passionate commitment, to its important social values. We strongly believe in the protection of individuals and the environment. We regard the value of human life and the environment as fundamental. The fact that we acknowledge the economic costs of achieving this protection does not lessen our commitment to protection. It does indicate that, as pragmatists, we understand the reality that no society can achieve absolute protection of its citizens or its environment. Thus pragmatism requires us to accommodate concerns about costs without giving up our strong belief in the intrinsic value of human life and protection of the environment, and to convince others to do likewise.

Further, pragmatism does not require a community of inquiry to regard every argument as worthy of its attention. Pragmatism entails practical discourse and practical judgment. Based on this process, a community is entitled to reject an approach, belief, or solution as inappropriate or unconvincing. While it is necessary to accommodate important social and conflicting values, a community is entitled to conclude that one way of reaching an accommodation is better than others. We strongly believe that the pragmatic method leads to the conclusion that the existing structure of risk regulation is a better way of accommodating concerns about the cost of risk regulation with conflicting social values than the economic approach favored by so many. We also strongly believe that the evidence cited by the economic critics of risk regulation, when carefully considered, is unpersuasive. Readers, of course, will reach their own conclusions.

Lisa Heinzerling acknowledges useful aspects of pragmatism, but she rejects it as the guiding ethic for protection of the environment because it cannot be "transformative." For Heinzerling, pragmatism is "just too calculating, too timid a word for the experimental, contextual, skeptical, and most of all transformative attitude that I have in mind." She therefore proposes a version of environmentalism that, while it shares many of pragmatism's traits, "would not shrink from encouraging adjustments, even radical adjustments, in human attitudes, habits and behavior." In the end, she notes, it is difficult to believe that "a 'transformative' environmentalism could call itself 'pragmatic' and still be transformative."[47]

Pragmatism can lead to transformation, but only through the process of debate and revelation by relevant critical communities of inquiry, and typically only on the basis of practical knowledge and experience. Thus pragmatism favors a more plodding approach to public policy than the radical transformations that Professor Heinzerling wishes to encourage. Despite this inherent caution, we believe that the transformation Heinzerling seeks can only come about in a pragmatic manner. It is no news that there are many strong opponents of risk regulation, and that they have mounted challenging arguments about the high costs and other dysfunctions of risk regulation which they perceive. We believe that the best way to refute these arguments is with the type of practical discourse and reason that we have undertaken in this book. Likewise, we believe that the best way to build the case for a strong commitment to risk regulation is in the same manner. The American political tradition is complex and multifaceted, and the discourse that best suits it is the one that was home grown: the American philosophical tradition of pragmatism.

3

The Structure of Risk Regulation

W hen Congress decided to address the risks of technology, it filled up thousands and thousands of pages in the U.S. Code with dense, turgid text that only a lawyer could love. Despite the level of detail, these laws have two common features that give them a similar and relatively simple structure. Risk regulation legislation can be characterized according to the choice by Congress of a "statutory trigger" and "statutory standard." As John Applegate has pointed out, these features are inevitable components of risk regulation, inasmuch as they define the situation that needs correction and the objective to be achieved by regulation. In Table 3.1 we organize most of the prominent examples of risk legislation according to these two aspects. Most of the statutes listed in the table were enacted during the 1970s, although some, such as the Safe Drinking Water Act (SDWA), have been amended since that time. A few statutes have been recently enacted, such as the 1990 ozone depletion amendments to the Clean Air Act (CAA) and the 1996 amendments to the Accountable Pipeline Safety and Partnership Act (APSPA).

Once the enormous detail of risk reduction legislation is stripped away, it is possible to see the two essential features of risk regulation. First, Congress has designed the statutory triggers in light of the "ignorance of mechanism" discussed in Chapter 1. As discussed earlier, when Congress adopted risk regulation, it rejected the common law paradigm in favor of a regulatory system that would reduce technological risks before they caused significant harm to individuals and the environment. Congress accomplished this goal by designing statutory triggers that permit the government to act on the basis of anticipated harm. This chapter identifies the nature of these statutory triggers and indicates why they have that effect.

TABLE 3.1

Structure of Regulation

			Statutory Standards		
Statutory Triggers	Risk- or Ambient Quality–Based	Phaseout	Constrained Balancing	Open-Ended Balancing	Cost-Benefit Balancing
No Threshold	*FDCA* Delaney Clause (1958) *FDCA* Pesticide Residues (1996)		*CWA* Existing Sources (1972, 1977) New Sources (1972)	*CWA* Ambient Quality Standards (1972)	
Risk Threshold		*CAA* Ozone Depletion (1990)	*CAA* Nonattainment (1977, 1990) PSD (1977) NESHAPS (1990) Mobile Sources (1970) New Sources (1970, 1990)	*CAA* NAAQS/ SIPs (1970)	
Significant Risk Threshold			*OSH Act* (1970) *SDWA* (1996) *RCRA* LDRs (1984)	*CERCLA* (1980, 1986)	
Unreason-able Risk Threshold	*TSCA* PCBs (1976)		*NTMVSA* (1966, 1994) *TSCA* (1976)	*FIFRA* (1972)	*CPSA* (1972, 1981) *APSPA* (1994, 1996)

SOURCE: Acts cited in the table (citations in the text).

Second, Congress in choosing statutory standards has almost universally rejected a cost-benefit test as the basis for setting the level of regulation.[1] Of the twenty-two laws we cover, only two set the level of regulation based on a cost-benefit standard, and only one of those requires a demonstration that the benefits of regulation exceed its costs. Instead, Congress relies primarily on two alternative methods of balancing costs and benefits: constrained and open-ended balancing. Sixteen of the twenty-two laws identified in Table 3.1 use one or the other of these alternative forms of determining the stringency of risk regulation. This chapter identifies the nature of these statutory standards and indicates how they balance regulatory costs and benefits.

Statutory Triggers

The statutory trigger establishes the evidentiary burden that an agency has to meet in order to regulate a toxic substance or other hazard.[2] Agencies operate under one of four triggers: "no threshold," a threshold based on the existence of a "risk," "significant risk," or "unreasonable risk."

No Threshold

An agency subject to a no threshold trigger is empowered to regulate once it establishes that a substance or other hazard has been introduced into the environment, workplace, or other location at which public exposure is possible. There is no requirement that the agency demonstrate that the public or the environment is exposed to the substance or hazard at a level (or to an extent) that causes some actual harm or risk of harm. For example, the Food and Drug Administration (FDA) is authorized to regulate color or food additives if they cause cancer in animals or humans, regardless of whether the substances pose a cancer risk that is above some threshold.[3] Thus, the FDA does not have to prove that an additive poses more than a *de minimis* risk in order to regulate.

Risk-Based Threshold

An agency operating under the next two thresholds, by comparison, must demonstrate that the risk to the public or the environment exceeds some threshold. Under a "risk-based threshold," an agency must prove that the public or the environment is exposed to a substance or hazard at a level (or to the extent) that is potentially dangerous. For example, the Environmental Protection Agency (EPA) is authorized under the CAA to regulate those new stationary sources of air pollution that may cause or contribute to "air pollution which may reasonably be anticipated to endanger public health or welfare."[4]

Significant Risk Threshold

A "significant risk-based threshold" further increases the agency's burden of proof. An agency operating under this third kind of statutory trigger must prove that the public or the environment is exposed to a substance or hazard at a level (or to an extent) that is "unacceptable." For example, the statutory trigger for the Occupational Safety and Health Act (OSH Act) requires that regulation be "reasonably necessary or appropriate to provide safe or healthful employment and places of employment."[5] Although this language is similar to the risk-based trigger in the CAA, described earlier, the Supreme Court interpreted the OSH Act to require proof of a "significant risk."[6] The Court did not give precise guidelines as to when such a risk exists, although it observed that a risk of one in a thousand of dying from exposure to a carcinogen is significant, whereas a risk of one in a billion is not.

Unreasonable Risk Threshold

The final category, "unreasonable risk threshold," reflects the most restrictive evidentiary requirement. An agency seeking to regulate under such a statute must do more than simply show that the quantum of risk posed by a targeted activity passes some threshold level of significance. Instead, the agency must demonstrate that any risk it desires to regulate is unreasonable in the sense that the activity generating it produces human or environmental costs that are not justified by the economic and social benefits it yields. For example, EPA cannot limit the use of a pesticide under the Federal Insecticide, Fungicide, and Rodenticide Act (FIFRA) if the pesticide will perform its intended function without "unreasonable adverse effects."[7] FIFRA defines "unreasonable adverse effects" as unreasonable risks to man or the environment, "taking into account the economic, social, and environmental costs and benefits of the use of any pesticide."[8]

Risk Prevention

The statutory trigger sets the evidentiary burden that an agency has to meet in order to be able to regulate a toxic substance or other hazard. Starting at the top of Table 3.1 with a "no threshold" trigger, the evidentiary burden increases as you move down the left column of the chart, with an unreasonable risk trigger constituting the heaviest evidentiary burden. Most of the laws (sixteen of twenty-two) use triggers that create less than the maximum evidentiary burden and, in particular, most fall in the middle categories—risk threshold or significant risk threshold.

Congress has not been consistent in choosing risk thresholds, but there is a clear pattern that reflects a preference for evidentiary thresholds that are easier, rather than more difficult, to meet. The critics of risk regulation blame this aspect of risk regulation for contributing to the irrational risk policies that they perceive. We will evaluate this claim in the next three chapters.

Statutory Standards

The second structural element consists of the statutory standard, or the standard that specifies the level or stringency of regulation.[9] The standards vary in terms of what factors an agency is to take into account in setting the level of regulation. In the first category, risk- or ambient quality–based standards, agencies can regulate without consideration of economic factors. In the second category, the cost of compliance may be at least an implicit justification for phasing out a risk-creating substance over time, instead of imposing an immediate ban. Under each of the remaining statutory standards, cost is an explicit factor that the regulatory agency must consider in determining the level of regulation, although the three standards vary concerning the nature of the relationship between regulatory benefits and the resulting costs of compliance. The last standard, cost-benefit balancing, requires the most finely tuned balancing of regulatory costs and benefits.

Risk- or Ambient Quality–Based Standard

If regulation occurs under a "risk or ambient quality–based" standard, an agency is empowered to impose such regulation as is necessary to achieve one of two related results. The level of regulation must be sufficient either to protect against a designated risk of harm to health or the environment (that is, risk-based) or to achieve some safety, health, or environment-based goal (that is, ambient quality–based), such as air or water clean enough to protect the public health. For example, the Delaney Clause of the Food, Drug, and Cosmetic Act (FDCA) bars the FDA from characterizing a food additive as safe if it has been found to induce cancer in humans or animals.[10] The 1996 amendments to the Delaney Clause establish a different, less absolute risk-based statutory standard for pesticide residues in food. Under the amendments, EPA is authorized to issue a tolerance (that is, an exemption) from a general statutory prohibition on adulterated food if there is a reasonable certainty that no harm will result from aggregate exposure to pesticide chemical residues.[11]

The category of risk- or ambient quality-based standards typically requires an agency to estimate the relationship between exposure to a risk and the harm that can result. A risk- or ambient quality–based standard requires the agency to construct a dose-response curve that indicates the relationship between the level of exposure and the extent to which the public or the environment is at risk of being harmed. These kinds of standards are the only ones reflected in Table 3.1 for which the cost of achieving the standard is irrelevant to its establishment.[12]

Phaseout

In a limited number of instances since the inception of risk regulation, Congress has ordered or mandated that a regulatory agency order the phased ban of a particular risk-creating substance. For example, the 1990 CAA amendments adopted a series of prohibitions on the production and consumption of chemicals harmful to the stratospheric ozone layer, prohibitions that were phased in over a period of years.[13] The statute itself designates some chemicals subject to the prohibitions,[14] and EPA is authorized to ban or phase out additional chemicals that meet the statutory trigger.[15] Unlike the first kind of standard, phaseouts take cost into account. By deciding to eliminate the regulated substance, Congress has recognized that it poses a risk level that warrants regulation. Instead of immediately banning the substance's manufacture or use, however, Congress phases it out over a period of time. In the case of the CAA's ban on the manufacture of ozone-depleting substances, that period extends for up to forty years. The reason for the delay is presumably the adverse economic impact and related practical difficulties (such as the unavailability of substitutes) of eliminating the substance more expeditiously. Congress thus considered cost to a degree that regulatory agencies may not when they promulgate risk- or ambient quality–based standards.

Constrained Balancing Standard

If regulation takes place under a "constrained balancing" standard, regulation is based on the balancing of potential harm attributable to the targeted activity and regulatory compliance costs in a manner directed by Congress. That directive, however, does not require the agency to refrain from regulating beyond the point at which regulatory costs and benefits are equivalent. Rather, in this category, Congress typically orders an agency to accomplish the chosen level of protection or precaution by identifying and patterning regulatory objectives upon some model technology. For example, the CAA specifies that each state containing a nonattainment area must require existing stationary sources of air pollution to implement all "reasonable available control technology" as expeditiously as practicable.[16] A nonattainment area is one that does not meet national ambient air quality standards (NAAQS) established by EPA. In addition, Congress often directs the agency to make adjustments in the level of regulation indicated by a model technology. The 1996 amendments to the SDWA,[17] for example, require EPA to set a maximum contaminant level (MCL) that comes as close as "feasible" to achieving the level at which no known or anticipated adverse health effects will occur, allowing an adequate margin of safety.[18] The statute then authorizes departures from the feasibility-based risk-management standard based upon comparative risk assessment and cost-benefit analysis.[19]

Like the second but unlike the first category of standard considered above, the constrained balancing approach limits the extent of permissible regulation based on its cost, although it does so more explicitly than the phaseout of a risk-creating substance. When Congress links the level of regulation to the existence of a model technology, it limits regulatory authority to impose abatement costs according to the availability of that technology. For example, consider the standard of "reasonably available control technology" mentioned in the last paragraph. That standard establishes a ceiling on the cost of abatement because a regulated entity can come into compliance by installing this technology, and the agency may not extract a more onerous commitment than that capable of being achieved by using that technology. The entity is also free to install a less expensive technology as long as it achieves the same level of pollution abatement.

In a sense, then, Congress itself balances the cost and benefits of abatement when it chooses a technology-based standard. Such a standard may be more protective than a standard that equates costs and benefits, because it seeks the maximum degree of protection that can be achieved by the model technology. The Supreme Court recognized this distinction when it decided that the OSH Act adopted a technology-based standard. Section 6(b)(5) of the act requires the Occupational Safety and Health Administration (OSHA) to reduce the exposure of workers to toxic substances. The level of exposure is to be reduced to the point that "most adequately assures, *to the extent feasible* . . . that no employee will suffer material impairment of health or functional capacity."[20] The Court explained:

> [A]ll parties agree that the phrase "to the extent feasible" contains the critical language in §6(b)(5) for purposes of these cases. . . . "[F]easible" means "capable of being done, executed, or effected." . . . In effect, as the Court of Appeals held, Congress itself defined the basic relationship between costs and benefits, by placing the "benefit" of worker health above all other considerations save those making attainment of this "benefit" unachievable. Any standard based on a balancing of costs and benefits by the Secretary that strikes a different balance would be inconsistent with the command set forth in §6(b)(5). Thus, cost-benefit analysis by OSHA is not required by the statute because feasibility analysis is.[21]

Similarly, the Fifth Circuit, in a 1998 case involving a challenge to effluent limitations issued by EPA under the Clean Water Act (CWA), explained that, in adopting regulations requiring a level of performance achievable through the application of the best available technology (BAT), "EPA is not obligated to evaluate the reasonableness of the relationship between benefits and costs. Indeed, the EPA may prescribe [limitations] whose costs are significantly disproportionate to their benefits, just as long as the BAT determination remains economically feasible for the industry as a whole." The industry petitioners asserted that the costs of control could not logically be considered without reference to the resulting amount of effluent reduction. But the court responded that "[t]he benefit to be achieved from adopting a particular pollution control technology is not an element of that technology's cost. The cost of complying with a BAT-based regulation can be gauged by reference to the cost of the technology itself, even if the benefits of using that technology are unclear."[22]

Open-Ended Balancing

In constrained balancing, Congress constrains or limits the manner in which an agency is to balance the costs and benefits of risk regulation, even though both factors bear on the selection of the appropriate level of regulation. By comparison, statutes containing an open-ended balancing standard require that agencies consider a variety of factors, including regulatory costs and benefits, before deciding how to regulate, but tend not to dictate the weight the agency must place on each factor. The process by which EPA classifies registered pesticides for restricted use under FIFRA provides an example of this type of standard. The agency may impose conditions on a pesticide's use to the extent necessary to avoid unreasonable adverse effects on the environment.[23] The statute defines unreasonable adverse effects as "unreasonable risk to man or the environment, taking into account the economic, social, and environmental costs and benefits" of the pesticide's use.[24]

Open-ended balancing standards make cost considerations an explicit aspect of setting a statutory standard without identifying precisely what role costs should play in relation to other factors. The absence of that kind of restriction on agency discretion distinguishes an open-ended from a constrained balancing standard. Unlike a cost-benefit standard, discussed next, the agency is not required to adopt the level of regulation that equates regulatory benefits and costs.

Cost-Benefit Standard

Finally, a statute containing a statutory standard that dictates cost-benefit balancing requires that the adopting agency directly compare the relationship between regulatory costs and benefits. The statute may require that costs bear a particular kind of relationship, such as a reasonable relationship, to regulatory benefits before regulation may be justified. Regulation by the Consumer Product Safety Commission (CPSC) of dangerous consumer products is an example.[25] Once CPSC identifies a dangerous product that meets the statutory trigger, it must make a finding that the benefits expected from a regulation bear a reasonable relationship to its costs.[26] It also must demonstrate that the regulation adopts the least burdensome requirement that prevents or adequately reduces the risk of injury for which the rule is

being promulgated.[27] Under a more rigorous version of a cost-benefit standard, sometimes referred to as "marginal cost-benefit analysis," the agency is
prohibited from imposing any regulation whose costs to regulated entities
exceed the benefits bestowed by the regulation on health, safety, or the environment. The adoption by the Secretary of Transportation of minimum
safety standards for pipeline transportation is subject to the mandate that
regulatory benefits justify regulatory costs.[28]

Summary

The pattern of statutory standards found in Table 3.1 clearly indicates
the general rejection by Congress of balancing costs and benefits. Only two of
the twenty-two statutes we analyzed use this method of establishing the level
of regulation. Many of the critics of risk regulation, as we have explained, seek
to have Congress adopt a cost-benefit standard for all risk regulation. We will
defend Congress's choice not to rely on a cost-benefit test in the next three
chapters.

Triggers and Standards

The previous analysis considered statutory triggers and standards in isolation.
The nature of a regulatory regime, however, depends on the combination of a
trigger and standard. In this section, we consider how Congress has matched
statutory triggers and standards. The results indicate that Congress generally
prefers a statutory trigger requiring evidence of risk or significant risk and a
statutory standard that involves constrained or open-ended balancing.

The Options

The statutory triggers and standards, and how they are combined, vary
the burden of proof that the government must meet before it can regulate. As
the reader moves from the top to the bottom of Table 3.1 and from left to
right, the burden of proof changes in two ways. First, it typically becomes
more difficult for the government to fulfill the evidentiary burden imposed
by the statutory trigger as one moves from the top to the bottom of the table.
If an agency cannot meet this burden, it cannot regulate at all. Second, as-

suming the agency can meet this evidentiary burden, the government is required to employ more cost-sensitive regulation, or regulation that requires a greater degree of demonstrated correspondence between regulatory costs and benefits as one moves from left to right on the table.

This design can be illustrated by considering the most extreme choices that Congress can make. Regulation under a statute appearing in the uppermost box on the left side of the chart is the easiest for an agency to promulgate and results in regulation that is cost-oblivious. An agency seeking to regulate under such a statute would not have to demonstrate any threshold of risk, and it would be empowered to adopt a risk- or ambient quality–based standard to address the targeted activity regardless of the cost of compliance. By comparison, a statute appearing in the lowermost box of the right-hand side of the chart imposes the most rigorous threshold showing upon the agency governed by it, and it imposes the most stringent constraint on the agency in terms of the level of regulation that it can impose. An agency seeking to regulate under such a statute would have to demonstrate that an activity poses an unreasonable risk (because the environmental costs resulting from the activity outweigh the economic and social benefits it bestows) before it could regulate at all. Even if the agency could make such a showing, it could regulate under a marginal cost-benefit standard only to the extent that the environmental benefits provided by the regulation exceeded its economic and social costs.

Risk- or Ambient Quality–Based Standards

Congress has avoided selecting risk- or ambient quality–based statutory standards in most of the risk regulation statutes. The 1958 Delaney Clause and the 1996 amendments to the FDCA, relating to pesticide residues in food, are the only important such regimes. Both the Delaney Clause and the 1996 FDCA amendments contain a no-threshold statutory trigger. As described earlier, the Delaney Clause requires the FDA to ban any color or food additive that causes cancer in animals or humans, regardless of whether the substance poses a cancer risk that is above some threshold.[29] For this reason, critics have picked out the Delaney Clause as the prime example of regulation that goes too far in regulating risk.[30] Congress reacted in 1996 by amending the clause to establish a risk-based standard for the regulation of pesticide residues in food. The amendment, also described earlier, authorizes EPA to permit pesticide residues in food as long as there is a reasonable certainty that no harm will result from aggregate exposure to these residues.[31] At first glance, the CAA's national ambient air-quality standard program appears to represent another example of a risk- or ambient quality–based statutory standard. We believe, however, that for purposes of our categorization scheme, it is more appropriate to place the NAAQS in the category of an open-ended balancing mechanism, because the NAAQS themselves are not self-implementing in the sense that they do not impose enforceable obligations on individual sources of air pollution. Rather, the states are responsible for adopting the individually enforceable controls necessary to achieve the NAAQS through state implementation plans, and the states may consider an open-ended array of factors, including cost, in adopting such controls.[32]

At one time, the CAA also relied on risk-based standards in regulating hazardous air pollutants. The pre-1990 CAA authorized EPA to establish emission standards for all hazardous air pollutants, defined as those that cause or contribute to air pollution which may reasonably be anticipated to result in mortality or serious illness.[33] Each national emission standard for hazardous air pollutants (NESHAP) had to be set at the level which, in the Administrator's judgment, "provides an ample margin of safety to protect the public health from such hazardous air pollutant."[34] In 1990, Congress replaced this approach with constrained-balancing,[35] because EPA had adopted NESHAPs for only eight pollutants in twenty years.[36]

Phaseout

Congress has generally avoided product or substance phaseouts. Only two examples could be found among the risk regulation statutes we surveyed, ozone-depleting substances and PCBs.[37] The first of these is tied to a risk-based threshold. The 1990 CAA amendments adopted a series of prohibitions on the production and consumption of chemicals that either Congress or EPA has determined to be harmful or to create a risk of harm to the stratospheric ozone layer.[38] The other phased-in prohibition, which contains an unreasonable risk threshold, applies to the manufacture, processing, distribution, and use of polychlorinated biphenyls (PCBs),[39] a chemical that is widely recognized as harmful to individuals and the environment.[40]

Constrained Balancing

Most legislation protecting humans and the environment involves constrained balancing, and almost all of the rest requires open-ended balancing. The regulation of point sources of pollution under the CWA occurs under constrained balancing.[41] So does regulation under the CAA of pollution located in attainment[42] and nonattainment[43] areas, and of pollution produced by select major new or modified stationary[44] and select mobile[45] sources (such as cars and trucks). EPA also uses constrained balancing to establish emissions standards for hazardous air pollutants,[46] and to regulate activities that threaten to contaminate drinking water under the SDWA,[47] land disposal of hazardous wastes under the Resource Conservation and Recovery Act (RCRA),[48] and the manufacture, distribution, and use of toxic chemicals under the Toxic Substances Control Act (TSCA).[49] Regulation of workplace health and safety by OSHA[50] and of automobile safety by the National Highway Traffic Safety Administration (NHTSA)[51] likewise involves constrained balancing. A significant number of other examples exist, but are not included for the sake of brevity.

The statutory triggers used in the legislation that relies on constrained balancing vary, but all except the CWA require some threshold finding. NHTSA regulation[52] and EPA regulation under TSCA[53] must be based on satisfaction of an unreasonable risk threshold, while the hazardous air pollutant provisions of the CAA,[54] the OSH Act,[55] the SDWA,[56] and RCRA[57] require a finding of either risk- or significant risk. Moreover, although the CWA legislation appears to lack a risk threshold, EPA policies have created one.[58] Thus most legislation involves a requirement of risk or significant risk.

Open-Ended Balancing

Congress has employed open-ended balancing for four areas of environmental and health regulation. The CWA requires states to set ambient water quality standards for all water bodies within their jurisdiction according to a mix of economic and environmental considerations. The statute provides no guidance concerning what weights to assign to any of the relevant factors.[59] Similarly, when states adopt plans (called SIPs) to regulate so-called criteria pollutants under the CAA,[60] they can choose the mix of emission controls, and, in making these choices, weigh economic considerations to whatever extent they deem proper.[61] EPA also engages in open-ended balancing under the Comprehensive Environmental Response, Compensation and Liability Act (CERCLA), also known as the Superfund law, because EPA must consider a variety of factors (such as cost-effectiveness and adequacy of public health and environmental protection), none of which are weighted in the statute.[62] EPA is in the same position regarding the regulation of pesticides under the FIFRA.[63]

Congress's choice of triggers in this category resembles the choices made in the statutes that require constrained balancing. Except for the CWA, Congress requires some type of threshold finding, and as noted earlier, EPA policies require a risk finding for the CWA.[64] There is an unreasonable risk trigger for FIFRA[65] and a risk-based trigger for the CAA[66] and CERCLA.[67]

Cost-Benefit Balancing

In all of risk regulation, only two statutes utilize a statutory standard of cost-benefit balancing, and both have an unreasonable risk trigger. The CPSC regulates the safety of consumer products[68] under a regime that requires that the agency demonstrate a reasonable relationship between regulatory costs and benefits. The pipeline regulation statute goes further, representing the only example of a mandatory marginal cost-benefit analysis standard.[69] The Department of Transportation regulates the safety of pipelines and pipeline facilities under a 1996 statute that replaced an earlier open-ended balancing standard for pipeline safety[70] with a cost-benefit standard.[71]

Summary

Once the entire pattern of risk regulation is considered, it is evident that Congress generally prefers a statutory trigger requiring evidence of risk or significant risk and a statutory standard that involves constrained or open-ended balancing. Sixteen of the twenty-two laws (or parts of laws) covered by Table 3.1 fit within these two choices, far more than in any other category.

It is also apparent that Congress has avoided the most extreme combinations available to it. There are only two statutes that fit in the uppermost left-hand box, which is the combination that imposes the least restrictive evidentiary burden on an agency. Likewise, there are only two statutes that fit in the lowermost right-hand box, which is the combination that imposes the most restrictive evidentiary burden on an agency, and only one of those requires proof that regulatory benefits will exceed costs as the ultimate standard for regulation.

Finally, it is noticeable that Congress generally requires an agency to take costs into account in establishing the level of regulation. Congress has authorized regulation without regard to the level of costs in only two of the twenty-two laws depicted in Table 3.1. Even laws such as the 1990 CAA amendments, which phase out the use of ozone-depleting substances, implicitly take cost into account by delaying the effective date of the ban by as much as forty years.

Conclusion

The two hallmarks of the structure of risk regulation are statutory triggers that authorize regulation on the basis of a reduced burden of proof and the rejection of a cost-benefit standard as the method to establish the level of regulation. Nevertheless, Congress has required agencies to take costs into account, although not in the manner that a cost-benefit standard would require.

As we have mentioned, many critics of risk regulation object to both the statutory triggers and standards that Congress employs. They would prefer statutory triggers that increase the level of evidence that an agency must have before it can regulate (by, for example, demanding proof of the unreasonableness of a targeted risk), and they would adopt a cost-benefit test to establish the level of regulation. For many critics, the objective is to move the existing structure down and to the right in the grid reflected in Table 3.1. We take the position that the current pattern of regulation is more pragmatic (as measured by the characteristics described in the previous chapter) than the one the critics prefer, and particularly, than one that relies on a cost-benefit statutory standard. The next two chapters defend the current structure of risk regulation on the basis of the pragmatic principles identified in Chapter 2.

Not all critics of risk regulation argue that the level of regulation should be based on a cost-benefit standard. They would retain the existing laws, but would expand the use of regulatory analysis, including cost-benefit analysis, as a prerequisite to regulation. We analyze that recommendation in Chapter 7.

4

The Rationale for Risk Regulation

Congress has almost always rejected a cost-benefit test as a regulatory trigger or regulatory standard in risk reduction legislation. Those who are critical of this pattern depend on economic theory to justify their preference for greater reliance on a cost-benefit test in triggering regulation or in setting the level of regulation. Alternatively, they support the use of cost-benefit analysis to analyze regulation before it is promulgated, even though regulators determine the level of regulation based on some other form of balancing or other standard. The equation of costs and benefits can be defended according to standard economic principles. By comparison, the rationale for risk regulation, as constituted by Congress, is not as obvious.

Pragmatic principles furnish this missing rationale. The current structure is pragmatic because, in comparison to a cost-benefit approach, it better reconciles important social values implicated by risk reduction. As Chapter 2 discussed, pragmatism requires the accommodation of important, widely held social values in risk regulation. The current structure is also more pragmatic than a cost-benefit standard because it better reconciles the bounded rationality of regulators with the goals of risk regulation. As Chapter 2 also discussed, pragmatism requires that the design of risk regulation take bounded rationality into account.

Regulatory Justifications

We begin by comparing the economic and pragmatic justifications for risk regulation. Pragmatic analysis reveals that a purely economic approach to risk regulation threatens two widely held social goals, which pragmatism attempts to accommodate. Risk legislation respects the integrity of human life and the

environment by refusing to view such protection solely in terms of the estimated dollar value of the protection. Current laws also reject the idea that the
amount of protection to which a person is entitled should be a function of the
person's wealth. At the same time, current laws also recognize that cost
should be an important consideration in regulatory policy. Accommodation
of these multiple goals is no easy matter, but the fact that current legislation
attempts to do so is what makes it pragmatic.

Economic Justification

The efficient operation of markets requires that those whose actions
injure humans or the environment take such costs into account when they
act. For example, if a chemical manufacturer does not pay for the environmental damage to nearby land that results from a manufacturing process, the
chemical will sell at a price that does not fully reflect its production costs. The
chemical will be priced too low, because one of the costs of production, environmental damage, is a cost that is external to the producer. Economic analysts describe such injuries as "externalities"—because the costs are not part
of the "internal" costs that the manufacturer must take into account in making its production decisions—or as "spillover costs"—because the costs spill
over to the persons who own the land damaged by the manufacturing process. If the manufacturer paid for the environmental damage, the price of the
chemical would be higher and, unless demand was completely inelastic, less
of it would be sold. The additional production of the chemical resulting from
a failure to internalize environmental costs is inefficient because it consumes
resources, such as raw materials and labor, that would be put to other uses
better matched to consumer preferences if the chemical were properly priced.

Until Ronald Coase published his famous article "The Problem of Social
Cost,"[1] economic analysts assumed that government intervention would be
necessary to require producers, such as the chemical manufacturer, to pay for
the damage caused by their activities. They favored taxing firms based on the
monetary value of the damage done to the environment. Professor Coase,
however, posited that, even absent the imposition of a tax, a free market exchange could result in the same reduction in pollution as the tax plan. Coase
pointed out that the neighbors of the factory had an incentive to pay it to reduce the environmental damage to their land. The amount that the neighbors

are willing to pay depends on the extent to which the pollution damages their land, which (in theory) is the same amount as the tax the government would assess if taxes were used to address this problem. The manufacturer is willing to reduce the level of pollution up to the point where the costs of doing so are greater than the payments it will receive from the neighbors.

Professor Coase acknowledged that this result required that no significant economic impediments prevent the neighbors from negotiating with the chemical manufacturer. When such "transaction costs" are present, they can prevent the negotiations from taking place or alter their outcome. This would occur, for example, if the manufacturing process damaged land owned by thousands of people because it would be prohibitively expensive, if not practically impossible, for all of the individuals experiencing harm to agree on the appropriate approach to negotiating with the manufacturer. When transaction costs have this impact, government intervention may be necessary to obtain an "efficient" outcome.

When the government intervenes, its goal is to replicate the result that would have occurred if the bargaining between the company and its neighbors had occurred in the absence of transaction costs. The government can do this by using a cost-benefit standard to establish the level of regulation. The amount of money that the neighbors are willing to pay to the manufacturer to reduce the environmental damage depends on the value of undamaged land to them. This is the "benefit" in a cost-benefit standard. The manufacturer's willingness to reduce the environmental damage is a function of the cost to it of reducing the damage. This is the "cost" in a cost-benefit standard. The manufacturer will reduce the environmental damage up to the point where the cost of any further reduction exceeds the amount of money that the neighbors are willing to pay. The government can replicate this result by requiring a reduction in environmental damage up to the point where the costs and benefits of such an action are equated.

Professor Coase supported this utilitarian approach by his insistence that there is no objective economic basis for blaming anyone for pollution or similar externalities. Although economists before Coase had identified the polluter as the source of the externality, he argued that the problem was "reciprocal" because the neighbors could equally be "blamed" for causing the externality. In this alternative view, the neighbors' demand for less pollution is an externality that the neighborhood imposes on the factory. Thus, the "problem we face in dealing with actions which have harmful effects," Coase argued, "is not simply one of restraining those responsible for them." Rather, "[w]hat has to be decided is whether the gain from preventing the harm is greater than the loss which [will] be suffered elsewhere as a result of stopping the action which produces the harm."[2]

Because economic theory eschews assessing blame for pollution and other externalities, it is the existence of transaction costs that justifies government action. The government intervenes because the market fails to achieve an "efficient" level of production. The government does not intervene because injury to the environment, or humans, is somehow "wrong." Instead, injuries to humans and the environment are simply production costs, and the goal is to achieve the "optimal" or most efficient level of human and environmental injury.

Pragmatic Justification

Economic theory seeks to maximize economic efficiency, and it would sanction government regulation if unregulated markets fail to produce an economically efficient level of harm to individuals or the environment. Unlike an economic approach, which focuses only on economic efficiency, risk regulation accommodates three widely held social values as presently constituted. While economic theory treats human life or the environment as merely a factor of production no different than any other factor of production, risk legislation respects the extraordinary value that many individuals attach to human life and the environment by refusing to view such protection only in terms of the estimated dollar value of the protection. Current laws also reject the idea that the amount of protection to which a person is entitled should be a function of the person's wealth, but without giving absolute protection to individuals. Thus, unlike an economic approach, current risk legislation does not deny protection to people because they cannot afford to pay for it. At the same time, because current laws take regulatory costs into consideration, risk legislation does not abandon the goal of economic development.

Extraordinary Value

Many people are troubled by the manner in which economic theory regards injuries to humans and the environment as simply production costs that are no different, in any fundamental sense, from the monetary cost to corporations of avoiding individual and environmental harm. For many, there is nothing admirable in the economic goal of seeking the "optimal" or most efficient level of human and environmental destruction. These reactions arise from society's commitment to individual and environmental integrity. In this section, we examine this commitment and explain how current risk legislation honors it.

Individuals

Utilitarianism diminishes the status of individuals, Christopher Schroeder explains, because anyone's claim to protection against technological risk can be overcome by society's pursuit of collective goals.[3] Since individuals can justifiably be inflicted with ever greater levels of risk in conjunction with increasing economic gains, Professor Schroeder finds that utilitarianism "ultimately denies each individual a primary place in its system of values." Thus, utilitarianism "obscures and diminishes the status of each individual" because it "reduces the individual to a conduit, a reference point that registers the appropriate 'utiles' but does not count for anything independent of his monitoring function." In the end, the individual's status under utilitarianism is preserved only so long as that status contributes to increasing total utility. When the individual no longer has that value, he or she can be "discarded." As a result, Professor Schroeder concludes, opposition to utilitarianism arises out of a desire to preserve "some fundamental place" that cannot be overrun by larger social considerations.

While regulation should preserve the extraordinary value of individuals, it is not socially possible to protect individuals against the imposition of all risks of injury or disease. A system of risk regulation that holds everyone harmless from technological risks would end economic development and the social wealth that it creates. Thus, while society has an important interest in protecting individuals, it also has an important interest in promoting economic and technological development. As Professor Schroeder concludes, what is necessary is a "nonabsolutist understanding of risk [that] preserve[s] the essential moral insight that individuals matter as autonomous moral agents worthy of respect."[4]

The Environment

The utilitarian character of establishing the level of regulation based on a cost-benefit test is inconsistent with recognizing the extraordinary value of humans. A similar problem arises concerning the protection of the environment. Environmental protection, like protection of human beings, has extraordinary value for many people. They believe that natural entities deserve to be the object of our moral concern irrespective of their use or value to us in meeting our day-to-day needs. For some, this innate value is to be preserved at all costs. In Aldo Leopold's famous statement of environmental responsibility: "A thing is right when it tends to preserve the integrity, stability, and beauty of the biotic community. It is wrong when it tends otherwise."[5]

Yet absolutism in behalf of the environment poses the same problem as absolutism in behalf of individuals: it fails to account for the consideration of other values that are impacted by efforts to protect the environment. What is necessary then is a nonabsolutist understanding of risk that preserves the essential moral insight that nature is worthy of our respect regardless of the value of natural resources for purposes of commerce.

Pragmatic Balancing

The pattern of risk regulation identified in Chapter 3 addresses the challenge of respecting the innate value of human life and of the environment in a non-absolutist manner. This is accomplished in two ways. The pattern reflects a goal of "doing the best we can" to protect individuals and the environment, and the goal is achieved without commodifying the value of individuals and the environment in order to determine the level of regulatory protection.

Do The Best We Can

Risk regulation balances the interests of risk creators and risk bearers, but not in the manner indicated by economic theory. As Chapter 3 discussed,

Congress has generally permitted regulation on the basis of a risk trigger that permits agency action on the basis of risk predictions, rather than requiring conclusive proof that harm will necessarily occur. Thus current risk laws respect the innate value of human life and of the environment by adopting evidentiary standards that make it easier for agencies to engage in protective actions. Moreover, as the last chapter explained, most risk regulation occurs under a constrained or open-ended balancing standard that allows regulation in instances in which a cost-benefit standard may not, or to a degree beyond that produced by a cost-benefit standard. Such statutes thus reflect an affirmative commitment to protecting humans and the environment. This commitment respects the innate value of human life and of the environment because it makes such protection a priority.

Although protection of individuals and the environment is a priority, costs are not ignored. With the four exceptions listed in the two left-most columns in Table 3.1, risk reduction laws require agencies to engage in some form of balancing of the costs of regulation (that is, the interests of risk creators) and the benefits of risk reduction (the interests of risk bearers). Moreover, as the last chapter indicates, even the phaseout of a toxic substance takes costs into account by creating exceptions, or by adopting a long period for the phaseout.

In this manner, current laws usually commit the country to "do the best that it can" to reduce human and environmental injury.[6] Under constrained balancing, for example, regulation is to occur, but only up to the point at which costs are disruptive or extraordinary. Congress normally identifies that point by requiring industry to limit its spillover effects to the level achievable through the use of some aspirational technology, such as "best technology economically achievable" or the technology capable of producing the "lowest achievable emission rate." Typically, Congress also requires regulators to consider the economic impact of achieving this level of performance along with other factors that may legitimately affect the regulatory entity's decision. "Congress has, in other words, announced to the world: 'If we cannot have a perfectly clean workplace and environment, then we shall do the best that we can.'"[7] Sometimes this commitment extends to forcing regulated entities to develop more effective technologies than those currently in use as a means of achieving desirable levels of risk reduction.[8]

OSHA's mandate is a good illustration of the ethical difference between the economic approach and Congress's commitment to "do the best that we can." As discussed in Chapter 3, Congress has said that OSHA must promulgate regulations that protect workers "to the extent feasible" from the harmful effects of toxic substances.[9] Under OSHA's mandate, a standard is technologically infeasible when it requires protective devices that are not generally available under existing technology. A standard is economically infeasible when regulation threatens the long-term profitability and competitiveness of regulated industries. A standard is not economically infeasible simply because it is financially burdensome or adversely affects profit margins.

Critics of risk regulation have criticized OSHA's mandate because it might be less expensive to compensate employees for occupational injuries or diseases in some cases than to spend money to prevent them. This argument, however, ignores the crucial ethical distinction between preventing fatalities or injuries and compensating the victim or his or her family for a death or disability. Protecting workers under a constrained balancing test may be somewhat more costly to society than after-the-fact compensation, because OSHA may act on incomplete information that overstates the degree of risk. This tilt in favor of protecting workers, however, respects the fundamental value of their lives. It aspires to something more than obtaining the "optimal" level of worker illnesses.

The same regard for human life is found in open-ended balancing. First, although an agency is required to balance costs and benefits, it is not required to equate them. Thus the agency is not committed to seeking an optimal allocation of injury to humans or the environment. Instead, the agency is free to protect individuals or the environment to an extent that exceeds the level of protection that a cost-benefit standard would provide if the agency determines that, in the particular circumstances, factors other than cost justify the higher protective level. Although this objective is not the same as a commitment to seek the greatest available protection, it still authorizes agencies to protect individuals or the environment in situations in which a cost-benefit standard may block, or at least weaken, such protection.

Second, an agency that operates under open-ended balancing is authorized to regulate even if it lacks sufficient information to quantify all benefits and ensure that they exceed costs. This tilts regulation in favor of protecting humans and the environment for a reason discussed later in this chapter. Because a cost-benefit standard requires more quantification of regulatory benefits than an open-ended balancing test, agencies will have greater difficulty defending their regulatory decisions when they are challenged in court. This difficulty hampers regulation and makes it less protective of humans or the environment. Finally, as discussed next, both constrained and open-ended balancing avoid commodification or the treatment of humans and the environment as commodities—"things" that people are willing to buy and sell.

Commodification

Prevailing methods of risk regulation respect the innate value of life and the environment in a second important way. They avoid what Margaret Jane Radin has described as "universal commodification."[10] In universal commodification, Professor Radin explains, "all things desired or valued—from personal attributes to good government—are commodities," and all social interaction is conceived of as free market exchanges. "In market rhetoric, under the discourse of commodification, one conceives of human attributes (properties of persons) as fungible with owned objects (the property of persons)."[11]

Cost-benefit analysis employs universal commodification because it "evaluates all human actions and outcomes in terms of actual or hypothetical gains from trade, measured in money."[12] In other words, a cost-benefit standard reduces all values to sums of money. Professor Radin identifies why, except for the deepest enthusiast of market rhetoric, this type of commodification "seems intuitively out of place" regarding most social policy:

> One basis for this intuition is that market rhetoric conceives of bodily integrity as a fungible object. A fungible object can pass in and out of the person's possession without effect on the person so long as its market equivalent is given in exchange; trading commodified objects is just like trading money. To speak of personal attributes as fungible objects—alienable goods—seems intuitively wrong to many people, because they do not conceive of bodily integrity as commodified. . . . Bodily integrity is an attribute and not an object. The effect of "detaching" it from the person is non-monetizable. We feel discomfort or even insult, and we fear degradation or even loss of the value involved, when bodily integrity is conceived of as a fungible object.[13]

For Professor Radin, "the way we conceive of things matters to who we are."[14]

Pragmatism takes this concern seriously. Because it focuses on the actual effects of social policies, pragmatism recognizes that "law, even if it begins as an instrument for the attainment of basic ends . . . can generate its own intrinsic values."[15] As Thomas Grey reminds us, "Dewey well understood this; that a good system of law was partly constitutive of, not merely instrumental to, a good society."[16]

The pattern of risk legislation identified in Chapter 3 respects the innate value of human life by refusing to treat human attributes—injury and death—as fungible with owned objects—the cost of abating risks. It does not reduce all values to money. Although the legislation does not ignore the cost of reducing risks, it conceives of the process of balancing risks and the costs of reducing them in other than market terms, and it thereby fosters the nonmarket significance of human life or the environment.

Equity

The current approach to risk regulation, unlike a cost-benefit standard, recognizes and seeks to protect the extraordinary value of life and the environment. Current laws are more consistent than a cost-benefit standard with another widely held social value. As a cost-benefit standard is usually employed, it bases the level of protection on a person's wealth. It therefore raises issues of justice and equity that the current system can avoid or minimize.

Economics and Equity

The agnostic position of economists concerning the distribution of wealth is related to Ronald Coase's article, discussed earlier. Professor Coase declared his indifference from the perspective of efficient resource allocation between two potential property rules. One rule gives a factory the legal right to pollute, while the other rule would give landowners adversely affected by the pollution the legal authority to stop the factory from polluting their land. Coase was indifferent because he assumed that the neighbors' "offer" price if the first rule were in effect would be identical to their "asking" price if the second rule were in effect. The "offer" price is the price that the neighbors would offer to the factory to reduce its pollution, which is based on the economic impact of the pollution on their property (or their health). If a reduction from 100 to 50 units of pollution would increase the value of the neighbors' land by $100,000, for example, they would be willing to pay the factory up to $100,000 to halve the pollution. The "asking" price is the price that the neighbors would demand to permit the factory to increase its pollution if they had the legal right to stop the factory from polluting. The neighbors would be willing to sell to the factory the right to increase its pollution from 50 to 100 units for $100,000, because that would allow them to recoup the money they will lose because of the decreased value of their land. When the neighbors and the factory bargain to shift the allocation of the legal right as initially provided by law, the result will be the same under either rule because the neighbors' offer and asking prices are the same.

Reliance on "willingness to pay" might provide a neutral method of measuring the costs and benefits of pollution if the offer and asking prices were identical, as Coase assumed for purposes of his article. The distribution of wealth that occurs in the real world, however, causes the two measures to diverge. A person's wealth will limit the amount that he or she can pay to purchase the right to be safe (or to reduce harm to the environment). For example, two economists, Marin and Psacharopoulos, found that the best estimate of the value of a life using the willingness to pay criterion was £0.619–0.686 million for manual workers and £2.245–2.259 million for nonmanual workers.[17] A person's wealth, by comparison, does not limit his or her "asking" price in the same manner. A poor person can demand the same amount of money to sell the right to be safe (or have the environment degraded) as a rich person.

A "willingness to pay" measurement of regulatory benefits biases a cost-benefit standard in favor of less protection because it ignores the impact of a person's wealth. A memorandum written by Lawrence Summers, then chief economist of the World Bank, vividly makes this point. Summers explained that economic analysis favors the relocation of polluting industries to the Third World. The relocation was advisable because the pollution would cause less harm in less developed countries. The pollution would make an equal number of persons ill, but, according to an economic measurement of the harm, lost earnings from morbidity and mortality would be less. In other words, because those who became ill and died would be poor, pollution would cause them less harm, as measured by their loss of income from illness and death, than it would to adversely affected individuals in the developed world. Thus, Summers concluded, the "economic logic behind dumping a load of toxic waste in the lowest-wage country is impeccable."[18]

Closer to home, economists suggest that when administrative agencies regulate risks that impact persons who are wealthier, they should use a higher economic value for each life saved. Kip Viscusi, for example, explains: "Whereas the average worker . . . has an implicit value of $4.1 million, for the income level of a typical airline passenger that value would be $5.7 million."[19] Viscusi therefore recommends that the Department of Transportation use a higher monetary value for calculating the potential loss of life from an airline crash than OSHA should use to calculate the potential loss of value from a workplace accident.

Pragmatism and Equity

Adoption of a cost-benefit standard to establish the level of regulation would generally require the measurement of regulatory benefits on the basis of an individual's willingness to pay for individual and environmental protection. The impact of wealth could be avoided if analysts measured regulatory benefits according to a "willingness to sell" measurement, but analysts generally lack reliable data concerning an individual's "willingness to pay" for individual or environmental protection. The problem is that there are few, if any, actual market transactions in which a polluter or similar entity must pay for the right to expose individuals or the environment to harm. Some analysts have attempted to overcome this limitation by relying on "contingent valuation" to measure the "willingness to sell," but that methodology is unreliable and controversial, as Chapter 5 will discuss.

Existing laws avoid the equity problem created by use of a cost-benefit standard to establish the level of regulation. For one thing, current regulation is not based on a measurement of benefits that is subject to wealth effects. Regulation under constrained balancing does not require the measurement of regulatory benefits. Instead, the outcome is tied to some existing or aspirational technology, such as "best available technology economically achievable" or the technology capable of producing the "lowest achievable emission rate," which may sometimes be adjusted in light of additional factors. Since regulators are not required to quantify the benefits of regulation in open-ended balancing, they can make adjustments for how wealth effects may bias efforts to measure benefits. For example, regulators can protect low-income populations in circumstances in which a health or safety measure would not pass a cost-benefit test because the affected persons cannot afford to pay more for an increased level of health or safety.

In addition, current regulatory standards make it possible to protect specific vulnerable populations. Both Congress and the risk regulatory agencies have taken steps to protect even the most susceptible individuals against environmental risk. For example, the 1996 amendments to the Food, Drug and Cosmetic Act (FDCA) require the Environmental Protection Agency (EPA) to provide an additional tenfold margin of safety in setting tolerance levels for pesticide residues in food as a means of taking into account the special susceptibilities of infants and children.[20] In establishing air quality standards under the CAA, EPA is obliged to "protect not only average healthy individuals, but also 'sensitive citizens'—children, for example, or people with asthma, emphysema, or other conditions rendering them particularly vulnerable to air pollution."[21] Likewise, EPA has adopted standards under other statutes that were designed to protect even the most sensitive segments of exposed populations.[22]

The current approach to risk regulation is also more protective of the interests of the potentially affected entities least able to protect themselves. These include future generations, whose interests may not be reflected at all in the valuation methodologies employed under an economic approach, as we explain in the next chapter. The current approach also enables protection of the politically as well as economically powerless low-income and minority groups. Open-ended balancing in particular leaves room for the agency contemplating the appropriate level of protection to consider (as one factor among many) the value of leaving the current generation's resource base intact for the benefit of future generations.

Cost-Benefit Defenses

Critics of risk regulation offer several responses to these objections to basing risk regulation on a cost-benefit standard. These answers, however, do not save a cost-benefit standard from the objections we have identified.

Altruism and Economic Value

A cost-benefit standard would measure the benefits of protecting individuals and the environment based on the willingness of individuals to pay for such protection in market settings. Supporters of this approach contend that such market prices reflect both an individual's self-interested and altruistic concerns. The neighbors in the hypothetical posited earlier in this chapter, for example, may be willing to pay the factory to reduce its pollution out of an altruistic concern for the environment or for animals that frequent their property. Thus the supporters dispute that a cost-benefit approach is inconsistent with other social values. To the extent that individuals are willing to pay to protect and promote such values, a cost-benefit test will reflect them.

This response, however, does not recognize protection of individuals or the environment as having extraordinary value because it still reduces such altruistic goals to market terms. For the same reason, the problem of commodification still exists. Using private values (revealed by market transactions) as the basis for public policy also ignores the impact of wealth on private choices. Individuals can give only as much protection to individuals or the environment as they can afford to pay for.

This response also assumes that there is no difference between the price people pay for things in private markets and the value they wish those same things to be assigned in public decisions. But, as Steven Kelman argues, "social decisions provide an opportunity to give things a higher valuation than we choose, for one reason or another, to give them in our private activities."[23] As consumers, we may dislike paying more for manufactured products because of the costs of protecting individuals or the environment, but as citizens we can rationally vote for outcomes that are costly and (by the economist's "willingness to pay" measure) irrational. Put another way, citizens have the opportunity in social decisions to establish a difference between private behavior and public responsibility. In Mark Sagoff's words, "We act as consumers to get what we want for ourselves. We act as citizens to achieve what we think is right or best for the community."[24] Sagoff is not the only one to recognize that individuals may have distinct and conflicting preferences in their roles as consumers and citizens. Several economic analysts have suggested that because individuals may have multiple preference orderings, they apply different preferences in different contexts.[25]

Reliance on private values to govern public decisions ignores another important aspect of social decision-making. Because this approach takes individual preferences as given, it ignores the potential for deliberation and debate to change individual preferences. By comparison, Dewey's conception of democracy as composed of critical communities of inquiry, discussed in Chapter 2, requires debate and deliberation. Similarly, as proponents of the civic republican conception of government remind us, public decisions should be regarded as valid only if they are related to public values, and public values are discovered through deliberation. Thus, for civic republicans, "government's primary responsibility is to enable the citizenry to deliberate about altering preferences and to reach consensus on the common good."[26] If public policy is based on private values, this opportunity is diminished, if not lost. By comparison, because political preferences involve opinions and beliefs, which may be true or false, "we may meaningfully ask the individual for the reasons that he or she holds them."[27]

Choices about tradeoffs between costs and benefits are made in risk legislation through public deliberation. In constrained balancing, Congress has made some tradeoffs, and agencies make additional decisions. In open-ended balancing, agencies make the tradeoffs. Some proponents of a cost-benefit standard misunderstand this advantage of risk legislation. They favor a cost-benefit approach on the grounds that it will better stimulate public debate about the tradeoff between cost and protection.[28] According to them, public deliberation will be improved through adoption of economic analysis as the test for regulation because a cost-benefit standard identifies the tradeoffs between technology and risk. But so does the existing legislation. Moreover, the cost-benefit framework makes it more difficult to debate public policy. As we elaborate at the end of this chapter, policy debates that take place under a cost-benefit standard revolve around economic estimates of costs and benefits. This orientation gives the upper hand to economic analysts and discourages noneconomic input. By comparison, existing legislation invites and facilitates input from all comers regardless of discipline or orientation. Risk legislation has this inclusive effect because it is based on logical reasoning and argument, rather than quantification and commodification.

Voluntary Choices

Critics of risk regulation favor a cost-benefit standard, despite the impact of wealth on the level of protection, because they regard market transactions as being based on voluntary choices. In economic theory, a person will enter into a market transaction only if it is beneficial for him or her to do so. Under this assumption, the results of market transactions concerning risk reduction accurately indicate the value that persons put on achieving more protection. Thus the higher value that richer persons put on risk reduction is simply a function of individual choice. Recall, for example, the finding of Marin and Psacharopoulos that the best estimate of the value of a life using the willingness to pay criteria was £0.619–0.686 million for manual workers and £2.245–2.259 million for nonmanual workers. Kip Viscusi surmises, without the benefit of empirical evidence, that the reason for this disparity is that "those prepared to work in exceptionally risky jobs may well have a lower dislike of danger and hence require less of a wage premium to compensate them more than average workers."[29]

Professor Frank Knight, founder of the Chicago School of Economics, has expressed a more famous version of the same thought. He once observed that the distinction between laborers and the owners of companies is that laborers have freely elected to risk their health and safety, whereas the owners have chosen instead to risk their capital.[30] As if to underscore Knight's claim, Professor Viscusi entitled his book on occupational safety *Risk by Choice*. Viscusi explains:

> Those individuals who are least adverse to [safety] risks are willing to accept a lower compensation per unit of risk than the rest of the working population. As a result, they are inclined to accept larger risks with lower wage premiums per unit of risk. . . . Those who price their life the cheapest are drawn into the market first; higher wages must be paid to lure additional workers into risky jobs.[31]

This explanation, of course, completely ignores the lack of choice of many poor workers, who accept riskier jobs because they lack the training and education to compete for safer ones. Not surprisingly, Professor James Robinson has found that hazardous employment pays 20 to 30 percent less than safe employment because persons with education and training will avoid the less safe jobs. According to Robinson, the labor pool for hazardous jobs therefore consists of "disadvantaged workers who are willing to accept health and safety risks in return for very modest amounts of compensation."[32]

Supporters of a cost-benefit standard elevate theory over reality. Pragmatic public policy, however, should not make the same mistake. First, wealth disparity exists, and pragmatism insists on creating public policies that reflect actual conditions. Second, in a country that holds equality of opportunity as a primary value, public policy ought not accept that safety should be a function of a person's wealth.

Efficiency as the Dominant Policy Value

While economic analysts concede that wealth disparities sometimes require government intervention, they normally would restrict those circumstances to a few narrow exceptions, such as selling votes and human beings.[33] They are reluctant to sanction the use of regulation to serve social values, such as equality of opportunity, because they see it as reducing economic efficiency. The title of Arthur Oken's book, *Equality and Efficiency: The Big Trade-Off*,[34] captures the economists' viewpoint. Peter Asch offers the following explanation:

> We cannot claim that even a perfectly efficient market is perfectly fair; and safety regulation might be supported on "equity" grounds even though the efficacy of affected markets is beyond reproach. What economists point out, however, is that even a patently unfair market does not argue against economic efficiency. Those who are "done dirty" by the system are not likely to be helped by rendering the system more wasteful. The venerable analogy is to the economic "pie." Efficiency maximizes the size of the pie. An unfair economy might give Ms. Jones too small a slice, but she is unlikely to be helped by inefficient policies that reduce the pie size.[35]

Asch's complaint is that society as a whole will be somewhat poorer if government pursues inefficient policies. Assuming there is an efficiency loss, the size of loss occasioned by particular regulatory programs and initiatives becomes crucial. The supporters of a cost-benefit standard argue that the losses are often quite large, which Chapter 5 disputes. For now, we acknowledge that voters (and their representatives) need to know the size of any efficiency losses, because they must decide whether the gains in fairness and equity are worth the loss in wealth. But this is a pragmatic analysis. It acknowledges that public policy may be supported by multiple social values, and it inquires what tradeoffs exist between or among those values. In Chapter 7 we support the sensible use of cost-benefit analysis to inform regulators, legislators, and the public about potential efficiency loses, but not as the governing regulatory standard.

A cost-benefit standard, as previously noted, will provide less protection for individuals than existing legislation. Nevertheless, economic analysts are content with the outcome, even though those who gain from less regulation do not compensate those who are worse off because of less protection. Consider, for example, John Mendeloff's comments:

> Those who die because society rejects inefficient lifesaving programs will not be around to benefit from the bigger pie. Does this fact require condemnation of any policy that stops short of a maximum effort to prevent deaths? No. It is inevitable that public policy will create losers who are beyond the reach of compensation. But this fact should spur thinking about who the losers are and how we feel about their plight.[36]

To begin with, Mendeloff's comments establish a false choice. Rejection of the economic justification for risk regulation does not necessitate "a maximum effort to prevent deaths." Current methods of risk regulation typically stop well short of a cost-oblivious blitzkrieg against risk-creating activities. Furthermore, unlike Mendeloff and other analysts, who consider distributional considerations to be beyond their bailiwick, pragmatism cannot ignore these impacts because it looks at the actual outcomes of social policy. In light of pragmatism's commitment to reflect important social values, the issue of "who the losers are and how we feel about their plight" is not something that should be set aside in the design of risk policy.

Preference for Fiscal Policies

Other critics of risk regulation acknowledge the distributional impacts of regulatory choices, but they still favor a cost-benefit standard in risk regulation. Instead of importing distributional concerns into risk policy, they would address these issues separately through fiscal policy, such as a pollution tax.[37] The proceeds from such a tax can be used to compensate those persons who bear the consequences of risks that are not prevented. As noted earlier, however, there is an important difference between compensating people for the illnesses and injuries they suffer as a result of externalities and pre-venting them in the first place. Moreover, although a tax-based approach might be a desirable policy in an ideal political world, there is little chance that it would happen in the real one we inhabit, which considers taxes, let alone redistribution (that is, welfare), as a political anathema.

Statistical Lives

Finally, supporters of a cost-benefit standard use the concept of "sta-tistical lives" to deflect criticism that this method of setting the level of regu-lation does not respect the intrinsic value of life. Professor Viscusi explains that economic analysts use the term "statistical lives" because regulatory ac-tion reduces the risk that someone will die, rather than protecting any identi-fiable person from a preventable death. He acknowledges that society does not condition the rescue of a child who falls down a well, or a man who is trapped under a collapsed freeway after an earthquake, on a positive cost-benefit ratio. He argues, however, that the situation is different when large numbers of people are exposed to small risks. Because the beneficiaries of risk reduction are not identified in risk regulation, Professor Viscusi claims that the issue is simply how much people are willing to pay to reduce units of risk. As he puts it, cost-benefit analysis simply "reflect[s] attitudes toward small probabilities" of risk reduction. Thus, valuation does not "imply" that an in-dividual would accept certain death in return for some payment, such as $2 million, or "even that we would accept a .5 probability of death" for some payment. Rather, all that analysts are asking "is how much the individuals themselves value a particular risk reduction."[38]

As a normative defense of a cost-benefit standard, the distinction between statistical and identifiable lives does not work. The fundamental problem with the characterization, as Lisa Heinzerling observes, is that "it implicitly assumes that statistical people do not die."[39] This fiction permits supporters of a cost-benefit standard to sidestep the "uncomfortable fact that most of us profess ourselves quite incapable of identifying the monetary equivalent of the lives of our sisters, daughters, mothers, and friends."[40] Because this fiction makes it more difficult to "understand, much less empathize," with the human damage that occurs, the use of statistical lives becomes a strategy to support the adop-tion of less protective regulation. Professor Heinzerling explains:

Describing pain and loss in statistical terms allows us to think coolly about them; it strips life-threatening risks of the moral and emotional texture that they derive from their association with real humans with real bodies and real loved ones. Describing human lives in statistical terms thus creates the conditions under which human suffering and loss can be conceived of in economic terms, and under which this suffering and loss can be allowed to continue simply because the monetary value we have attached to them is lower than the costs of avoiding them.[41]

Bounded Rationality

Assessed by a pragmatic yardstick, current approaches to risk reduction are preferable to a cost-benefit standard because they do a better job of accommodating important noneconomic social values with the goal of economic efficiency. There is a second pragmatic reason to prefer the existing approaches: they work better in the actual conditions in which risk policy is implemented. Because pragmatism addresses the world as it exists, pragmatic risk regulation acknowledges "bounded rationality" in the protection of the public and the environment. As Chapter 2 discussed, regulators are subject to "bounded" rationality because of significant time, resource, and cognitive constraints, which usually make it impossible to identify the optimal solution to a problem. Instead, regulators employ heuristics or rules of thumb that are responses to limitations concerning knowledge and understanding.

The existence of bounded rationality detracts from the value of a cost-benefit standard as a decision-making device in the context of risk regulation. When economic analysts argue that risk reduction should employ a cost-benefit standard, they cannot claim as an advantage that this methodology leads to an optimal allocation of resources. If Congress required regulators to employ a cost-benefit standard, regulators would be subject to bounded rationality in the same manner as they currently are. Thus the issue of whether to adopt a cost-benefit standard is a pragmatic one: under conditions of bounded rationality, is a cost-benefit standard more likely than current approaches to improve the policy process in terms of the aims that Congress has adopted for risk regulation?

We offer three arguments why the current system is better than a cost-benefit standard under conditions of bounded rationality. First, current laws are a more appropriate response to regulatory constraints that arise from bounded rationality. Second, in light of bounded rationality, current laws establish an evidentiary burden that is more consistent with the preventative goals of risk regulation. Third, current laws better foster a multidisciplinary approach to risk regulation and broad public participation in decision-making.

Regulatory Constraints

Pragmatism determines the value of an approach or policy by looking at its success under actual conditions. For this reason, we argued in Chapter 2 that risk regulation should recognize the work of the "behavioral" school of organizational decision-making, led by Herbert Simon and Charles Lindblom, among others, who discussed how institutions can make rational decisions under conditions of bounded rationality. In this section, we turn to the new institutional economics, originated by Oliver Williamson,[42] which builds on this earlier literature. On the basis of this newer literature, we identify the regulatory constraints that flow from bounded rationality and indicate how risk regulation is structured to overcome those constraints.

New Institutional Economics

The new institutional economics began as a study of the conditions under which economic actors will join together in business firms, and it progressed to studying how firms overcome collective action problems that prevent mutual gains in trade. A collective action problem exists when one firm (or person) is reluctant to cooperate with another firm (or person) because the second firm may take advantage of the first one by some type of opportunistic behavior. The possibility of opportunism arises because each firm is subject to bounded rationality—which Williamson describes as the "mind as a scarce resource."[43] Neither firm is in a position to predict accurately the future behavior of the other, and each is limited in its capacity to monitor the behavior of the other. Following its self-interest, either firm may find it advantageous to "mislead, distort, disguise, obfuscate, or other[wise] confuse."[44] Thus neither firm will be willing to engage in collective action unless it can find some structure that will permit credible commitments before it engages in such action and mutual compliance during it. Economic actors employ a variety of structures for this purpose, such as incentive schemes, monitoring, or enforcement mechanisms. In choosing among various options, they will adopt the business arrangement that addresses potential collective action problems in a manner that yields the greatest economic benefit at the lowest cost.[45]

Positive political theorists use the same concepts to study the structure of governmental institutions. According to this viewpoint, political actors seek to adopt structures which address collective action problems that prevent the realization of collective goals or the ends that citizens seek through the collective action of government. Thus, as Douglas North notes, "political institutions constitute *ex ante* agreements over cooperation among politicians."[46] The collective action problems that political actors confront are similar to those that economic actors must overcome. Governmental actors, like economic actors, are subject to bounded rationality, which invites opportunistic behavior by those with whom they seek to cooperate.

Regulatory Design

The previous analysis suggests that the design of regulation is rational if it reflects the behavioral and informational constraints under which an agency is likely to operate. Table 4.1 identifies the relationship between bounded rationality and opportunism and the regulatory standards that Congress can choose. The "+" in the table indicates that an attribute is present and a "o" indicates that is it absent. Bounded rationality may or may not exist concerning the agency's capacity to determine the extent of the "risk" posed by a substance or hazard or the degree of the "cost" imposed on regulated entities engaging in preventive activities. We assume that opportunism will exist regarding any regulatory standard that Congress might choose. We make this assumption for purposes of this analysis because we assume that people who furnish information to the regulator will act opportunistically by presenting information in a manner that best serves their regulatory preference. The choice of regulatory standard is nevertheless capable of reducing the degree to which this opportunistic behavior contributes to a regulator's uncertainty. In addition, the table indicates that certain regulatory standards match up with different attributes of bounded rationality better than do other standards.

TABLE 4.1

Attributes of Risk Regulation

Bounded Rationality			
Risk	Cost	Opportunism	Standard
0	+	+	Risk-Based
+	0	+	Constrained Balancing
+	+	+	Open-Ended Balancing
0	0	+	Cost-Benefit

SOURCE: Chapter 4.

Risk-based standards are preferable when regulators are subject to bounded rationality concerning calculations of abatement costs, but are not subject to it concerning calculations of risk. In this circumstance, a risk standard will minimize transaction costs because abatement costs are not relevant to setting the level of regulation. Instead, regulators seek to achieve some "safe" level of exposure. Moreover, the fact that the parties furnishing information to the agency may act opportunistically will not prevent the agency from regulating because it has its own risk information.

A constrained balancing standard is appropriate when regulators are subject to bounded rationality concerning risk calculations, but not concerning cost information. In this situation, a constrained balancing standard will minimize transaction costs because risk information is not necessary to establish the level of regulation. Instead, regulators identify what technologies are currently in use (or could be in use) for purposes of abatement. A regulated entity is then required to reduce exposure to a hazard to the level of protection produced by the technology, although this determination can be subject to additional adjustments. The availability of such technologies means that an agency can relatively easily obtain information about them. The fact that industry might supply cost data that overestimate compliance costs does not matter, because the regulatory standard does not require a calculation of such costs.

An open-ended balancing standard is the best choice when regulators are subject to bounded rationality concerning both costs and benefits. This standard recognizes and accommodates the bounded rationality because it does not require that a regulator prove that such costs and benefits are precisely and quantitatively balanced. Instead, the regulator must compare such costs and benefits and balance them in a way that can be defended as reasonable.

Finally, a cost-benefit standard is appropriate when regulators are not subject to bounded rationality concerning risk and cost information. Because this standard requires regulators to measure both the benefits and costs of reducing risk, it assumes that regulators do not operate under conditions of bounded rationality in terms of such measurements. Where such conditions do not exist, some other regulatory standard will produce lower transaction costs.

Current Law

As Table 3.1 illustrates, very few of the current risk regulation statutes are based on either the risk-based or cost-benefit model. The new institutional economics generally justifies this outcome. Although not every choice that Congress has made matches Table 4.1, an analysis of the bounded rationality that affects risk regulation supports the rationality of the pattern of congressional choices in risk regulation.

The infrequent appearance of risk-based legislation, which proceeds without regard to the cost of compliance, is consistent with a lack of sufficient information about the scope of the risks being targeted or about the effect of various levels of control on reduction of those risks. In a few instances in which Congress has phased out use of a risk-creating substance or activity, the phaseout in effect amounts to a determination that the substance or activity posed unacceptable levels of risk. Although bounded rationality typically prevents drawing confident conclusions about the economic impact of much risk-based regulation, in these instances Congress has taken cost into account in blunt fashion in its determination of the phaseout period, as we explained in Chapter 3. The provisions of the CAA that eliminate over a forty-year period substances that pose threats to the integrity of the stratospheric ozone layer provide an example.

Similarly, analysis based on the new institutional economics suggests that a cost-benefit standard, which requires an agency to have sufficient information to find the optimal level of regulation, is an appropriate choice only under conditions in which an agency is unlikely to be subject to bounded rationality concerning either risk or cost assessments. Under conditions of bounded rationality, another choice is more appropriate. Given the difficulties of ascertaining and quantifying both the costs and benefits of regulation, which we describe in the next two chapters, the decision by Congress to avoid a cost-benefit standard is appropriate.

Thus, institutional economics justifies the popularity of the remaining two options, constrained and open-ended balancing standards. Each reduces the cost of regulatory decision-making by assigning regulators a burden of proof that recognizes and seeks to mitigate the adverse consequences of bounded rationality and opportunistic behavior. As Table 3.1 demonstrates, the great bulk of risk reduction legislation is based on either a constrained or open-ended balancing model.

Evidentiary Burden

The new institutional economics focuses on the relationship between collective action problems and decision-making structures. The pattern of risk regulation is generally consistent with an attempt to minimize transaction costs associated with bounded rationality and opportunistic behavior. Bounded rationality justifies the current pattern of risk regulation in another, but related, way. Because current risk legislation imposes a lesser evidentiary burden on agencies than a cost-benefit standard, it makes it possible for agencies to overcome successfully the legal opposition of regulated entities.

The importance of burden of proof to successful regulation can be illustrated by comparing recent developments in antitrust enforcement. At one time courts employed so-called per se tests that reduced a plaintiff's burden of proof to establish some violations. Like per se standards in antitrust law, regulatory triggers and standards eschew comprehensiveness in order to serve the underlying policies of risk legislation. They permit costs to be taken into account, but in a manner that is less likely than a cost-benefit standard to stymie regulation through judicial review. Critics objected that per se tests did not require a plaintiff to prove that the costs of the defendant's behavior exceeded its benefits, which is known as the "rule of reason." They argued that courts should adopt a rule of reason approach because it was more likely to produce an accurate decision about the net economic impact of the defendant's behavior.[47] The federal courts generally substituted rule of reason for per se analysis and, not surprisingly, antitrust enforcement declined. Of course, a decline in antitrust enforcement is not necessarily bad public policy, and the decline cannot be attributed entirely to the demise of the per se rule. But assuming that more regulation is appropriate, the antitrust analogy indicates how increasing the burden of proof imposed on government regulators can decrease regulatory output.[48]

The validity of the antitrust analogy is suggested by EPA's experience under the Toxic Substances Control Act (TSCA) and the record of the Consumer Product Safety Commission. EPA has found it well nigh impossible to regulate under TSCA, which one court has interpreted to include a cost-benefit regulatory trigger.[49] The Commission, which has the burden of meeting both a cost-benefit trigger and standard, is viewed by many as ineffectual.[50]

A lesser burden of proof permits more regulation than a more difficult burden of proof. In risk regulation, a lesser burden of proof enables regulators to make regulation more preventative than they could if the burden of proof were higher. A pragmatic inquiry, however, must ask about results. As we have mentioned several times, opponents of risk regulation claim that the current regulatory scheme—with its reduced evidentiary burden—has resulted in regulations whose costs are greatly in excess of benefits. We address their evidence for this claim in the next chapter.

Conclusion

Unlike the rationale for a cost-benefit standard, the reasons that support the current structure of risk regulation legislation do not constitute an integrated social theory. Following the tradition of philosophical pragmatism, these arguments are drawn from different normative and disciplinary perspectives, and they favor institutional realism over (economic) theory as a guide to social action. This complexity is both a disadvantage and an advantage. The disadvantage is that, in comparison to economic theory, there is no set of cumulative and relatively simple definitive principles that explain risk policy. The advantage is that risk policy reflects the messy realities of the world in which we live.

One of these realities is that risk regulation implicates widely shared social values besides economic efficiency. Unlike economic theory, pragmatism requires that regulation seek to accommodate all widely shared social values implicated by risk reduction. In light of this goal, the structure of risk regulation makes sense. Risk regulation rejects a cost-benefit standard because it is inconsistent with recognition of the extraordinary value that many individuals assign to protection of life and the environment and with social equity. Instead, it substitutes other forms of balancing prevention and regulatory costs that seek to reconcile multiple social goals.

Another one of these realities is that risk regulation takes place under bounded rationality. Once this limitation is acknowledged, the structure of risk regulation makes sense. In economic theory, the argument for a cost-benefit standard is that it produces the optimal level of human and environmental injury. Even if this were a socially appropriate goal, the identification of the optimal balance of costs and benefits is not actually possible. Further, a cost-benefit standard is less likely to achieve the preventative goals of risk regulation because it requires levels of information that are difficult for regulators to obtain. This constraint opens regulators to legal attack for not meeting the statutory standard for regulation. By comparison, risk regulation is currently structured to prevent the lack of some types of information from defeating the preventive goals of risk regulation.

5

The Critique of Risk Regulation

Risk reduction legislation satisfies pragmatic principles that regulation should reflect important relevant social norms and be formulated in light of bounded rationality. To accomplish these goals, regulation takes costs into account, but not in the manner prescribed by economic theory, which would establish the level of regulation by a cost-benefit standard. The critics of regulation contend that the failure to use a cost-benefit standard has produced excessive and irrational regulation, and they cite a few key studies to back up this claim. The studies, however, employ methods of analysis that raise questions or that are based on methodological assumptions that are controversial. Other studies, which employ different methods and assumptions, find that most regulation is reasonable.

The problem with efforts to calculate the costs and benefits of regulation is that they are often subject to substantial uncertainty because of bounded rationality. In order to plug gaps in our understanding of regulatory effects, analysts employ various methods and assumptions. The next chapter considers the difficulty of estimating regulatory impacts and how the results are heavily influenced by methodological choices. In this chapter, we explain why the key evidence relied upon by critics of risk regulation cannot be accepted at face value.

Aggregate Studies

The effort to quantify the consequences of risk regulation involves two types of studies. Aggregate studies measure the total benefits and costs of regulation. Individual studies measure the costs and benefits of specific regulations. We first consider aggregate studies and then individual studies.

Some critics of risk regulation point to the extremely high cost of risk regulation as evidence of its irrationality, but the studies that they cite are not very reliable. In any case, any assessment of the value of regulation must look at both costs and benefits. These studies establish that aggregate benefits exceed aggregate costs, probably by a considerable extent, but the reliability of these studies is hampered by the lack of relevant data. Nevertheless, Congress has mandated that the Office of Management and Budget (OMB) prepare yearly aggregate estimates of regulatory costs and benefits, which will focus attention on aggregate accounting.

Aggregate Cost Estimates

Some critics of current risk legislation cite cost estimates as evidence that there is too much risk regulation. This was a popular tactic of the Reagan administration, which repeatedly used a 1980 estimate by Murray Weidenbaum that all federal regulation cost $120 billion.[1] More recently, publications of the Heritage Foundation and the Cato Institute cite with alarm estimates by Professor Thomas Hopkins.[2] Professor Hopkins estimates that the total regulatory "burden" in the United States is $700 billion, while the annual cost of environmental and other risk reduction regulation is $223 billion.[3]

These studies provide a dubious basis upon which to criticize the rationality of risk regulation for two reasons. To begin with, their definitions of cost are questionable. Consider Professor Weidenbaum's estimate of $120 billion. A 1976 paper by Weidenbaum and Robert De Fina was the first effort to estimate total regulatory costs. They estimated that all federal regulation had a total cost of $63 billion.[4] Instead of updating his prior study, Professor Weidenbaum derived the $120 billion estimate based on the ratio of administrative and compliance costs identified in the earlier study. Because compliance costs exceeded administrative costs in the first study by a ratio of approximately twenty to one, Weidenbaum derived his $120 billion estimate by multiplying administrative costs in 1980 by twenty.[5] Other analysts have objected that "there is no reason to believe that there is a constant relationship between the costs of administrative and direct compliance." They also pointed out that paperwork costs constituted almost 40 percent of Weidenbaum's original estimate, that his estimates of paperwork costs had a "tenuous empirical footing," and that the paperwork requirements were "tied only loosely to regulatory activities."[6] Professor Weidenbaum responds that the "magnitude of the figures here outlines the need for increased attention to the problem from scholars, regulators, and policymakers."[7]

Professor Hopkins follows Weidenbaum's lead by including the cost of complying with paperwork requirements, such as filling out income tax forms. As noted, critics regard such expenses as remotely, if at all, connected to government regulation and as empirically suspect. Hopkins also includes transfer payments, such as farm subsidies, as regulatory costs. As the OMB has noted, the inclusion of these two types of costs does two things: "It produces large numbers and creates confusion" by "including 'costs' that are not normally considered as part of the regulatory reform debate."[8]

An even more significant objection is that attention to regulatory costs, without consideration of regulatory benefits, is obviously misleading. If risk regulation generates greater total benefits than total costs, then it contributes to total economic welfare no matter how high the total cost might be. For example, assume that risk regulation generates $250 billion in total benefits for a total cost of $200 billion. In light of a net benefit of $50 billion, regulation cannot be considered to be a "bad thing" in the aggregate, even though it imposes high regulatory costs.

Aggregate Net Benefit Estimates

There have been four prominent aggregate estimates of regulatory costs and benefits. Table 5.1 summarizes the results. The three most recent of the studies find that aggregate benefits exceed aggregate costs by billions of dollars.

Hahn and Hird

Robert Hahn and John Hird were the first analysts to publish quantified estimates of total costs and benefits. In 1991 they estimated that regulation in seven areas had total benefits of $41.9 billion to 181.5 billion and total costs of $78.0 billion to 107.1 billion, producing a net benefit range of $(65.2) billion to $103.5 billion. In light of the overlap between the range of costs and benefits, the authors' "best guess" was that the costs and benefits were "roughly comparable."[9]

TABLE 5.1

Total Annual Regulatory Benefits and Costs

	Environment ($ billions)	Transportation ($ billions)	Labor ($ billions)	Other ($ billions)	Total ($ billions)
HAHN AND HIRD (1988 DOLLARS)					
Benefits	16.5–135.8	25.4–45.7	negligible	n.a.	41.9–181.5
Costs	55.4–77.6	6.4–9.0	8.5–9.0	7.7–11.4	78.0–107.1
Net Benefits	(38.9)–58.2	18.5–36.7	(8.5–9.0)^a	(7.7–11.4)	(65.2)–103.5
HAHN (1995 DOLLARS)					
Benefits	764.2	997.4	138.2	48.8	1,948.6
Costs	283.6	53.1	28.5	30.6	395.8
Net Benefits	480.7	944.3	109.8^a	18.2^b	1,552.8
EPA: CLEAN AIR ACT^c (1997 DOLLARS)					
Benefits	5,600–(49,400)				
Costs	500				
Net Benefits	5,100–(48,900)				
OMB 2000 (1996 DOLLARS)					
Benefits	97–1,595	84–110	28–30	55–60	264–1,795
Costs	124–175	15–18	18–19	17–22	174–234
Net Benefits	(78)–1,471	66–95	9–12	33–43	30–1,621

SOURCE: Studies cited in the table (citations in the text).
^{a}OSHA health and safety standards.
^{b}CPSC, HHS, HUD, and USDA regulations.
^{c}For period 1970–90.

These estimates have limited relevance today, for two reasons. First, although the authors estimated regulatory costs for seven areas of regulation, they estimated benefits for only two of those areas—environmental protection and highway safety regulation. Second, their calculation of the benefits of environmental protection greatly underestimates its value. This estimate is based on empirical work done in the 1970s that fails to reflect the benefits associated with either programs developed later, such as the clean air initiatives of the Environmental Protection Agency (EPA) in the 1980s, or the scientific knowledge indicating the existence of newly recognized risks from polluted air, and that does not recognize the benefits associated with preventing degradation in air quality.[10] An EPA study, discussed later in this section, suggests that the benefits of the Clean Air Act (CAA) alone total hundreds of billions of dollars more than the estimate by Hahn and Hird.

Although the Hahn and Hird study is outdated, we mention it because OMB has relied on it in making its congressionally mandated estimate of aggregate net regulatory benefits. OMB relies on this study because, despite is considerable flaws, it is the only available study measuring regulatory benefits during the time period covered by the study.

Hahn

Robert Hahn has compiled a more recent estimate of aggregate costs and benefits using a methodology different from the one he relied on for his earlier study. Using data that agencies supplied to OMB or that they published in the *Federal Register*, Hahn compared the costs and benefits of 106 final regulations promulgated between 1982 and mid-1996. He estimated that the net benefit of regulation in these cases was $1.5 trillion (1995 dollars), based on benefits of $1.95 trillion and costs of $395.8 billion.[11]

Hahn made two types of adjustments that reduce the size of his net benefit estimate. The first adjustment was to exclude two EPA regulations on stratospheric ozone that have a net benefit of trillions of dollars according to EPA. The two regulations phase out the use of chlorofluorocarbons (CFCs) and hydrochlorofluorocarbons (HCFCs), which cause a depletion of ozone in the atmosphere. In a footnote, Hahn explains: "While these rules probably have positive net benefits, the EPA's estimates probably overstate the actual benefits significantly. I therefore did not include these rules."[12] In an earlier version of his estimates, Hahn explained the omission on different grounds. He noted that EPA's calculations were based on a "large number of deaths caused by skin cancer," and "[it] is quite possible that a cure will be developed."[13]

In a second adjustment, Hahn supplied his own estimate of the value of the benefits when agencies failed to monetize the value of the lives that a regulation was projected to save. This adjustment also decreased his net benefit estimate for the reasons discussed later in this chapter when we take up Hahn's calculations regarding individual regulations.

Section 812 Study

In 1997, EPA published a study of the total costs and benefits of the CAA from 1970 to 1990, known as the "Section 812 study," in response to a congressional mandate that it periodically make such estimates. Although the study is limited to one area of risk regulation, it is worth considering because it is the first and only effort to undertake a comprehensive measurement of the costs and benefits of an entire regulatory program over time. Reflecting this commitment, the study took seven years to complete and cost millions of dollars.[14] EPA estimated regulatory benefits ranging from $5.6 trillion to $49.4 trillion, in comparison to regulatory costs of approximately $0.5 trillion.[15] Moreover, EPA pointed out that a number of benefits could not be quantified because of limitations in risk data or the unavailability of reliable economic methods to assign a monetary value.

Critics argue that EPA's upper bound estimate of benefits—$49.4 trillion—is "implausible," "doesn't pass a common sense test," and "stretches the credibility of the report because the benefits are as much as one-sixth of the gross national product of the United States."[16] The vast range of benefits reflected EPA's difficulty in making precise estimates of regulatory benefits. Nevertheless, the upper bound estimate may not be too wide of the mark. An emerging literature on the value of "nature's services" places the value of these services at a level higher than the *world's* GDP,[17] which suggests that EPA's estimate of the value of clean air is not necessarily inaccurate because it is one-sixth of the domestic gross national product. Moreover, EPA's report was the subject of intensive peer review by an independent, external panel of well-known economists, health scientists, and environmental scientists, known as the Science Advisory Board Council on Clean Air Act Compliance Analysis (the "Council"). The peer reviewers found the report to Congress to be a "serious, careful study [that] employs sound methods along with the best available data," and that EPA's findings are "consistent with the weight of the available evidence."[18]

OMB

As noted earlier, OMB has estimated the total costs and benefits of environmental and safety regulation in response to a congressional mandate to make such an assessment. In 2000, OMB estimated that the net benefit of regulation was $30 billion to $1.62 trillion per year, based on benefits of $264 billion to $1.8 trillion and costs of $174 billion to $234 billion. In earlier estimates, OMB found net benefits of between $34 billion and $3.38 trillion per year (1998) and $100 billion (1997).[19]

As the variation in these estimates might indicate, OMB's calculations are subject to numerous potential sources of error. Two such problems illustrate the difficulty of making accurate estimates of total regulatory costs and benefits. First, OMB uses Hahn and Hird's estimates of regulatory costs and benefits for regulations promulgated as of 1988, except for environmental regulations. As discussed earlier, Hahn and Hird underestimated regulatory benefits because they made no estimate of benefits for regulations in five areas, although they calculated costs for those activities. OMB, however, had no choice but to rely on their study because there is no alternative source of data concerning these early regulations. Second, OMB based its lower bound estimate of the value of environmental benefits on the Hahn and Hird study. Hahn and Hird estimated the value of *all* environmental regulation to be $22 billion.[20] The Section 812 study, by comparison, had a lower bound estimate of $378 billion for the benefits of *only* the Clean Air Act.[21] OMB's use of the Hahn and Hird estimate produces a range of net environmental benefits from a negative $78 billion to a positive $1.5 trillion. In other words, OMB's lower bound estimate implies that the country might have been better off during the last three decades if no environmental law had ever been passed, a conclusion entirely at odds with EPA's CAA study.

Individual Regulations

The high aggregate costs of risk regulation cited by some critics obscure the fact that risk regulation appears to have generated aggregate benefits in excess of aggregate costs and probably greatly in excess of its costs. The fact that risk regulation produces aggregate net benefits, however, does not mean that individual regulations are not excessive or irrational. Criticisms to that effect are based on two types of studies. In the first type, analysts rank the cost-effectiveness of individual regulations, according to how much money it costs to prevent a premature death. In the second type, analysts calculate and compare the benefits and costs of individual regulations.

As mentioned, a few key studies have been widely cited by critics of risk regulation to establish that individual regulations are often excessive and irrational, but other evidence finds risk regulation to have produced reasonable results. This evidence is sufficient to suggest that the key studies relied on by regulatory critics should not be automatically accepted as valid estimates of regulatory outcomes.

Cost-Effectiveness Studies

Almost everyone who has argued that risk regulation produces irrational outcomes has relied on cost-effectiveness studies by one or both of two analysts. The first is a 1986 article by John Morrall, a well-known economist at OMB,[22] that was twice updated by OMB during the Reagan and the first Bush administration.[23] The OMB-Morrall estimates have become "Exhibit A in the academic and political case for regulatory reform."[24] Such prominent analysts as Justice Stephen Breyer and Professors Cass Sunstein (University of Chicago) and Kip Viscusi (Harvard University) are among those reprinting the results of these studies. Analysts critical of risk regulation also commonly cite research conducted by John Graham of the Harvard Center for Risk Effectiveness, who is President George W. Bush's choice to head up the Office of Information and Regulatory Affairs in the Office of Management and Budget.[25]

OMB-Morrall

John Morrall's 1986 article analyzed the cost-effectiveness of forty-four proposed, final, or rejected regulations on the basis of data that agencies had submitted to OMB as adjusted by him for purposes of his analysis. He estimated the regulatory costs of preventing one death by dividing the cost of the regulation by the number of lives it was estimated to save. The results demonstrate a stunning variation in the regulatory cost of saving a life. The three least-cost regulations had a cost of $100,000 per life saved, while the most expensive regulation had a cost of $72 million per life saved. In addition, many of the regulations came with a high price tag. Twenty-four of the regulations cost more than $7 million per life saved, and seventeen regulations cost more than $50 million per life saved.

OMB published a revised version of Morrall's analysis in its annual report on regulation in 1988 and again in 1992. The 1992 study, which analyzed fifty-three final regulations, found even more widely disparate results. The five least-cost regulations had a cost of $100,000 per life saved, while the most expensive regulation had a cost of $5.7 trillion per life saved. Twenty-five of the regulations had a cost of more than $6 million per life saved, twenty of the regulations had a cost of more than $20 million per life saved, and fourteen had a cost of more than $50 million.

Based on these studies, these critics have reached one or both of two conclusions. First, many regulations are grossly inefficient because they spend
much more money to save a human life than the conventional value that
economists place on saving one life.[26] Economists conventionally use a value
of human life of $3.0 million to $7.0 million for purposes of analyzing the
benefits of regulation. Second, regulatory priorities are not set in a rational
manner because the nation could purchase more safety and health protection
by refocusing regulatory efforts on hazards that cost far less to prevent. Justice
Breyer, for example, concludes on the basis of the 1992 OMB data, that
"[t]hese estimates suggest that the nation could buy more safety by refocusing its regulatory efforts."[27]

Wood Preserving Chemicals Rule

We begin our analysis of this evidence with the regulation that the 1992
OMB-update indicates is the most expensive regulation promulgated by any
agency. According to OMB, EPA's Hazardous Waste Listing for Wood-
Preserving Chemicals has a stunning cost of $5.7 trillion per life saved. We
analyze this estimate in detail because it illustrates why the Morrall-OMB results cannot be accepted at face value.

The regulation requires firms that apply wood preserving chemicals to
lumber in an out-of-doors location to place a cement pad under coating ma-
chines in order to prevent the chemicals from dripping on the ground. The
rule also requires that such firms take other modest actions to prevent environmental contamination, such as the safe removal of chemicals collected on
the drip pads.[28] EPA estimated that the total annual cost of this regulation was
$11 million to $14 million per year. How, then, did OMB assign an extraordinary $5.7 trillion price tag to a regulation that does not cost in absolute terms
more than $14 million per year?

EPA's intention was to protect the environment. Prior to the rule, the
agency had listed fifty-four locations where there had been outdoor wood
treatment on the Superfund National Priorities List (NPL), and it had ordered corrective actions under the act for numerous other facilities because
of "extensive groundwater and soil contamination." Although EPA intended
the rule as an environmental protection initiative, it did not provide any
monetary estimates of the value or benefits of the environmental protection

that would result. Further, although the agency was highly uncertain about the extent to which humans would drink water contaminated by wood-preserving operations, it estimated that the rule might save one life every three hundred years.[29]

OMB attributed the entire $14 million cost of the regulation to reducing health risks, which ignores the fact that the compliance costs also pay for environmental protection. If the rule results in at least $11 million to $14 million of environmental protection benefits—a likely result in light of the number of contaminated sites involved and EPA's description of the benefits of the rule as including elimination of soil erosion with adverse effects on ground-water quality and aquatic life in nearby streams—there is little or no cost to any additional health benefits that the rule might have. Even if the environmental benefits do not equal the cost, inclusion of those benefits necessarily reduces the cost per life saved by the regulation.

OMB also discounted the value of the health benefits, which reduced the number of lives saved from one per year to an infinitesimally small number. Because OMB discounted the benefit of one life saved per year and because this benefit occurred over a three-hundred-year time horizon, the cost of the rule became $5.7 trillion. We discuss in the next chapter the controversy surrounding the use of discounting in estimating the number of lives that a regulation might save. For now, we would point out that the total cost of the regulation is as low as $11 million per year, which produces considerable environmental protection and may produce some small health benefits as well. The use of a discounted estimate, without a comparison of the annual costs and benefits, even if they cannot be quantified, is quite misleading.

Mythic Costs

A closer look at Morrall's article confirms that the results should not be automatically accepted. In *Regulatory Costs of Mythic Proportions*, Lisa Heinzerling concluded that most of the "fantastic costs" in Morrall's article are "open to question."[30] Table 5.2 compares Heinzerling's analysis with Morrall's.

Professor Heinzerling identified two aspects of Morrall's methodology that impacted his results. First, Morrall included a significant number of proposed and withdrawn rules for purposes of demonstrating that many government

TABLE 5.2

Competing Estimates of Cost-Effectiveness

(Millions of Dollars)

	Annual Cost per Premature Death Avoided	
	Morrall's 1986 Cost Estimates (Discounted 10%)	Heinzerling's Estimates (Not Discounted)
Formaldehyde (OSHA 1985)	72,000	21.8
Land Disposal (EPA 1986)	3,500	2.38
Arsenic/Low-Arsenic Copper (EPA 1986)	764	4.17
Arsenic (OSHA 1978)	92.5	10.0
Asbestos (OSHA 1986)	89.3	2.8
Coke Ovens (OSHA 1986)	61.8	4.5
Uranium Mill Tailings/Active (EPA 1983)	53.0	2.5
Acrylontrile (OSHA 1978)	37.6	3.5
Uranium Mill Tailings/Inactive (EPA 1983)	27.6	1.57
Ethylene Oxide (OSHA 1984)	25.6	2.03–3.88
Arsenic/Glass Plant (EPA 1986)	19.2	4.8
Benzene (OSHA 1985)	17.1	1.8
Asbestos (OSHA 1972)	7.4	0.19

SOURCE: Lisa Heinzerling, "Regulatory Costs" (citation in text).

regulations are not cost-effective. She found that eight out of the eleven most expensive regulations listed by Morrall, and several other regulations, were rejected by the government precisely because of their excessive costs—or the regulations did not take effect for other reasons. "By the regulatory reformers' lights," Heinzerling notes, "the rejection of such rules should be viewed as a success story."[31] Although Morrall disclosed that the regulations had been rejected, some subsequent citations to the table have not made this disclosure. Regardless, one cannot prove that government regulation is too expensive by citing regulations that were never adopted.

Second, Heinzerling found that Morrall's estimates of cost per life saved are "strikingly different from—and inevitably higher than—the agencies' estimates."[32] She attributed the differences to two sources. Morrall sometimes substituted his own lower estimate of the number of deaths that a regulation prevents for the estimate made by agency risk appraisers. He also discounted the number of future lives that the regulation would save by 10 percent per year. When Heinzerling used the agency's own risk estimates and did not discount the number of lives saved in the future, the cost per life saved for all but two of the regulations fell to less than $5.0 million. Since, as noted earlier, economists generally consider a cost of $3.0 million to $7.0 million as reasonable, the cost of regulations according to Heinzerling falls "well within the bounds of reasonableness."[33]

Economic analysts object to cost estimates that do not discount the value of lives saved in the future, and Heinzerling's estimates have been criticized on that basis.[34] As the next chapter discusses, the use of discounting reflects an economic perspective about the goals of regulation that is controversial. For now, we compare Heinzerling's results to a study that we undertook of OMB's update of the Morrall list of regulations.

OMB Update

In 1992, OMB published an update of Morrall's study that contained twenty-three regulations that had a cost of $8.0 million or higher. Of the fifteen regulations that did not appear in Morrall's original study, we were able to analyze the cost of nine regulations based on relevant available agency data. Our results, which are summarized in Table 5.3, confirm Heinzerling's conclusions. Our cost estimates are millions of dollars less than the OMB estimates for seven of the nine regulations. Five of these seven regulations cost less than $6.0 million for each premature death avoided. A detailed explanation of our calculations can be found in Appendix I.

Moreover, it is likely that we have overestimated the cost of two of the four regulations that cost more than $6.0 million per life saved. As discussed earlier, OMB's estimate of the cost-effectiveness of the Wood Preservative Chemical Rule ignores the benefits gained from environmental protection. Our estimate likewise does not include those benefits, although we identify their existence. As also noted in Table 5.3, our estimate of the cost of the Hazardous Waste Listing for Petroleum Sludge does not include both health and nonhealth benefits produced by the regulation.[35]

The difference between our results and those of OMB is apparently attributable to methodological choices. First, like Heinzerling, we did not use discounting in Table 5.3. As noted, the use of discounting is controversial, as we will discuss in the next chapter. Second, Professor Heinzerling found that Morrall made his own estimates of the number of lives that a regulation might save, rather than accepting the agency's estimate. Likewise, she was able

TABLE 5.3

Competing Estimates of Cost-Effectiveness

(Millions of Dollars)

Regulations	Annual Cost per Premature Death Avoided		Additional Considerations
	OMB's 1992 Estimates (Discounted 10%)	Agency Data (Not Discounted)	
Hazardous Waste Listing for Wood-Preserving Chemicals (EPA 1990)	5,700,000	$11.0–14.0	—Benefits do not include environmental protection
Atrazine/Alachlor Drinking Water Standard (EPA 1991)	92,069.7	1.81	—Benefit and cost estimates for 37 substances including Atrazine and Alachlor
1,2 Dichloropropane Drinking Water Standard (EPA 1991)	653.0	1.81	—Benefit and cost estimates for 37 substances including 1,2 Dichloropropane
Benzene NESHAP (Revised: Waste Operations) (EPA 1990)	168.2	164.68	
Asbestos Ban (EPA 1989)	110.7	3.33–5.86	
Lockout/Tagout (OSHA 1989)	70.9	0.19–1.2	
Benzene NESHAP (Revised: Transfer Operations) (EPA 1990)	32.9	33.0	
Hazardous Waste Listing for Petroleum Refining Sludge (EPA 1986)	27.6	9.0–131.0	—Benefits do not include environmental protection —Agency could not quantify additional health benefits
Benzene Occupational Exposure Limit (OSHA 1987)	8.9	3.31	—Agency could not quantify additional health benefits

SOURCE: For sources and methodology, see Appendix I.

to document examples of OMB reducing agency estimates of the number of lives that a regulation is likely to save.[36]

We also made discounted estimates for eight of the regulations that OMB studied for which we could obtain the necessary data. The results can be found in Table 5.4. Six of the eight regulations cost millions less than OMB's estimate. Moreover, we have likely overestimated the costs of Formaldehyde, which is one of the three regulations that had costs greater than $7.0 million. Our estimate is based on data available to the Occupational Safety and Health Administration (OSHA) at the time it promulgated the regulation, but later

TABLE 5.4
Competing Estimates of Cost-Effectiveness
(Millions of Dollars)

Regulations	Annual Cost Per Premature Death Avoided		
	OMB's 1992 Estimates (Discounted 10%)	Agency Data (Discounted 2%)	Additional Considerations
Formaldehyde Occupational Exposure (EPA 1991)	86,201	21.7–164	—OSHA underestimated the number of lives saved —Costs are significantly overstated
Benzene NESHAP (Revised: Waste Operations) (EPA 1990)	168.2	170.3	
Asbestos Ban (EPA 1989)	110.7	3.1–5.45	—Agency could not quantify additional health benefits —Based on 3% discount rate
Lockout/Tagout (OSHA 1989)	70.9	1.23	
Benzene NESHAP (Revised: Transfer Operations) (EPA 1990)	32.9	35.14	
Cover/Move Uranium Mill Tailings (Inactive Sites) (EPA 1983)	31.7	3.37	
Arsenic/Copper NESHAP (EPA 1986)	23.0	4.7	
Ethylene Oxide Occupational Exposure Limit (OSHA 1984)	20.5	3.29–6.25	—Agency could not quantify additional health benefits —Retrospective study indicates that costs are "modestly" underestimated

SOURCE: For sources and methodology, see Appendix II.

information indicates that the costs of the regulation are overstated and the benefits understated.[37]

The difference between OMB's estimates and our own is again attributable to different methodologies. As the next chapter discusses, there are a number of methodological choices concerning discounting, such as the size of the discount rate, that greatly impact the results of a study. For example, OMB used a 10 percent discount rate, which is considered by many analysts to be too high for the purpose of estimating regulatory costs. As explained in the next chapter, a high discount rate will greatly increase the cost of regulation. Thus, we achieved lower costs in part by use of a 2 percent discount rate. Our methodology is explained and documented in Appendix II. We discuss and defend our methodology in the next chapter.

John Graham

John Graham has produced two studies that are popular citations of regulatory critics. As with the OMB-Morrall estimates, Graham's results depend on methodological choices and assumptions that tend to raise the cost of the regulations that he studied. In light of these choices and assumptions, his results are also open to question.

In a 1995 study,[38] Graham and his coauthors estimated the cost-effectiveness of 587 life-saving interventions organized into three categories: fatal injury reduction, the control of toxins, and medical interventions. Slightly less than half of the interventions (250) involved risk regulation. Graham measured cost-effectiveness according to the cost per life-year saved, which is the cost per year of preventing a premature death. Graham and his coauthors found vast disparities in life-saving costs across interventions and across categories of interventions, particularly in the category of toxic control, where the costs ranged from zero or less than zero, because the intervention saved more money than it cost, to $99 billion for each life-year saved.

In 1996, Graham and Tammy Tengs estimated the "opportunity cost" of pursuing more expensive life-saving interventions instead of less expensive choices.[39] They calculated that there would be an additional 60,200 lives saved if the annual resources then devoted to saving lives were directed toward life-saving interventions that cost $7.57 million or less. This step would, the analysts concluded, more than double the life-saving potential of current interventions. Or, as Graham has said, the country is committing "statistical murder" by missing the opportunity to save the lives of a large number of unidentified persons.[40]

Like the OMB-Morrall studies, Graham's work suggests that something may have gone terribly wrong with current regulatory approaches to risk regulation. But Graham, like the OMB-Morrall studies, employs methods of analysis that are questionable or involve assumptions that reflect controversial political value choices.[41]

First, like Morrall, Graham cites regulations that were never implemented. Of the ninety EPA interventions included by Graham, Professor Lisa Heinzerling has found that only eleven were ever promulgated by EPA. Many of the ninety were never even proposed by the agency. As we stated earlier, one cannot prove that government regulation is too expensive by citing regulations that were never adopted, let alone never proposed. Moreover, the implication of Graham's second study is that we are wasting money on regulations that are not very cost-effective when we could be investing the same money in regulations that are more cost-effective. But if a regulation was never adopted, it is not wasted resources that prevent us from pursuing a more cost-effective regulation.

Second, Graham's estimates of cost-effectiveness are drawn from dozens of studies conducted by others, and the cost per life-year saved of the very same regulatory strategy varies, sometimes greatly, according to the source.[42] For example, the cost per life-year saved of a ban on urea-formaldehyde foam insulation in homes is either $11,000, if you accept an estimate by EPA, or $220,000, if you accept an estimate by Professor Kip Viscusi.[43] More dramatically, the cost per life-year saved of regulation of low-arsenic copper smelters ranges from $2.6 million to $890 million, and the cost per life-year saved of regulation of arsenic emissions from glass plants ranges from $2.3 million to $51 million.[44] As stated earlier, estimates of regulatory costs and benefits can vary widely, depending on the assumptions underlying the numerical estimates, yet Graham's confident conclusion that more lives can be saved by switching to lower cost regulations assumes that the higher cost estimates are accurate.

Third, Graham used discounting to measure cost-effectiveness. As in the OMB-Morrall studies, this technique has the impact of reducing the cost-effectiveness of risk regulations. The reader will recall that nondiscounted estimates of the regulations studied by OMB and Morrall were millions of dollars less than discounted estimates. Moreover, as we discuss in the next chapter, Graham uses a form of discounting that is at odds with his measurement of the effectiveness of regulation according to how many years of life it prolongs.

Finally, as noted, Graham uses the number of years that a regulation prolongs a life as the measure of its effectiveness. As a result, a life-saving intervention that saves an older person's life is less cost-effective than one that saves a younger person's life. Thus Graham and his coauthors assume that saving the life of the young is more beneficial to society than saving the life of the middle-aged or elderly. The impact of this controversial assumption is to increase the cost of regulations that protect persons when they get older. Most cancer protection regulations have this impact, because cancer generally occurs years after exposure to carcinogens. Since Graham's methodology is biased against cancer protection, it is not surprising that he finds that toxin protection is generally less cost-effective than medical and safety interventions that tend to protect younger persons from more immediate deaths.

Cost-Benefit Studies

The studies just discussed are of cost-effectiveness, which determines how much money it takes to prevent a premature death. Other studies of regulation utilize a cost-benefit methodology that assigns an economic value to the benefit of saving lives in the future, and to other benefits, such as a reduction in illness, and compares that benefit to the cost of the regulation. This second approach has also led critics of risk regulation to conclude that many regulations are grossly inefficient because the cost of the regulations far exceeds the benefits. Other studies, however, dispute that conclusion.

A 1999 study by Robert Hahn, mentioned earlier in the discussion of aggregate costs and benefits, illustrates the cost-benefit approach. Hahn began with data that agencies had submitted to OMB on 106 final major regulations promulgated by agencies between 1981 and mid-1996. Where agencies failed to monetize the value of the lives that a regulation would save, Hahn used a $5.0 million measurement of the value of a statistical premature death avoided and a 5 percent discount rate. He valued injuries using conventions such as counting a chronic disease or disabling injury as one-third of a life and workday-lost-injuries as one-hundredth of the value of a life. As noted earlier, Hahn found that the rules produced $1.6 trillion in net benefits. He also found, however, that only 57 percent of the individual regulations had positive net benefits. Federal regulations had a total net benefit because the positive net benefits of the regulations that passed a cost-benefit test were greater than the negative net benefits generated by regulations that did not pass the test.[45]

Critics of risk regulation have used Hahn's data as the basis for recommending greater reliance on a cost-benefit standard in risk regulation. Citing an earlier version of Hahn's 1999 study, for example, six prominent economists, including Hahn, concluded: "While some regulations pass a cost-benefit test according to agency estimates, most do not. Balancing the incremental benefits and costs could help reduce waste and inefficiency and improve economic welfare."[46]

A 2000 OMB study comes to a remarkably different conclusion than Hahn's cost-benefit estimates. The study was undertaken as part of OMB's effort, described earlier in the chapter, to estimate aggregate costs and benefits for all regulation. OMB considered all of the major final regulations it had reviewed between April 1, 1995, and March 31, 1999, for which the agencies provided quantified estimates of costs and benefits. In cases in which the agency both quantified and monetized fatality benefits, OMB made no adjustments in the agency's estimate. In cases in which an agency provided only a quantified estimate of fatality risk, but did not provide any method of monetizing the benefit, OMB used a value of $5.0 million per life saved.[47] OMB provided a range of benefit and cost estimates for most regulations. Estimates were made on an annualized basis and based on net present value. OMB also described some benefits that agencies could not, or did not, quantify.

According to the OMB data, benefits exceeded costs for about 80 percent of the final regulations based on annualized costs and benefits and about 75 percent of the final regulations based on the net present value of costs and benefits. For purposes of this comparison, we counted a regulation as having positive net benefits if the lower bound estimate of benefits was higher than the upper bound estimate of costs. We also counted a regulation as having a positive net benefit if 70 percent or more of the net benefit range was positive because the net benefit range is significantly positive.[48]

Whereas the OMB data indicate that 75 to 80 percent of the regulations studied had benefits that exceed their costs, Hahn found that only 43 percent met this mark. One potential explanation for this result is that OMB studied regulations that were finalized from mid-1995 to mid-1998, and Hahn studied regulations that were promulgated between 1981 and mid-1996. Criticisms of risk regulation by analysts like Hahn may have led agencies to do a better job equating costs and benefits in the later regulations studied by OMB. A more likely explanation is that OMB and Hahn used different valuation methods. Efforts to measure the benefits of risk regulation are fraught with uncertainty, as the next chapter discusses. These uncertainties require evaluators to make assumptions and policy choices that can greatly impact the calculations that are being made.

Conclusion

Some critics of risk regulation point to the high aggregate regulatory costs as evidence that something is amiss, but aggregate net benefits total billions of dollars. Thus risk regulation makes a large positive contribution to economic welfare in the aggregate. A more relevant consideration for policy purposes, however, is the impact of individual regulations. The OMB-Morrall, Graham and Hahn studies, which are widely cited by regulatory critics, find that many individual regulations are excessive and irrational. These results, however, are attributable in many instances to their methodological choices and assumptions. Different results can be reached by employing different choices and assumptions.

Thus, whether risk regulation is reasonable or not turns on how it is analyzed. The next chapter considers how methodological choices and assumptions impact the results of studies of risk regulation, and whether the choices and assumptions of the critics should be accepted.

6

Valuation Methods

There is nothing simple about estimating the impact of most regulations. This chapter describes and analyzes the difficulties in making such estimates. More specifically, we consider how the choices and assumptions that analysts employ affect the estimates that they make. Since the outcome of a study can turn on how regulations are analyzed, pragmatic policy-makers should avoid indiscriminate reliance on studies critical of risk regulation for sweeping policy-based reforms.

Some of the choices that analysts employ are dictated by limitations in data or existing analytical methods. Once these limitations are understood, they suggest that regulatory estimates may not be accurate depictions of actual outcomes. In theory, analytical choices can produce estimates that overstate or understate the reasonableness of risk regulation. In practice, studies critical of risk regulation tend to employ choices that understate the value of regulation. In light of our bounded rationality, estimates more favorable to risk regulation are equally plausible.

Analytical techniques, such as cost-effectiveness and cost-benefit analysis, are built on economic principles and assumptions. Yet, as Chapter 3 discussed, Congress has almost universally rejected economic principles as the sole basis of risk legislation. As Chapter 4 discussed, risk legislation instead reflects multiple, widely held social values. Thus, although regulatory analysis might inform us of the extent to which risk regulation is consistent with economic principles, it does not measure the extent to which risk regulation is consistent with the multiple social values that risk regulation serves. There is no mathematical, analytical tool to which one can turn for such an assessment. This does not mean that policy-makers and researchers should not perform such assessments, but it does mean that careful, qualitative analysis will be necessary.

Regulatory Analysis

As the last chapter discussed, regulatory analysis is of two types: cost-effectiveness and cost-benefit analysis. Both techniques require an estimate of the number of lives that a regulation will save as well as other protective consequences that will result. For this purpose, analysts rely on risk assessment, a process that uses available scientific evidence to define the effects of exposure of individuals or the environment to hazardous materials and situations.[1] This chapter begins with a description and analysis of risk assessment and of the choices and assumptions that underlie this process.

Under cost-benefit analysis, the analyst establishes the economic value of the benefits identified in risk assessment. This requires that the analyst have a quantified estimate of such benefits. As the last chapter discussed, one serious limitation of many studies is that analysts ignore benefits that cannot be quantified. We will discuss this and other methodological choices and assumptions that impact the effort to monetize the benefits of risk regulation.

Under both forms of analysis, the analyst must estimate the cost of regulation. Under cost-effectiveness analysis, the analyst divides an estimate of the number of premature deaths that a regulation may prevent by the cost of such prevention. Under cost-benefit analysis, the analyst compares estimates of the monetary benefits of regulation with the estimate of costs. The estimation of regulatory costs also involves complicated methodological choices and assumptions, and that is the third subject covered by this chapter.

Finally, we discuss a methodological issue that arises in both forms of analysis: how to discount future benefits and costs. As with the previous issues, the choices and assumptions employed by analysts affect their estimates. Indeed, as the last chapter indicated, the use or nonuse of discounting greatly impacts estimates of cost-effectiveness. The Morrall–Office of Management and Budget (OMB) studies, which employed high discount rates, identified regulations that had extraordinary costs. Efforts by Lisa Heinzerling and ourselves to recalculate these estimates without discounting found the same regulations mostly had reasonable costs. The final section of this chapter discusses this issue and other issues that arise from the use of discounting.

Risk Analysis

Although risk assessment is based on scientific evidence, it is not a precise scientific prediction because information about the risks being studied is usually limited. Cancer and other health risks are difficult to estimate, for example, because so few substances have been subjected to full-scale toxicological testing in laboratory animals, and even fewer have been studied in statistically valid epidemiological studies.[2] In light of the limited data, it is inevitable that the results will be influenced by the methodological choices and assumptions made by the analyst.[3] For example, the estimates of exposure risks produced by cancer risk assessment models can vary by five to ten orders of magnitude, depending on the models selected and the exposure assumptions that are plugged into those models.[4] Translated into economic terms, differences of this magnitude are analogous to the difference between the price of a cup of coffee and the size of the national debt at its peak.[5]

Most risk assessments are subject to uncertainty, but the degree can vary. Some safety studies may be more accurate than estimates of cancer risk, for example, because there is better evidence about cause and effect relationships between risk and injuries and about the size of the exposed populations. By comparison, determining ecological effects may be an even more daunting task than estimating cancer risks, because so little is understood about the relationship between human activity and environmental outcomes.[6]

Default Assumptions

In light of the many uncertainties, risk assessors must interpret the existing data, draw inferences from those interpretations, and make assumptions to fill the gaps between data and predictions. Some methodological choices are informed by scientific judgment about which there may be disagreement among the experts. Other choices reflect policy preferences about which there is invariably disagreement among regulators and interested parties.

Opponents of risk regulation particularly object to one policy preference typically used by agency risk assessors concerning cancer risks. Agencies usually assume in the absence of conclusive evidence to the contrary that a carcinogen has no "threshold" concentration below which it poses no risk of causing cancer. Similar assumptions are built into the conversion factor for translating the results of animal testing to humans.[7] Since such assumptions are made in the absence of definitive scientific proof, they have become known as "default" assumptions. As the Environmental Protection Agency (EPA) has explained:

> [D]efault assumptions are necessarily made in risk assessments in which data gaps exist in general knowledge or in available data for a particular agent. These default assumptions are inferences based on general scientific knowledge of the phenomena in question and are also matters of policy concerning the appropriate way to bridge uncertainties that concern potential risk to human health (or, more generally, to environmental systems) from the agent under assessment.[8]

The use of conservative default assumptions is in keeping with the protective mandate of risk regulation because it minimizes the danger to the public if the agency underestimates a risk. As John Applegate argues:

> [T]here is nothing inherently wrong with choosing conservative or protective scenarios or assumptions. After all, environmental legislation has at its heart the prevention of harm before it occurs. This certainly implies erring on the side of safety when uncertainty exists. If an estimate turns out to be erroneous, surely we would rather be in the position of relaxing unneeded restrictions than apologizing to victims' families.[9]

These assumptions promote the preventive function of risk regulation and are based on the premise that it is typically worse to fail to regulate based on an erroneous determination that a risk was not serious enough to warrant regulation (a false negative) than it is to regulate based on an erroneous determination that a risk was serious enough to warrant regulation (a false positive).

Because agencies employ conservative risk assumptions, critics of risk regulation contend that agencies overstate the benefits of risk regulation. Since agencies lack proof that risks are as great as assumed, the critics argue that monetary estimates of benefits by agencies, which are based on these risk assessments, are overstated. There is no clear evidence, however, that risks are in fact overstated. If anything, the available evidence, although fragmentary, indicates that regulators have not overestimated the extent of environmental and health and safety risks.[10]

Because of their opposition to conservative risk assumptions used by agencies, some of the critics of risk regulation have made their own risk assessments.[11] In John Morrall's original article, for example, he acknowledges adjusting agency estimates of the number of lives that a regulation will save.[12] Likewise, it appears that OMB made adjustments to agency risk estimates for purposes of its 1992 cost-effectiveness study.[13] Similarly, as documented earlier, Robert Hahn failed to include two significant EPA regulations in his calculations of net regulatory benefits because the regulations protected against skin cancer, and he believed that a cure will be developed.[14] It does not appear, however, that these adjustments were made according to the practices and methods of risk assessors.

Critics of risk regulation, such as John Graham, have proposed that Congress eliminate the use of default assumptions by requiring agencies to use the "best" or "most likely" estimate of the risks posed by a particular activity.[15] This proposal is not pragmatic because it erroneously assumes that there is sufficient risk information to achieve such an estimate. The uncertainties that becloud risk assessment, discussed earlier, are simply too large in most cases to support "best estimates."[16] Moreover, it is simply not feasible to "average" risk estimate studies because studies that reach different results typically utilize different methodological choices and assumptions. As Elaine Silbergeld points out, calculation of a "central" estimate of risk in this circumstance, is like "averag[ing] the winning percentage of all Los Angeles sports teams—basketball, football, hockey and baseball—to derive a central estimate of likely success for an athlete playing in that city."[17]

A better reform is to require that agency risk assessments be transparent. The choices and assumptions used by risk assessors should be clearly explained. Moreover, if different risk assessment models yield different predictions, the predictions should be displayed and explained in a comprehensible fashion. These are pragmatic requirements because such transparency is a necessary foundation for two-way communication between government and the public it serves.[18]

Regulatory Benefits

Analysts attempting to compare the costs and benefits of a regulation must assign an economic value to the benefits identified in the risk assessment. Just as in the risk assessment context, analysts end up plugging holes in the data with methodological choices. We discuss three such choices and why each tends to understate the value of regulatory benefits. The value of benefits is affected by the use of a "willingness to pay" measurement of benefits, the assumption that market prices are an accurate reflection of preferences for additional safety, and the failure to include difficult-to-measure regulatory benefits. Analysts are working on improving analytical methods, which should make the monetization of regulatory benefits more accurate. As of yet, however, these methods have not been perfected, and it is not clear that they will be perfected any time soon. Other evaluation problems, however, are inherent in monetizing benefits, and these cannot be overcome.

Chapter 4 explained that economic theory determines the value of human life, reduction of injury, and disease and environmental protection according to how much the beneficiaries of regulation are willing to pay for a reduction in risks. Willingness to pay is ascertained indirectly through the "revealed preferences" of individuals in market transactions. Thus the value of protecting human life from workplace risks is based on how much money workers are willing to pay to reduce small safety risks at work.[19] Similarly, the value that consumers assign to the reduction of safety risks is determined from how much money consumers pay for safer products.[20] To measure the value of environmental amenities like national parks, economists consider the amount of money that people spend to travel to such places.[21]

The use of revealed preferences to estimate individuals' willingness to pay for more protection and less risk is subject to a number of potential errors, which cause regulatory benefits to be understated. This section considers these problems and the extent to which analysts are likely to overcome them.

"Willingness to Pay" versus "Willingness to Sell"

As Chapter 4 discussed, economic theory assumes that the amount that someone is willing to pay to purchase some additional level of protection is equal to the amount that the person would demand in order to receive less protection, if the person ends up at the same level of risk in either case. Pragmatism, however, is concerned with real world outcomes, where it is less likely that the willingness to sell is impacted by a person's wealth than the willingness to buy. Since willingness to pay is a function of a person's wealth, a person's wealth will limit the amount that he or she can pay to be safer or to reduce harm to the environment. By comparison, if regulatory benefits were measured by a "willingness to sell," the value of regulatory benefits undoubtedly would be higher.

Since the market system works as a "willingness to pay" system, any preferences revealed by the market system will necessarily be "willingness to pay" measurements. As Chapter 4 discussed, that is one reason why it is not pragmatic to base the level of regulation on a cost-benefit test. If regulatory decisions were made on the basis of people's willingness to pay for protection, equitable considerations would be ignored.

When cost-benefit analysis is used to evaluate the extent to which risk regulation as presently constituted is consistent with economic efficiency, there is still a problem. Criticism of current regulatory programs on the basis of willingness to pay measurements assumes that the existing distribution of wealth did not affect the measurement of regulatory benefits, which is unlikely.

Market Flaws

The next problem is the assumption that revealed preferences used by analysts to determine the benefits of regulation are accurate reflections of individual preferences. This assumption is valid, however, only to the extent that markets function without imperfections, which are known as "market flaws." In economic theory, a market will function in this "perfect" manner only if certain crucial conditions are met, such as accurate and complete information for buyers and sellers.[22] When market transactions occur without complete information, market prices are not accurate reflections of buyers' preferences.

The use of wage premiums to estimate the benefits of workplace safety illustrates this difficulty. Economic theory predicts that workers will seek safer jobs unless employers compensate them for the workplace risks that accompany a more dangerous job.[23] Thus workers will seek a wage premium sufficient to reimburse them for the costs of any future accidents, including the loss of any compensation. Since a worker gives up the "wage premium" to work in a safer place, the worker who leaves a risky job is "willing to pay" (in terms of forgone compensation) the amount of the premium to work in safer conditions.

Consistent with this theory, some studies have found that workers in dangerous jobs receive higher wages after controlling for education, experience, and other market characteristics of safety hazards.[24] The size of wage premiums is typically small. Professor Viscusi, for example, has found that annual compensation for all job safety risks equals about $400 per worker.[25] Although the compensation is low, analysts extrapolate from such data that workers are willing to pay between $3.0 million and $7.0 million to prevent one premature death.[26] A small wage premium is the equivalent of this much larger amount because the premium is paid for a relatively small risk. For example, if one worker out of ten thousand workers will die annually from a particular safety risk, a $400 wage premium is the equivalent of a $4.0 million value of life. The value of a life is calculated by dividing the $400 wage premium by the fatality risk (.0001), which results in a $4.0 million valuation for a life saved.

The existence of wage premiums would seem to indicate that workers have some knowledge of workplace risks, but a study by Peter Dorman and Paul Hagstron disputes that conclusion. They found that, although wage premium studies control for education, experience, and other market characteristics of safety hazards, these studies did not control for labor market imperfections in the industries being studied. When they accounted for such imperfections in their correlation studies, they found no evidence that workers receive compensation for the risk of fatal and nonfatal injuries except for one weak measure of fatality risk. They concluded that "[t]hese results cast doubt on the very existence of compensating differentials for all workers, union and nonunion alike."[27]

Even if the additional wages paid to workers in dangerous industries are actually wage premiums, they are an accurate reflection of the workers' preferences only if workers had an adequate understanding of existing risks.[28] Workers' knowledge, however, may be limited. Using national survey data, James Robinson found that 33 percent to 50 percent of workers in occupations with high rates of disabling injuries and illnesses reported that they faced no significant safety or health hazards. Although workers were more likely to recognize cancer risks in industries where such risks were high, only 12 percent to 33 percent considered that they were exposed to a significant risk.[29] Moreover, it is not enough that individuals know that working in a steel mill is more dangerous than working for an insurance company. To bargain for appropriate wage premiums, workers must be able to discern marginal differences in risk between jobs within the same firm or between two firms in the same industry.[30] Workers are hampered in obtaining accurate information about workplace risks because existing data significantly understate the extent of such risks.[31] A worker's evaluation of risk may also be distorted by psychological defects in the way that risk information is processed by individuals.[32] Younger workers, for example, are likely to undervalue low probability and high consequence risks based on the familiar "it-can't-happen-to-me" theory.

There is another market flaw that impacts the reliability of wage premium studies as an indication of workers' preferences. The additional compensation that a worker can obtain for hazardous work is a function of the worker's bargaining power. That is especially true in jobs in which employees can be easily replaced and for which alternative jobs are not readily available. Many hazardous jobs have these characteristics. Dorman and Hagstron found evidence of a negative correlation—that is, relatively high risk and low wages—for nonunion workers.[33] James Robinson found that if education and skill levels are ignored, hazardous jobs pay 20 percent to 30 percent less than safe employment. This discrepancy indicates that persons with training and education avoid such jobs because safer employment pays more. The pool of labor for hazardous jobs therefore consists of "disadvantaged workers who are willing to accept health and safety risks in return for very modest amounts of compensation."[34] "In plain terms," Dorman and Hagstron explain, "nonunion workers in dangerous jobs are, in many cases, simply unlucky: they have found their way into situations of high risk and low pay and would presumably move to a better job if they could."[35]

Extrapolation from Safety Studies

Analysts use wage premium studies for purposes other than estimating the benefits of workplace regulation. For example, researchers have been unable to test for the existence of risk compensation for occupational illness, such as cancer, because there is little reliable data about the risk of occupational diseases.[36] In light of the lack of evidence concerning how much workers are willing to pay to reduce health risks, analysts assume that it is the same amount that they are willing to pay to reduce safety risks.

This assumption leads to a likely understatement of the value of workplace and environmental health protections, for several reasons. Benefits are likely to be understated because analysts fail to take into account the impact of wealth and the context in which the risk occurs.

Wealth Effect

This extrapolation ignores the impact of wealth on willingness to pay. Individuals who take risky workplace jobs generally have lower than average incomes. Environmental protection, however, generally protects a larger and wealthier population, who presumably could and would pay more for a reduction in health risks than workers can afford to pay for a reduction in workplace risks. Thus, as Richard Revesz notes: "[An] appropriate correction needs to be made when extrapolating from the workplace to the environmental arena." The problem, he continues, is that "[no] empirical literature ... sheds light on the magnitude of the correction."[37] Thus we can anticipate that the cost-benefit analysis undervalues the health benefits that result from environmental protection, but analysts as of yet lack the information to overcome this problem.

Contextual Effects

Extrapolation from workplace safety studies to estimate other regulatory benefits presents another problem that affects the reliability of such estimates. The use of revealed preferences in a different context assumes that individuals will assign the same value to protection in other contexts. But revealed preferences are likely to be context specific. As Richard Pildes and Cass Sunstein note: "We cannot get a good sense of what people value simply from choices, since choices are a function of context and since they are inarticulate—poor predictors of future behavior—without an account of what lies behind them."[38] Thus "[s]moke alarm purchases, cap safety expenditures, and use of suntan lotion cannot plausibly be said to reflect general judgments about the value of life."[39] Similarly, "a willingness to spend $X to eliminate a 1/10,000 risk of death does not necessarily entail a willingness to pay $10X to eliminate a 1/1000 risk of death, a willingness to pay $100X to eliminate a 1/100 risk of death, or a willingness to pay $1,000X to eliminate a 1/10 risk of death."[40]

The problem of context shows up in several ways. As noted, wage premiums concern safety risks, but researchers use the information to estimate the willingness of individuals to pay for reductions in health risks. Individuals, however, are likely to view the two situations differently.[41] Whereas deaths from industrial accidents occur instantaneously and without warning, deaths from environmental exposures to carcinogens often occur after a long and agonizing ordeal. "All deaths are bad," Cass Sunstein notes, "[b]ut some deaths are worse than others."[42] Analysts have begun to study how this difference impacts willingness to pay. One study finds that the valuation of life in the case of carcinogenic exposure is twice as high as the valuation of life for an unforeseen, instantaneous death.[43]

Another contextual problem arises from the difference in valuation of voluntary and involuntary incurred risks. Research suggests that people assign a higher value to avoiding a risk that is thrust upon them involuntarily than risks that they voluntary incur.[44] The revealed preferences indicated by wage premiums, however, are supposed to relate to voluntarily incurred risks. In economic theory, market transactions involve voluntary transactions because no one will enter into a transaction unless it makes the person better off. If that is accurate, it is unreliable to estimate the value of avoiding involuntary risks, such as risks posed by air and water pollution, on the basis of wage premiums, which reflect voluntary risks.[45] In fact, as discussed earlier, it is not clear the extent to which workplace risks are voluntarily incurred.[46] Analysts are attempting to estimate the impact of voluntariness on willingness to pay. Professor Revesz interprets one such study as suggesting that individuals may be willing to pay twice as much to avoid a death from an involuntary risk as from a voluntary one.[47]

Contextual factors other than the voluntary or involuntary nature of risks also affect individual perceptions of the acceptability of risk. Such factors include whether a risk produces catastrophic or diffuse consequences, whether the consequences involve irretrievable or permanent losses, the social conditions under which a particular risk is generated and managed, the nature of the death that the risk creates, how much suffering is entailed, and equity among groups and between generations.[48]

While it is clear that context affects how people value the avoidance of risks, "further research on such matters is clearly needed."[49] In the meantime, we do know that existing estimates of the benefits of environmental health protection likely understate the amount of benefit, although no one knows by how much.

Nonquantified Benefits

The effort to estimate regulatory benefits understates such benefits for yet another reason. In order to quantify the monetary value of a regulatory benefit, the analyst must start with a quantified estimate of that benefit, such as the number of premature deaths that a regulation is estimated to prevent. Analysts therefore tend to ignore benefits that are difficult or impossible to quantify, which means that the monetized benefit estimate does not accurately reflect the actual regulatory benefits.[50] If analysts attempt quantification, they often use rough estimates that may bear no realistic relationship to actual benefits. Recall, for example, that Bob Hahn treated a chronic disease or disabling injury as having the same economic value as saving one-third of a life.[51] This problem is unavoidable because, as discussed earlier in this chapter, many human and environmental risks are not very well understood. As a result, analysts lack empirical estimates of them.

The fact that benefits cannot be quantified does not mean that they should not be considered in any effort to assess the benefits of regulation. Yet because these benefits cannot be quantified, they do not play a role in efforts to quantify benefits for purposes of a cost-benefit test. In Laurence Tribe's famous observation, modelers tend to "dwarf soft variables."[52] In turn, critics of risk regulation likewise ignore such benefits. The Morrall-OMB studies discussed in the previous chapter are a good example. Although these studies have been cited by regulatory critics dozens of times, the critics have generally failed to note, as we did, the nonquantified environmental benefits that resulted from the regulations studied by Morrall and OMB. Once these benefits are taken into account, there is a more complete picture of the rationality of some of the regulations that appear to be the most unreasonable. Although these regulations were intended primarily to protect the environment, OMB attributed the entire cost of the regulations to the reduction of health risks.

Contingent Valuation

As noted, analysts have begun to address defects in the manner in which regulatory benefits are calculated. The most significant such effort is to use survey evidence. For example, one such technique, contingent valuation, has become popular with analysts to estimate environmental benefits.[53] Although this approach permits analysts to monetize what are now nonquantified benefits, the reliability of such estimates is open to question.

In contingent valuation, economists ask a representative sample of individuals how much money they would be willing to pay for an environmental outcome, such as how much money they would pay in higher electricity rates to ensure clean air over the Grand Canyon. The advantage of this method over using revealed preferences is that it can account for nonuse or existence value. If the analyst uses revealed preferences, such as how much money people are willing to pay to travel to the Grand Canyon, the analyst fails to account for the amount of money that persons are willing to pay to ensure pristine air over the Grand Canyon even though they have no plans to visit the area. Some people are willing to make such a payment because they derive value from the mere knowledge of the existence of unique assets such as the Grand Canyon, scenic wilderness, or the preservation of endangered species.[54] Analysts have also used survey data to obtain information about individual preferences concerning health benefits. The study discussed earlier about how much more individuals are willing to pay to avoid death from an involuntary risk used this technique.[55] In particular, this approach has been used to attempt to value classes of risks not captured in labor market risk data, particularly nonfatal health risks.[56]

Besides plugging data gaps, a survey approach has several other advantages.[57] With contingent valuation, analysts do not have to abstract and generalize from context-based choices because hypothetical questions can be designed for virtually any context. Because they are context-based, surveys usually yield monetary values that are higher than those produced by economists' measures of revealed preferences concerning risks for which context is an important consideration for people. For example, we noted earlier that Professor Revesz interpreted one such study as suggesting that individuals may be willing to pay twice as much to avoid a death from an involuntary risk as from a voluntary one.

Despite these advantages, the data revealed by such studies may not be very reliable. The results vary depending on how the questions are framed, because it is the survey question that supplies "both the context and definition of the relevant task to which participating individuals are expected to respond."[58] In addition, the very advantage of such studies is a disadvantage: the answers are hypothetical, and respondents "do not have to put their money where their mouths are by making choices constrained by real budgets."[59] Because respondents know the effect that their answers have on the assigned values, they may answer questions dishonestly or strategically.[60] Finally, contingent valuation methods cannot escape some of the important limitations on the use of revealed preferences. If individuals lack information or experience concerning what they evaluate, their answers will not be informed.[61]

Answers are also subject to wealth effects. If contingent valuation answers are accurate, the amount that people are willing to pay (that is, state they would pay) is still bounded by their wealth. Analysts can seek to minimize the impact of wealth by asking questions of an appropriately representative pool, and average the answers to produce an average, hypothetical willingness to pay to avoid various conditions. That solution, however, does not solve the problem, identified earlier, that if regulatory benefits were valued by a person's willingness to sell, the price would be higher.

Regulatory Costs

The monetization of regulatory benefits is subject to data and methodological limitations that limit the reliability of benefit estimates, and most of these problems lead to an understatement of benefits. There are also valuation problems in estimating the compliance costs of regulation. The problem is that regulated industries are often the only source of information about the costs of complying with a proposed regulation, and regulated firms have an incentive to overstate such costs in order to persuade agencies to weaken proposed regulations. Although there have been only a few attempts to validate cost projections in light of subsequent experience, the available evidence suggests that agencies overstate compliance costs more often than they understate them.

Critics of risk regulation do not deny this result, but they do contend that regulation costs more than the studies estimate because most studies do not include some significant regulatory costs. In particular, they argue that there is a "health-health" tradeoff, in which regulatory expenditures create health problems by reducing social wealth. There is only weak evidence, however, to support these claims.

Compliance Costs

The few studies that have compared estimated and actual costs are summarized in Table 6.1. The studies have identified three reasons why contemporary agency cost estimates apparently are often too high.

One reason why contemporaneous cost estimates tend to be too high is that agencies rely heavily on information provided by regulated entities that have an obvious stake in the outcome of the proceedings.[62] As a result, "firms have an incentive to overstate their pollution control costs as a way of reducing the possibility that they will be saddled with additional regulatory costs in the future."[63] This phenomenon is illustrated by some of the examples that the retrospective studies cite. Car manufacturers, for example, estimated in 1993 that EPA regulations limiting the use of CFCs in automobile air conditioners would increase the price of a new car by $650 to $1,200, but a 1997 estimate established the actual cost as between $40 and $400 per car.[64] The costs of installing emission control equipment on stationary sources of nitrogen oxides to reduce acid deposition turned out to be 20 percent to 50 percent of the amounts initially predicted.[65] And when the Occupational Safety and Health Administration (OSHA) proposed to adopt a 1 ppm exposure limitation for vinyl chloride, the president of Firestone's plastics division warned that it would put the vinyl plastics industry "on a collision course with economic disaster."[66] OSHA promulgated a 1 ppm standard anyway, and actual compliance costs were about 7 percent of the predicted amount.[67]

Agency estimates also tend to be too high because forecasters fail to anticipate that competitive pressures will cause firms to find less expensive methods of compliance. OSHA's formaldehyde standard is an example. The industry's actual cost was about half of the agency's estimate, because regulated entities were able to use low formaldehyde resins to meet the exposure limitation, rather than install expensive ventilation and control equipment.[68] OSHA's cotton dust standard offers another example of technological inno-

TABLE 6.1

Retrospective Studies of Regulatory Costs

Study	Subject of Cost Estimates	Results
PHB, 1980	Sector level capital expenditures for pollution controls	—EPA overestimated capital costs more than it underestimated them, with forecasts ranging 26 to 126 percent above reported expenditures
OTA, 1995	Total, annual, or capital expenditures for occupational safety and health regulations	—OSHA overestimated costs for 4 of 5 health regulations, with forecasts ranging from $5.4 million to $722 million above reported expenditures
		—OSHA underestimated cost for 1 safety regulation by $0.3 to $2.1 million
Goodstein and Hodges, 1997	Various measures of cost for pollution regulation	—Agency and industry overestimated costs for 24 of 24 OSHA and EPA regulations, by at least 30 percent and generally by more than 100 percent
Resources for the Future, 1999	Various measures of cost for environmental regulations	—Agency overestimated costs for 12 of 25 rules, and underestimated costs for 2 rules

SOURCE: Studies cited in the table (citations in the text).

vation. The actual cost of compliance was about $82.8 million, in comparison to OSHA's pricetag of $280 million. The textile manufacturers spent much less because competitive pressures forced them to build new plants, which allowed them to avoid the more costly job of installing abatement equipment in their older facilities.[69] There is a similar story concerning the development of acceptable substitutes for CFCs. At the time of the adoption of the phaseout of the manufacture and use of CFCs in the 1987 Montreal Protocol and the Clean Air Act (CAA) amendments, the cost, efficacy, and environmental acceptability of chemical substitutes for CFCs were anticipated to create serious obstacles to the achievement of the phaseout. Instead, industry quickly developed substitutes that cost less and performed better than CFCs.[70]

There is a debate in the literature about the extent to which environmental regulation triggers innovation that can offset some or all of compliance costs.[71] Based on their retrospective review of twenty-four regulations, Goodstein and Hodges are optimistic: "When pollution regulation makes a certain type of production more expensive, markets adjust—in fairly rapid order, uncovering substitute methods of production, and developing cheaper cleanup technologies."[72]

A study done for Resources for the Future (RFF) suggests a third reason why agency cost estimates may be too high: there can be less regulatory compliance than an agency estimates.[73] Industry compliance with OSHA's regulation on occupational lead exposures provides an example. Industry compliance costs have been about one-sixth as much as OSHA had estimated, and one reason is that airborne levels of lead, while lower now than at the time OSHA promulgated its regulation, remain above the emission level mandated by the regulation.[74] If an agency overestimates the quantity of pollution reduction, the regulation may also produce lower benefits than anticipated. Thus the RFF study concludes that the overestimation of costs in such cases "does not imply that the regulation *as envisioned* was less expensive than predicted."[75]

Missing Costs

Estimates of regulatory costs can go astray because they are based on industry-supplied data, fail to account for innovation, or overestimate the quantity of pollution reduction. The first two sources of error, other things being equal, will cause cost-effectiveness studies to be overstated and net regulatory benefits to be understated. Critics of risk regulation respond that estimates of regulatory costs may also be too low because they fail to account for equilibrium costs and the possibility that regulation creates regulatory costs as well as benefits.

Equilibrium Costs

The regulatory impact assessments that agencies prepare do not estimate general equilibrium effects of regulation, such as product substitution, or discouraged or retarded investment, and they estimate transition costs, such as unemployment or plant closures, only sometimes. The RFF study, mentioned above, notes that although the additional management resources required to comply with regulations or disrupted production are "plausibly important," there are no *ex ante* estimates of such costs.[76] Agencies fail to make such estimates because there is a lack of credible information or because they have insufficient analytical resources to apply to whatever data or models do exist.

Some information suggests, however, that indirect regulatory costs are not excessive. The prior discussion noted that innovation reduces, sometimes significantly, regulatory costs, which will likewise decrease equilibrium costs. Further, the Office of Technology Assessment (OTA) study compared *ex ante* and *ex post* information available about equilibrium effects and found that industry predictions of significant indirect costs were not borne out. For example, OSHA rejected predictions by the formaldehyde industry of significant financial disruption, and OTA found no evidence that more than a few foundries closed as a result of the regulation.[77] Likewise, contrary to industry estimates, "few if any" grain-handling facilities closed as a result of an OSHA regulation that required the abatement of grain dust to reduce the risk of explosions.[78] Finally, agencies can and usually do go to extreme lengths to phase in or avoid entirely job losses that might result from their regulations.[79]

Health-Health Tradeoffs

Analysts also argue that cost estimates are too low because agencies fail to take into account "health-health tradeoffs" that occur when the abatement of one health risk increases another health risk. For example, John Applegate and Steven Wesloh established that EPA officials generally failed to take into account short-term remediation risks in the remedy selection process for Superfund sites.[80] The authors identified a number of such risks, including death and injuries resulting from transportation accidents related to a cleanup operation. Although critics of risk regulation, such as Cass Sunstein, claim that the agency's failure to analyze "health-health" tradeoffs is a "pervasive" problem,[81] there is little empirical evidence concerning the extent to which regulators fail to take into account such tradeoffs in other contexts or how important these are.

Another claim of a "health-health" tradeoff is based on the "richer is safer" argument first advanced by Aaron Wildavsky.[82] In an "enormous expansion of the classic concept of opportunity cost,"[83] Wildavsky argued that any regulation that imposes costs necessarily results in some death. This tradeoff is said to occur because regulations, particularly when they cost substantial amounts of money, cause unemployment and greater poverty. Citing evidence that people who are poor or unemployed tend to have worse health and live shorter lives, some analysts conclude that costly regulation increases health risks by virtue of reducing wealth. Consider, for example, Judge Williams's exposition of this argument in the context of an OSHA regulation:

> More regulation means some combination of reduced value of firms, higher product prices, fewer jobs in the regulated industry, and lower cash wages. All the latter three stretch workers' budgets tighter (as does the first to the extent that the firms' stock is held in workers' pension trusts). And larger incomes enable people to lead safer lives.[84]

Kip Viscusi predicts that "every time we spend $50 million on a life-saving effort, the income loss that will result will generate a statistical death because of the income-mortality linkage."[85] Other analysts claim that the expenditure of as little as $7.25 million to save a statistical life leads to the loss of another life.[86]

Studies of the relationship between poverty and morbidity and mortality demonstrate a reasonably strong correlation between income and mortality.[87] As a general matter, richer persons live longer and healthier lives than poor persons. The connection between cost-imposing regulations and the health of poor persons, however, is far from established.[88] First, there are no studies that correlate the lost income attributable to a particular regulation or group of regulations with deaths among populations that have lost income. Second, while poor persons tend to die sooner than rich people do, it is not clear why this is the case, and the available empirical evidence does not show a cause-effect relationship.[89] The relationship is likely a complex one explained by factors such as health, education, and good eating habits, which are roughly correlated with wealth but do not depend on it. Third, as discussed earlier in this section, there is no reason to believe that regulations often lead to significant economic dislocations, while there is considerably more evidence that regulations lead to increased productivity, which creates new jobs.[90] Further, agencies go out of their way to avoid unemployment.

Finally, "while groups of poor individuals may have a higher mortality risk than groups of wealthier individuals, it does not follow that the risk of any individual would increase if a marginal sum of money was taken away from him or her."[91] For example, OSHA estimated that its air contaminant rule would increase compliance costs for the construction industry by $145 million. According to Professor Viscusi, the regulation would therefore result in the death of three workers. As we discussed earlier, he predicts that every time the country spends $50 million on a life-saving effort, there will be the loss of one life because the regulation will increase the level of poverty. Even if one assumes that employers reduced the wages of workers by $150 million to pay for the regulation, each worker would lose very little money. The construction industry, for example, employs about five million workers. The average worker would therefore lose only about twenty-nine dollars per year.[92]

Agencies undoubtedly fail to account for some regulatory costs, but it is difficult to conclude on the basis of available evidence that the missing costs result in significant regulatory excesses. In particular, the idea that regulations cause an income loss that results in a health-health tradeoff remains entirely unproven.

Discounting

Estimates of regulatory costs and benefits often involve methodological choices that are open to question. The same is true regarding discounting, which is employed by analysts to determine the present value of the regulatory costs and benefits that they have derived. Analysts use discounted estimates because economic theory requires that future expenditures or income be measured according to their monetary value today, which is their "present value."

As with the estimates of regulatory benefits and costs, discounting involves methodological choices, which have the impact of decreasing the value of risk regulation, although other choices that increase the value of regulation arguably are as or more valid. This section considers these choices and assumptions and how they affect benefit and cost estimates.

The use of discounted estimates to claim that risk regulation is excessive and irrational poses an additional problem. Discounting has the effect of shrinking the monetary value of future costs and benefits, often by substantial amounts. While this reduction may be appropriate under economic theory, it does not follow that it is appropriate in terms of evaluating the success of risk regulation. Discounting reflects one social value, economic efficiency, but risk regulation attempts to balance multiple social values. Thus what may be "irrational" from an economic perspective may not be "irrational" from a pragmatic perspective. This section also considers the normative implications of discounting.

Discounting Theory

Economic theory offers two justifications for discounting the value of regulatory benefits and costs that occur in the future. One justification is the time-value of money. The other is the rational comparison of benefits and costs that occur in different years.

According to the time value of money principle, a dollar today is worth more to an individual than a dollar available to the person some time in the future.[93] The reason is that a person with a dollar today can invest the money and, because of interest payments, it will be worth more in the future. Assume, for example, that an individual invests $1,000 and that at the end of ten years the investment is worth $2,592, which equates to a 10 percent rate of return. The value of $2,592 today, however, is only $1,000 because the individual will discount the future amount by 10 percent. In economic terminology, $1,000 is the "present value" of $2,592 conferred at the end of a ten-year period. Thus, everything else being equal, the individual is indifferent between having $1,000 today and $2,592 in ten years if the money can be invested to earn a 10 percent rate of return. Similarly, an individual will be indifferent between paying a cost (for example, a tax) of $1,000 today or $2,592 ten years from now, assuming that the $1,000 can earn a 10 percent rate of return in the ten-year period before the tax is paid.

Since regulatory benefits and costs occur in the future, the time value of money principle justifies the use of discounting to determine the value today of those future benefits and costs. A regulation is analogous to an investment in the sense that it produces future results that have a monetary value, and the value of those future benefits is less today because of the time value of money. Thus if a 10 percent discount rate is appropriate, regulatory benefits of $2,592 at the end of ten years have a present value of $1,000. The same theory applies to regulatory costs. If the cost to comply with a regulation is $2,592 at the end of ten years, the present value of the cost is $1,000, using a 10 percent discount rate.

A related economic justification for the use of discounting is that it permits the comparison of benefits and costs that occur at different points in time. If, for example, a regulation produces $1,000 in benefits for each of ten years and $1,000 in costs for each of five years, a nondiscounted measurement yields benefits of $10,000 (10 x $1,000) and costs of $5,000 (5 x $1,000), or a net benefit of $5,000. Economists object that these costs and benefits cannot be directly compared because this ignores the time value of money and the fact that the benefits and costs occur over different periods of time. Assuming a 7 percent discount rate (the rate OMB uses), the benefits have a present value of $7,024 and the costs have a present value of $4,100, which produces a net benefit of $2,924. Since the present value of the discounted net benefit is about 60 percent of the nondiscounted net benefit, economic analysts argue that the failure to discount overvalues regulatory benefits.

The use of discounting, and the choice of a discount rate, have a significant impact on estimates of regulatory benefits. Assume, for example, that a regulation will prevent a premature death from cancer twenty-five years from now, and that the life has a nondiscounted value of $7.0 million. If it is assumed that the benefit of saving the life occurs twenty-five years from now, the present value is $4.27 million if a 2 percent discount rate is used and $1.29 million if a 7 percent discount rate is used.

Discount Rate

As the previous hypothetical illustrates, the choice of the discount rate has a significant impact on estimates of regulatory benefits. There was a $3.0 million difference in the estimate depending on whether a 2 or 7 percent rate is used. Despite the importance of choosing an appropriate rate, there is considerable uncertainty about what rate should be used.

Assumptions about Preferences

Analysts discount future regulatory benefits according to discount rates used for financial transactions. In other words, to determine the discount rate that individuals use to avoid death or illness in the future, analysts use the discount rate which markets reveal that individuals prefer concerning future costs or income. This methodology involves two assumptions. First, it assumes that individuals actually discount future life relative to present life. Second, it assumes that, if they do, the discount rate they employ is the same discount rate that individuals use to make financial investments.

As to the first assumption, it seems implausible that individuals value future health according to some type of discounting. As Lisa Heinzerling observes:

> Imagine the person who, before quitting smoking or embarking on an exercise program or switching to a low-fat diet, first considered whether Alan Greenspan and the Federal Reserve Board might soon raise or lower interest rates, and how this might affect investment returns. Wouldn't that person seem just a little crazy? Yet, this is exactly the line of reasoning implied by [the analysts'] approach to the future.[94]

It seems even more implausible that individuals engage in the type of discounting used in cost-effectiveness analysis. In cost-effectiveness analysis the analyst is discounting the number of premature deaths that are prevented, not the monetary value of those deaths. For example, if one life is saved fifty years from now, it has a present value of 0.37 life today at a 2 percent discount rate. It seems unlikely that individuals think in such terms. After all, "You cannot put a life—or a life-year, for that matter, in the bank and earn money on it."[95] And lives do not come in fractions. "If a person dies 30 years from now due to cancer caused by exposure to arsenic, a whole life is lost."[96]

An economic analyst would respond that if discounting is established as an empirical matter, then the accuracy of its assumptions are sufficiently established. There is only limited and highly varied empirical evidence, however, on people's revealed preferences concerning future risk-related effects.[97] The limited evidence does suggest that a majority of people value future risk events in a manner that reflects discounting. Kip Viscusi and Michael Moore, for example, examined wage premiums and concluded that they contained an implicit discount rate ranging from 2 to 12 percent.[98]

The lack of evidence that people behave in the manner that discounting assumes is not the only problem with discounted estimates. The existing evidence "does not bring us anywhere close to being able to identify a single *rate* at which people discount future risk-related effects."[99] Consider the Viscusi and Moore study. The difference between a 2 and 12 percent discount rate has a significant impact on regulatory estimates. If one hundred lives are saved fifty years from now, the result is the equivalent of thirty-seven lives saved today at a 2 percent discount rate. By comparison, it is the equivalent to one-third of a life at a 10 percent discount rate, a difference of over two orders of magnitude.

Moreover, the effort to calculate a discount rate based on revealed preferences is subject to the same problems identified earlier that make market behavior an imperfect indicator of people's preferences. In addition, as Chapter 4 discussed, citizens may have different preferences when they make decisions about public policy, in comparison to decisions they make as market participants. The existence of the risk regulation legislation, which rejects economic principles as the basis for regulation, supports this argument. As Lisa Heinzerling notes, one

> can make a very plausible argument that the existence and widespread popularity of dozens of federal statutes ensuring a high level of environmental protection belie the claim, implicit in discounting, that the future matters relatively little to the ordinary person. Closer to home, most parents, I think, are at least as concerned about their children's future, and as anxious to make it good, as they are concerned about their own present well-being.[100]

Assumption of a Constant Rate

Analysts apply financial discount rates in estimating regulatory benefits and costs because they do not have good evidence of what rates individuals actually use. Another problem is that analysts use a constant discount rate, which makes two assumptions about individuals' behavior. First, it assumes that individuals discount the utility of avoiding death or illness in the future at the same rate regardless of whether the risk-related event occurs sooner or later in their life. In fact, there is some evidence that individuals' discount rates tend to decline the further into the future the relevant effects would occur.[101] This limited evidence suggests that the use of a constant rate would understate the value of regulatory benefits that occurred in later periods. Second, it assumes that individuals discount every risk of death or illness in the same manner regardless of the nature of that risk. As discussed earlier, however, individuals appear to vary their risk preferences based on the context of the risk. There is some empirical evidence that an individual's risk-related discount rates depend on the nature of the risk in question, but that issue has not been thoroughly tested.[102]

Which Discount Rate?

As a proxy for individuals' actual discount rates, the financial discount rate may or may not be accurate. When it comes to choosing the financial discount rate, analysts are in disagreement. Some analysts propose that a 1 to 3 percent discount rate should be used to measure regulatory benefits. Other analysts, including OMB, use a 7 percent discount rate.

The lower rate is the historical real rate of return on riskless investments, such as U.S. Treasury bonds.[103] It therefore indicates what return an individual can expect to earn if the person trades off consumption today for consumption in the future.[104] The real rate of return refers to the rate of interest that the investor earns after paying taxes. Other investments may pay a greater return after taxes than 1 to 3 percent, but the additional amount reflects a payment for the risk assumed by the investor.

The argument for the higher rate is that by engaging in regulation society deprives itself of the opportunity to invest the money in some income-generating opportunity. As a result, the discount rate should reflect the rate of return that is lost, which is the historical rate of return on private investments before taxes and inflation. Prior to 1992, OMB determined that this rate of return was 10 percent, but it has since lowered its estimate to 7 percent.[105]

The opportunity cost argument assumes that there is only a fixed amount of money available for regulatory compliance or investments, and if money is spent on regulation, it is not available to be spent on investments. There is a growing consensus, however, that this displacement does not occur.[106] Analysts question the displacement idea because money is available in today's worldwide investment markets for new investments even if agencies adopt new regulations.

OMB's use of the higher discount rate has the impact of lowering the value of regulatory benefits by a considerable amount. Indeed, the OMB-Morrall studies discussed in the previous chapter painted a dismal picture of regulation in part because they apply a 10 percent discount rate. Likewise, Bob Hahn's estimates of regulatory benefits are lowered by his choice of a 5 percent discount rate, which is greater than the 1–3 percent discount rate that reflects the consumption rationale. Given a choice between the consumption and opportunity cost rationales, the consumption approach is more appropriate. A higher rate assumes that each dollar spent on regulation prevents a dollar of investment, which is clearly misleading. By comparison, the lower discount rate measures the time value of money, which is the basic reason for discounting.

Discounting Period

The choice of a discount rate can raise or lower estimates of regulatory benefits by orders of magnitude. The value of regulatory benefits is shrunk by another methodological choice. Analysts assume that regulations which reduce the risk of cancer produce no benefits until the end of the latency period. In other words, if a regulation will reduce the number of cancer cases that would otherwise occur in twenty years, they measure the benefits as starting twenty years hence. The magnitude of this adjustment is suggested by the following example. Assume that a life is worth $7.0 million and that there is a thirty-five-year latency period before someone will die from cancer. Under this approach, it would not be worth more than $656,000 to prevent one death if the discount rate is 7.0 percent. In other words, preventing a premature death in thirty-five years is worth less than 10 percent of the value of preventing such a death today.

As Lisa Heinzerling has identified, the assumption that cancer prevention produces no immediate benefits is inconsistent with the rationale offered for cost-benefit analysis. As we discussed in Chapter 4, economic theory determines the value of a life by how much individuals demand in payment to accept a slightly increased risk of death. In other words, the benefit under cost-benefit analysis is the reduction of risk, not the avoidance of death.[107] But when analysts use discounting, the benefit switches and becomes the occurrence of the death itself. Heinzerling concludes that "[if] a reduction in risk is the relevant benefit for purposes of valuation, it must also be the relevant benefit for purposes of discounting."[108]

Our calculation of discounted estimates in Chapter 5 assumes that the regulatory benefits began immediately. The results are presented in Table 5.4. In our approach, discounting allows the comparisons of costs and benefits that occur in different years, but it does not treat the benefits as being delayed for years after the costs occur. Our results indicate that the regulations studied cost millions of dollars less than the OMB estimates for the same regulations. The difference is that OMB assumed the benefits did not start until after the latency period. Although our approach is not standard practice, it does indicate that arguments that risk regulation is wildly unreasonable are a result in large part of the assumption that any health benefits are delayed for twenty, thirty, or more years.

Critics can respond to Heinzerling by arguing that there is an immediate benefit, but it does not justify measuring the value of risk reduction as of the time a regulation is promulgated. According to this argument, there are two benefits to risk reduction. An immediate "benefit" is that people have to worry less about getting cancer from exposure to some hazard. The long-term benefit is that fewer people will become ill from cancer at some distant date. In other words, risk regulation yields both a psychological benefit (which occurs now) and a benefit of preventing premature deaths (which occurs in the future). This explanation justifies the assumption that a regulation produces no benefits in terms of lives saved until the end of the latency period, and it measures the psychological benefit of risk reduction as of the time the regulation was promulgated.

One important difficulty with this response is that critics of risk regulation fail to include such a psychological benefit when they calculate the benefits of regulation. This is another soft variable that is dwarfed by cost-benefit analysis and cost-effectiveness analysis. As a result, existing studies undoubtedly understate the value of health regulations. Our approach, according to the conventional methodology, would overstate the benefits. The true discounted value of such benefits is simply unknown.

Discounting and Regulatory Rationality

The use of discounted estimates of regulatory benefits, based on high discount rates and delayed benefits, provides the primary evidence upon which the critics base their claims that risk regulation is irrational and unreasonable. As we have seen, these claims are open to question. The criticism of risk regulation is troubling for another reason other than the empirical weakness of critical studies. As Chapter 4 discussed, there are pragmatic reasons for not making economic efficiency the sole guide to risk policy decisions. Such a narrow approach ignores the extraordinary value that most people place on protecting people and the environment. It also conflicts with social understandings of fairness and equity. Discounting presents special problems regarding these noneconomic social goals.

Existing laws commit the country to reconcile, as best we can, the cost of human and environmental protection with the recognition that protecting human life and the environment has an extraordinary value. Discounting is inconsistent with this commitment because it considers lives saved in the future (or protection of the environment in the future) to be intrinsically less valuable than saving lives (or the environment) today. Moreover, because discounting reduces the value of saving lives (or the environment) in two or three decades to near zero, it justifies doing little or nothing to address risks that occur in the future. For this reason, discounting commits us to do little to protect today's workers against the risk of getting cancer in twenty-five or thirty years. Discounting also means that society today should not undertake most regulations that produce benefits for future generations. The failure to protect workers or the environment from risks that occur in three decades is hardly consistent with a commitment to do the best we can to reconcile regulatory costs and the protection of individuals and the environment.

Some analysts, who favor discounting regarding risks that the present generation will confront, oppose its use when evaluating risks that will impact future generations.[109] This opposition reflects the fact that discounted estimates of benefits in future generations have an almost insignificant present value today. This refusal recognizes the folly of deciding a difficult ethical issue—what obligation does this generation have to future generations?—by a mathematical formula which assumes that the rate of return on government bonds should dictate the relative value of present and future life.

It is not clear why this same reluctance should not extend to intragenerational impacts. The failure to protect individuals or the environment within the lifetime of this generation likewise reduces a difficult moral question—to what extent should we reduce risks in the future?—to a simple, one-dimensional consideration: the discounted value of reducing or abating those risks. Public policy need not be reduced to this single calculation, and pragmatism instructs that it should not be. At the same time, because pragmatism rejects essentialism, it has no basis for completely excluding discounted estimates as part of the debate over risk regulation. Policy-makers, however, should be careful to consider the multifaceted implications of reducing future risks.

Conclusion

The divergence among the results of cost-effectiveness and cost-benefit studies described in Chapter 5 is now understandable. The vagaries in the calculation of costs and benefits permit estimates that can differ significantly, sometimes by orders of magnitude, depending on the methodological choices and assumptions used to make such estimates. Critics of risk regulation often employ choices and assumptions that reduce the value of regulation, but estimates more favorable to regulation can be equally plausible in light of bounded rationality.

Despite this state of affairs, many of the opponents of risk regulation have simply assumed the accuracy of studies critical of risk regulation. Once the limitations are acknowledged, however, it is clear that current studies do not justify sweeping reforms of risk regulation. The last two chapters support another conclusion first mentioned in Chapter 4. We noted that, in light of bounded rationality, current laws establish an evidentiary burden that is more consistent with the preventative goals of risk regulation. If agencies were required to use a cost-benefit test to establish the level of regulation, there would be endless litigation over the accuracy of the agency estimates because of the difficulty of making such estimates.

Although cost-benefit and cost-effectiveness analysis are not suitable to set the level of regulation, they can be employed to measure the extent to which risk regulation is inconsistent with economic efficiency. In the next chapter, we consider the current use of these forms of analysis for that purpose.

7

Regulatory Impact Analysis Requirements

As we have seen, most risk regulation laws require that agencies demonstrate the existence of risk or significant risk before they may regulate and that they take cost into account through the use of either constrained balancing or open-ended balancing as a standard-setting device. The previous evidentiary requirements, however, are not the only fact-finding mandates to which agencies are subject. As Chapter 1 identified, they must also comply with a series of regulatory impact analysis requirements established by presidential order and by legislation. An Executive Order issued by President Clinton requires that agencies compare the costs and benefits of proposed significant regulations before they are promulgated. The order is similar to one issued by President Reagan and continued by the first President Bush. Additional orders and legislation require agencies to study the potential impact of proposed significant regulations on children, environmental justice, federalism, paperwork burdens, property owners, small businesses, and the fiscal burdens of state and local governments, among others. The totality of these requirements adds dozens of analytical steps to the regulatory process.

As Chapter 1 also identified, critics of risk regulation would like to add to these existing requirements to study potential regulatory impacts. They have attempted to pass new legislation that would codify and extend the regulatory impact analysis requirements imposed by presidential order. In particular, they would establish detailed procedural requirements for comparing the costs and benefits of regulation, including procedures for conducting risk analysis. The ostensible purpose of these analysis requirements is to measure the extent to which risk regulation is inconsistent with economic efficiency. The study of potential regulatory impacts can also identify ways in which the same regulatory goal can be met with lower costs. These requirements, how-ever, have been opposed on the grounds that the analytical burdens they im-pose outweigh the value of the information that is produced. Given this negative payoff, the opponents claim that the real purpose of these analytical requirements is "paralysis by analysis."

This chapter considers the extent to which agencies should prepare regu-latory impact studies before they impose risk regulation. Since pragmatism encourages challenges to entrenched thinking and analysis, the idea of ana-lytical impact studies has pragmatic merit. As we indicated in Chapter 4, cost-benefit analysis in particular may perform a useful function by informing regulators and the public about the potential efficiency losses that would re-sult from a decision to pursue social values other then efficiency. Because pragmatism acknowledges that public policy may be supported by multiple social values, information about such tradeoffs can provide valuable input. At the same time, pragmatism judges such input by the value it adds to the regulatory process. In light of bounded rationality, we are skeptical of exten-sive analytical requirements to study the impact of proposed regulations. The huge uncertainties that pervade this area make it difficult to justify commit-ment of extensive resources to perfecting estimates of regulatory impacts. While some study of regulatory impacts is appropriate, efforts to achieve comprehensive analysis are likely to be counterproductive because they slow the regulatory process without producing offsetting benefits in terms of in-creased knowledge.

More specifically, we join Professors Celia Campbell-Mohn and John Ap-plegate in recommending that regulatory impact requirements be modeled on the analysis of environmental impacts of government actions mandated by the National Environmental Policy Act (NEPA),[1] although we would stress the pragmatic aspects of NEPA as the reason for this recommendation. NEPA is designed to regulate agencies that might otherwise be inclined to ignore en-vironmental considerations, to identify them before irreversible resource commitments are made, and to provide for public disclosure of the results of those deliberations. Unlike more recent regulatory impact analysis require-ments, NEPA does not aim for comprehensive analysis, requires multidisci-plinary input, does not require cost-benefit analysis, and discourages moneti-zation even if a cost-benefit analysis has been prepared in which there are important qualitative considerations. The one aspect of NEPA that we deem inappropriate for the risk regulation process relates to judicial review. While NEPA provides for independent judicial review of analysis studies, we endorse judicial review of risk regulation impact studies only as part of court review of a final regulation.

National Environmental Policy Act

NEPA was prompted by the public's growing concern about the inclination of federal agencies to give short shrift to the potential adverse environmental consequences of their decisions.[2] It was also meant to function as an "environmental full disclosure" law by requiring that federal agencies circulate environmental assessment documents to other federal and state agencies and make those documents available to the public.[3] Opening up agency decision-making processes to the light of day in this manner would provide opportunities for other agencies, legislators, or the public to mobilize opposition to decisions that apparently had been made without sufficient consideration of environmental factors.

The principal mechanism for achieving these objectives is the environmental impact statement (EIS), which an agency must prepare for all major federal actions significantly affecting the quality of the human environment.[4] The EIS must include, among other things, discussion of the environmental impact of the proposed action, any unavoidable adverse environmental effects attributable to implementation of the proposal, and alternatives to the proposed action and their environmental consequences.

Some of NEPA's supporters envisioned the EIS as "a comprehensive analytical document, . . . intended to change fundamentally agency thinking processes."[5] Lynton Caldwell, a professor of government at the University of Indiana who was instrumental in the drafting of NEPA, envisioned the act as a means of inducing agencies to engage in "rational-comprehensive analysis proceeding from a clear objective through identification of all relevant alternatives and analysis of all consequences (environmental impacts, as well as economic and technical considerations) to an optimum decision."[6] According to one early decision interpreting the statute, NEPA was meant "to ensure that, with possible alterations, the optimally beneficial action is finally taken."[7]

The text of NEPA, however, does not support the conclusion that Congress had that intent. Instead, the statute appears to recognize bounded rationality because it commits agencies to complying with environmental assessment procedures only "to the fullest extent possible."[8] Even if the statute's drafters modeled the NEPA process on comprehensive rationality, it has not been implemented that way.[9] NEPA is interpreted and enforced by the Council on Environmental Quality (CEQ) and the courts. Both have adopted a pragmatic stance concerning NEPA's implementation.

CEQ Regulations

CEQ regulations point the way for pragmatic implementation of NEPA. Under NEPA, the CEQ is responsible for promulgating procedural regulations that establish how agencies are to prepare an EIS. As the reader will recall, a hallmark of pragmatism is its willingness to consider a plurality of traditions, perspectives, and academic orientations. CEQ requires that EISs be prepared using an interdisciplinary approach that will ensure integrated use of the natural and social sciences. Pragmatism acknowledges the constraints placed by bounded rationality on efforts to ascertain what actions are necessary to protect the environment, and it seeks to accommodate widely held social values, particularly including the intrinsic value of protecting the environment. CEQ's regulations recognize the difficulty of capturing the benefits of environmental protection through monetization, as well as the undesirability of doing so. While CEQ requires agencies to "rigorously explore and objectively evaluate" on a comparative basis the environmental impact of alternative plans of action, it does not require agencies to use cost-benefit analysis as the basis of comparison. Moreover, if an agency uses cost-benefit analysis, its weighing of the comparative costs and benefits of a proposal and its alternatives need not be expressed in monetary terms, "and should not be when there are important qualitative considerations." Finally, the regulations require agencies to acknowledge and explain the impact of bounded rationality. When information about a proposal's reasonably foreseeable adverse effects on the environment is incomplete or unavailable because the costs of obtaining it are exorbitant, an agency is required to "make clear that such information is lacking."[10]

Judicial Review

An important question that arose shortly after NEPA's adoption was how the duties it imposed on federal agencies would be enforced. In particular, the role of the courts in enforcing NEPA was at first unclear. NEPA's drafters expected Congress and the executive branch, through agencies like the Office of Management and Budget, to take the lead in supervision of agency compliance with NEPA.[11] Indeed, NEPA contains no provisions authorizing judicial review of agency compliance.[12]

In the landmark *Calvert Cliffs'* case, the Court of Appeals for the District of Columbia Circuit concluded that it "is the responsibility of the courts to reverse" a decision that "was reached procedurally without individualized consideration and balancing of environmental factors."[13] Thus litigants who can show that they will be adversely affected by agency-endorsed projects can solicit the aid of the federal judiciary in seeking to enjoin implementation of decisions that have been reached without compliance with NEPA's environmental assessment processes.[14] Since *Calvert Cliffs'*, the courts have routinely halted projects and remanded to the agencies to remedy such procedural defects.[15]

The court in *Calvert Cliffs'* also speculated that NEPA probably does not authorize reviewing courts to reverse an agency decision on the basis of its substantive merit,[16] and the U.S. Supreme Court subsequently confirmed that interpretation of the statute.[17] Accordingly, as long as an agency fully complies with the statute's procedural dictates either by justifying its decision not to prepare an EIS or by preparing an adequate EIS, the courts may not invalidate the resulting decision on the grounds that the EIS revealed that the project's environmental costs will outweigh its economic benefits, or that an environmentally preferable alternative was available but not chosen by the agency.[18]

Like CEQ, the courts have adopted a pragmatic approach to NEPA. In light of bounded rationality, the courts charged with determining whether agencies have complied with NEPA have not insisted that agencies adhere to a comprehensive rationality model. Instead, according to Professor Rodgers, they have settled for a "pragmatic rationality."[19]

Several aspects of judicial review demonstrate its pragmatic character. Agencies engaged in environmental evaluation under NEPA rarely consider alternatives antithetical to their missions,[20] and reviewing courts have largely endorsed their authority to take that approach.[21] Moreover, although CEQ describes the comparative discussion of alternatives to be "the heart of the [EIS],"[22] courts tend to reject assertions that agencies have considered an inadequate range of alternatives, as long as the agency has considered the "no action" alternative (that is, maintenance of the status quo) and does not appear to have been biased in favor of the proposed action or to have ignored comments submitted in response to the draft EIS.[23] Finally, the courts typically afford agencies considerable leeway in their descriptions of the likely adverse impacts attributable to implementation of a proposal.[24] EIS adequacy is by and large measured against a "rule of reason," such that a reasonably thorough discussion of probable adverse consequences is likely to pass judicial muster.[25]

Judicial review of alleged agency noncompliance with NEPA procedures has tended to be more rigorous than has scrutiny of the contents of agency impact statements. An agency's blatant failure to respond in a final EIS to comments submitted on a draft is likely to trigger a remand.[26] Similarly, a failure to solicit comments from the public or other agencies is likely to meet with a frosty judicial reception.[27] Even when an agency is alleged to have run afoul of such NEPA procedures, however, the courts by and large have refused to block agency action based on what they perceive to be minor procedural flaws.[28]

In short, while NEPA seeks to enhance the rationality of agency decisionmaking by fostering consideration of potential adverse environmental consequences, and their relationship to anticipated project economic and social benefits, its implementation reflects a recognition that agencies face limits in the degree to which they can engage in that kind of analytical endeavor. Both the CEQ and the courts have been willing to accommodate these practical realities.

The Impact of NEPA

Although CEQ and the courts have implemented NEPA in a pragmatic manner, few would disagree with the conclusion that it has enhanced agency consideration of the environmental impacts of proposed actions.[29] In Professor Caldwell's assessment, NEPA has caused reconsideration, redesign, and at times even withdrawal of projects with potentially damaging environmental consequences.[30] Another observer has remarked that "[e]nvironmental impacts *are* now considered in making natural resources decisions. . . . NEPA's action-forcing mechanism forced agencies to think about environmental consequences."[31] That kind of consideration rarely occurred before 1970.

In a related vein, NEPA, by all accounts, has succeeded in fostering an interdisciplinary approach to decision-making.[32] The statute mandates that agencies rely on "a systematic, interdisciplinary approach" to decision-making by integrating use of both natural and social sciences.[33] That mandate had forced agencies to diversify their staffs in performing tasks such as EIS preparation, review of the EISs of other agencies, and advocacy in internal agency decision-making processes.[34]

Likewise, the dissemination of draft EISs for public comment has resulted in increased public participation in agency decision-making processes and, to a certain extent, a resulting increase in the accountability of decision-makers.[35] The NEPA process appears to have provided new opportunities for environmental groups, concerned citizens, and individual scientists previously underrepresented in agency consultation networks to influence agency decisions.[36]

Despite these accomplishments, the NEPA process has not escaped criticism. On the one hand, some have criticized NEPA for not going far enough. The absence of a judicially enforceable substantive component has prompted some observers to attack it as a statute that requires nothing specific in the way of altering environmentally damaging behavior. These critics note that agencies can avoid the statute's sting simply by generating sufficient paperwork to satisfy their procedural obligations.[37] On the other hand, NEPA has also been criticized for going too far. The principal upshot of the NEPA environmental evaluation procedure, in this view, has been delay and frivolous litigation. By one account, NEPA has been "regularly and often frivolously exploited by supporters of the status quo and opponents of proposed actions."[38] By another account, the EIS process creates unnecessary paperwork that delays or kills useful and beneficial projects.[39]

Regulatory Impact Analysis

The critics of federal risk regulation, like the advocates of NEPA's adoption, have complained that agencies fail to take into consideration information

TABLE 7.1

Requirements for Federal Administrative Rulemaking

	APA	Statutory Mandate	Reg Neg	Regulatory Flexibility	SBREFA	Congressional Review	Unfunded Mandates	Paperwork Reduction	FACA	NEPA	Trade Agreements	Technology Transfer	NAFTA	E.O.12866	E.O.12988	E.O.12630	E.O.12898	E.O.13045	E.O.13084	E.O.13132
Get an idea for a rule and establish a regulatory program	✓	✓			✓		✓	✓						✓			✓			
Consider alternatives to usual development of a rule			✓				✓		✓		✓	✓		✓		✓		✓	✓	✓
Determine if analyses and/or procedures required before Notice of Proposed Rulemaking (NOPR) published			✓	✓		✓	✓	✓		✓	✓			✓						
Internal checks and/or procedures for determining whether analyses required			✓	✓						✓										
External checks for the above determination						✓								✓						
Prepare draft (pre-NOPR) analyses				✓						✓				✓		✓	✓	✓		
Internal checks/procedures for draft analyses				✓			✓			✓				✓		✓		✓		
External checks for draft analyses							✓			✓				✓						
Analyze public input regarding analyses			✓	✓						✓										✓
Prepare final analyses (if required prior to NOPR)			✓					✓												

Internal checks or procedures for final analyses

External checks for final analyses

Draft and issue Notice of Proposed Rulemaking

Allow for public input on proposed rule

Internal checks and/or procedures for public input

External checks regarding public input

Prepare final analysis (if required after NOPR)

Internal checks and/or procedures for final analyses

External checks for final analyses

Analyze public input

Draft and issue final rule

Procedural checks and/or requirements for final rule

Substantive checks and/or requirements for final rule

Submit rules for mandatory review

Defend rules against discretionary rule challenges

SOURCE: Mark Seidenfeld (citation in chapter).

that is of central relevance to informed resource allocation decision-making. There is a fundamental difference, of course. Those who favored passage of NEPA on the whole supported risk regulation and sought to educate agencies and the public about the potential deleterious effects of economic development on the environment. Those who support impact analysis for risk regulation typically oppose risk regulation (at least as it is currently designed) and seek to educate agencies and the public about the potential deleterious effects of risk regulation on economic development and other important considerations.

If the critics of risk regulation received inspiration from their environmentalist predecessors, they have learned their lesson well. Over the last two decades, both Congress and the executive branch have adopted an assortment of substantive and procedural obligations applicable to agencies engaged in the adoption of regulations. The volume of this body of analytical consideration law is considerable. Professor Mark Seidenfeld of the Florida State University College of Law has calculated that an agency engaged in rulemaking may have to run the gamut of some 120 different procedural or analytical steps. Table 7.1, based on Professor Seidenfeld's compilation, summarizes these analytical responsibilities. Some of these obligations require agencies to undertake a cost-benefit analysis of their proposed and final actions, while others require agencies to study the potential impact of proposed and final regulations on other considerations.[40]

Analysis Requirements

As Professor Seidenfeld's table indicates, agencies are currently subject to numerous requirements to analyze the impacts of regulations before they are adopted. Congress has been poised for several years to add even more such requirements. The existing and proposed requirements are described next.

Current Requirements

Every president since President Reagan has endorsed the use of cost-benefit analysis in some form in agency rulemaking.[41] The latest order, President Clinton's Executive Order No. 12,866,[42] is similar to those of his predecessors. It requires agencies in the executive branch of government to assess the benefits and costs of proposed and final "major" rules and to "assess all costs and benefits of available regulatory alternatives, including the alternative of not regulating." A "major" rule is one with an annual economic impact of $100 million or more on the economy, or one with other significant effects on individuals, businesses, governments, or the economy. Although the order pertains only to executive branch agencies, almost all risk regulators are in such agencies. In addition, in choosing among regulatory alternatives, the order requires agencies to "select those approaches that maximize net benefits (including potential economic, environmental, public health and safety, and other advantages; distributive impacts; and equity), unless a statute requires another regulatory approach." Finally, the order permits agencies to adopt major regulations "only upon a reasoned determination that the benefits of the intended regulation justify its costs." That mandate, however, is subject to its being overridden by contrary substantive enabling legislation. Since most risk regulation statutes reject the use of a cost-benefit standard to set the level of regulation, the order does not override the nonutilitarian basis of risk regulation.

The Unfunded Mandates Reform Act (UMRA) of 1994 also aims at producing both cost-efficient and cost-effective regulation. UMRA requires each federal agency, unless otherwise prohibited by another statute, to assess the effects of its regulatory actions on state, local, and tribal governments and the private sector. Before an agency issues regulations that include any "federal mandate"[43] that may result in the expenditure by governments in the aggregate or by the private sector of $100 million or more in any one year, it must prepare a written statement that includes a qualitative and quantitative assessment of the anticipated costs and benefits of the mandate. It also must estimate the future compliance costs of the mandate and any disproportionate budgetary effects on particular regions or on particular segments of the private sector, and it must estimate the effect of the rule on the national economy if it is feasible to do so. The UMRA also requires that, before issuing a rule for which a written statement is required, the agency identify and consider a reasonable number of regulatory alternatives. It must then select from among them "the least costly, most cost-effective or least burdensome alternative that achieves the objective of the rule" for state and local governments and the private sector.[44]

Besides cost-efficiency and cost-effectiveness, agencies are also required to analyze a number of other potential impacts of proposed and final regulations. President Clinton issued Executive Orders that require agencies to identify regulatory impacts on civil justice reform, property rights, environmental justice in minority and low-income communities, protection of children from environmental health and safety risks, coordination with Indian tribes, and federalism.[45] Pursuant to legislation, agencies analyze the potential regulatory impact of proposed and final regulations on small businesses,[46] paperwork requirements,[47] and trade.[48] Congress has proposed, but not yet enacted, legislation that would require agencies to prepare a federalism assessment to ascertain the impact of all federal rules, not just major rules, on state and local regulation.[49]

Proposed Requirements

Critics of risk regulation have sought the adoption of legislation that would establish even more rigorous and more extensive cost-benefit mandates. In March 1995, for example, the House of Representatives passed the Job Creation and Wage Enhancement Act, a component of the Republican leadership's effort to implement the Contract with America. That bill contained detailed analytical and substantive requirements for agency rulemaking.[50] The Senate's version of regulatory reform took the form of the Comprehensive Regulatory Reform Act of 1995, also known as the Dole Bill because its primary sponsor was Senator Robert Dole of Kansas.[51] Adoption of the Dole Bill was blocked by a filibuster that Senate Republicans failed to end by two votes.

The 1995 proposed legislation, like the Executive Orders, would have mandated the preparation of rulemaking analyses for all "major" rules, but it was more extensive in three ways. First, the proposed legislation prescribed detailed requirements concerning how agencies were to undertake cost-benefit analysis. The Dole Bill, for example, exceeded one hundred pages in length. Second, some versions of the proposed legislation defined what was a "major" rule by reference to a much lower threshold dollar figure than those contained in presidential Executive Orders. Finally, agencies would have had to conduct rulemaking analyses not only for new rules but also for selected existing rules. Some versions of regulatory reform legislation included a "sunset" provision that would have resulted in the termination of any "major" rule that was not reviewed by an agency within a prescribed period of time.

Since 1995, similar reform legislation has been introduced in each subsequent Congress. In May 1999, for example, the Senate Governmental Affairs Committee voted to send comprehensive regulatory reform legislation, sponsored by Senators Fred Thompson (R-TN) and Carl Levin (D-MI), to the floor of the Senate. The approach of the bill, entitled the Regulatory Improvement Act of 1999,[52] was similar to that of the 1995 Dole Bill, although it was not as prescriptive concerning how agencies are to conduct impact assessments. The legislation, however, would have required that agencies undertake "independent" peer review for both cost-benefit and risk assessments of certain major rules.

Impact

NEPA requires agencies to study the potential environmental impacts of their proposed actions on the assumption that development-oriented agencies are inclined to ignore such impacts. The same logic would appear to apply to agencies whose primary mission is the reduction of health, safety, and environmental risks. Requirements to study economic and other potential impacts would appear to have the beneficial effect of forcing agencies to consider factors that they might otherwise be inclined to ignore. The defenders of risk regulation, however, have objected on the grounds that subjecting agencies to the plethora of analytical requirements described above will produce adverse consequences of both a procedural and a substantive nature.[53] In this section, we consider the impact of regulatory assessment requirements.

Reducing Tunnel Vision

Professor Tom McGarity has identified a number of ways that analysis requirements can improve agency decision-making.[54] By asking the right questions, regulatory analysts can "frame old questions in ways that suggest novel solutions." This may prompt regulators to think in new ways about their regulatory mission. Risk analysts can also identify fresh options and then become an institutional voice for pursuing those options. A well-prepared impact analysis can organize data and information for agency decision-makers in a coherent and systematic fashion. Since a good analysis should also identify information gaps and assumptions, agency managers can use regulatory analysis as a management tool to ensure bureaucratic accountability. Because impact analysis furnishes managers with information about regulatory impacts and options, they can avoid efforts by agency staff to limit the information they receive. Finally, regulatory analysis documents can be a vehicle for making agencies accountable to the President, Congress, and the public by alerting readers to the potential impacts of proposed and final regulations.[55]

Regulatory Delay

For some critics of risk regulation, regulatory impact analysis requirements may have one more advantage. The plethora of regulatory requirements has undoubtedly slowed regulatory output and perhaps weakened regulation. According to Professor McGarity:

> The existing analytical requirements for rulemaking are already a significant contributor to the current virtual paralysis of the existing rulemaking process. Adding more requirements for analysis and explanation is certainly not a prescription for clearing up the regulatory log jam. It will, however, indirectly reduce the burdensomeness of regulation on affected industries. Regulations that are never promulgated are not at all burdensome, and agencies will predictably reduce the stringency of the regulations they do write in the (perhaps naive) hope of reducing the intensity of the attacks on their analyses.[56]

Proponents of regulatory analysis, of course, disagree with this assessment. On balance, it is difficult to determine whether the reduced flow of regulation attributable to regulatory impact analysis requirements is the unfortunate but appropriate price society must pay for adopting more rational regulation. After all, proponents of NEPA justify the delays in development that it causes as the inevitable consequence of forcing agencies to consider environmental consequences they are prone to ignore. We think it is more likely than not, however, that regulatory impact analysis requirements have gone too far.

While both NEPA and impact analysis requirements address tunnel vision, NEPA is more pragmatic. For one thing, NEPA is less prescriptive concerning how agencies are to conduct impact analysis. The portion of the legislation requiring an EIS is composed of only about one hundred words.[57] By comparison, agencies are subject to dozens of requirements concerning regulatory impact analysis. Critics of risk regulation would go further. As mentioned, the Dole Bill contained more than one hundred pages of instructions to agencies concerning how to conduct impact analyses. NEPA, as pointed out earlier, only commits agencies to study potential impacts "to the fullest extent possible," and CEQ regulations specify that agencies identify what information is lacking. The same qualifications are missing from most of the regulatory impact analysis requirements. Indeed, Congress has continually sought to be more prescriptive concerning how studies are conducted, which indicates a commitment to comprehensive rationality. In addition, NEPA reflects a commitment to giving appropriate consideration to "unquantified environmental amenities and values," along with economic and technical matters. Similarly, as discussed earlier, the CEQ regulations are skeptical about the value of cost-benefit analysis, particularly when it is difficult to monetize important benefits, and they require an interdisciplinary approach. By comparison, regulatory impact analysis is primarily the domain of economic analysts.

We also question the benefits of the current level of impact requirements because of the failure of Congress to fund agencies adequately to undertake their many analytical burdens. Performing a comprehensive cost-benefit analysis in a conscientious fashion is not inexpensive. The Environmental Protection Agency (EPA) has spent tens of millions of dollars on cost-benefit analysis over a fifteen-year period.[58] Yet, as Professor Richard Pierce has observed, Congress appears to be more interested in slashing agency budgets than supplying the funds necessary to cover the increased costs of undertaking analysis requirements. As Pierce notes, reductions in discretionary spending, which is the portion of the federal budget that supports administrative agencies, reduced the number of federal employees by 250,000 between 1992 and 1996, and the rate of staff reductions was expected to increase significantly between 1996 and 2002.[59] Inadequate funding has been endemic in federal agencies whose responsibilities include health, safety, and environmental protection. Among the agencies whose efforts have been hampered are EPA, OSHA, the Forest Service, the Fish and Wildlife Service, the National Park Service, and agencies responsible for compliance with the Endangered Species Act.[60]

The failure of Congress to reconcile and rationalize the thicket of regulatory impact analysis requirements is another indication that critics have

regulatory delay, not improvement, as their objective. The analysis requirements have been added over the years, layer after layer, by Congress and the
President, until they constitute a crazy quilt of obligations that are cumulative and overlapping. Yet members of Congress have indicated little or no
interest in reducing the number of separate analytical requirements by combining them into one coherent statute, such as NEPA. Instead, critics of risk
regulation appear prepared to create additional layers of mandatory analysis,
as the proposed federalism legislation discussed earlier illustrates.

Cost-Effectiveness

Besides efforts to estimate costs and benefits, regulatory impact analysis
is particularly concerned with requiring that agencies identify various regulatory options and their cost. Studying regulatory alternatives has several
virtues. As Chapter 8, below, indicates, agencies may have the opportunity to
choose regulatory instruments (such as performance standards instead of design specification standards or market-based techniques instead of or in
conjunction with performance standards) that permit regulated entities to
choose the least-cost means of compliance.[61] Moreover, unlike cost-benefit
analysis, cost-effectiveness studies are less likely to result in the exclusion or
soft-peddling of values that are hard to quantify. Cost-effectiveness analysis
has this virtue because it compares only the costs of various risk management
standards. The benefits of regulation need not be compared with the costs.
Finally, while cost calculations are subject to myriad uncertainties, many of
which are described in Chapter 6, above, these calculations generally tend to
be less subject to bounded rationality than efforts to quantify benefits.

Still, a mandate to study cost-effectiveness has the potential to impose the
same kinds of onerous analytical burdens on agencies that a cost-benefit consideration requirement does. To begin with, bounded rationality problems
may prevent agencies from calculating with anything approaching precision
the comparative costs of achieving a particular regulatory objective. As Lisa
Heinzerling has recognized, "ensuring that market-based regulation," for example, achieves the same degree of environmental protection as technology-
based regulation is complicated, because it requires a prediction in the face of
"profound scientific uncertainty, of human health effects and ecological consequences, and also a means of comparing one type of impact with another."[62]

The problem with expecting too much from cost-effectiveness analysis is illustrated by the decision in the *Corrosion Proof Fittings* case,[63] in which the federal Court of Appeals for the Fifth Circuit invalidated EPA regulations phasing out the use of asbestos in a variety of consumer products under the Toxic Substances Control Act (TSCA). EPA had issued a notice of proposed rulemaking that asked for comments on four options concerning banning the manufacture and use of asbestos according to various phased schedules for different uses. It also raised the possibility of requiring warning labels on certain asbestos-containing products. EPA received more than two hundred comments from the public, held informal hearings, gathered additional data, and permitted extensive cross-examination of agency personnel and contractors. EPA recognized the burden that a ban on most products containing asbestos posed for industry, but it decided that the ban was the only alternative that would adequately protect against the risks posed by human exposure to asbestos. It attempted to ease the regulatory burden by providing a process through which companies that wished to continue to manufacture and use particular products containing asbestos could obtain an exemption from the ban. Despite this extensive attempt to choose an appropriate regulatory policy, the Fifth Circuit detected a plethora of deficiencies, including that EPA failed to demonstrate to the court's satisfaction that the public could not be adequately protected by a less burdensome regulatory alternative than a ban on the use of asbestos.[64]

The difficulty with the Fifth Circuit's decision is that the judges sought a level of analytical perfection that fails to recognize either bounded rationality or limits on the agency's resources. As Thomas McGarity concludes, the court "sent EPA on a potentially endless analytical crusade in search of the holy grail of *the* least burdensome alternative that still protected adequately against unreasonable risk."[65] While such comprehensive rationality may be attractive as a theoretical matter, it is simply not possible in the real world and thus amounts to what Professor Lynn Blais has referred to as "superficial rationality."[66] Since the *Corrosion Proof Fittings* case, EPA has not even attempted to use TSCA to impose regulatory requirements of the type in that case,[67] and it is unlikely to do so until Congress amends the act to overrule the court's opinion.

Conclusion

NEPA is based on the premise that government can benefit from studying the potential impacts of its actions before they occur, and the various impact requirements established by the President and Congress adopt that premise in the context of risk regulation. The regulatory assessment requirements, however, are more numerous and detailed than NEPA, and opponents of risk regulation favor even more detailed requirements. In light of bounded rationality, the crazy-quilt pattern of impact analysis requirements, a number of them overlapping, appears to be counterproductive by slowing the regulatory process without an offsetting benefit in terms of improved regulation. If this point has not been reached already, the accretion of still more layers of regulatory impact analysis is likely to impose a "brake" on risk regulation without significantly improving the substance of regulation.

Judicial Review

The discussion of the *Corrosion Proof Fittings* case in the preceding section raises the question of what role the courts should play in ensuring that agencies comply with regulatory impact analysis requirements. Some of the regulatory impact analysis requirements contain judicial provisions that essentially duplicate the opportunities to seek judicial review of NEPA compliance, while other requirements authorize more limited judicial review of agency compliance with analytical obligations. We believe that the limited judicial review approach is a more pragmatic approach.

Forms of Review

Judicial review of existing regulatory impact requirements is of two forms. In "independent review," a court is authorized to enjoin agency action to which the analysis pertains if the agency fails to comply with one of its analytical obligations. Judicial review under NEPA is of that type. A court is authorized to review the adequacy of an EIS, and it can stop the development action to which the EIS pertains if it deems the EIS to be inadequate. Independent review is also mandated by the Regulatory Flexibility Act, which requires agencies to assess the impact of regulations on small businesses and other small entities. Any small entity that is adversely affected or aggrieved by final agency action is entitled to judicial review of agency compliance with the requirements of the act, and the courts may order a noncomplying agency to take "corrective action," including remanding the rule to the agency or deferring enforcement of the rule against small entities.[68] Finally, agency noncompliance with the Paperwork Reduction Act does not prevent promulgation of a rule that establishes a paperwork requirement, but it may prevent enforcement of the obligation.[69]

In "nonindependent" review, a court is not authorized to enjoin enforcement of a regulation if an agency fails to comply with an analytical obligation that pertains to the regulation. The results of the analysis, however, are part of the rulemaking record. For example, there is no judicial review of agency compliance with Executive Orders,[70] but a court will consider the results of the study, along with all of the other information in the rulemaking record, when it reviews the legality of the regulation to which the analysis pertains. The Unfunded Mandates legislation also provides for nonindependent judicial review.[71]

The regulatory reform proposals considered in the mid-1990s included both forms of judicial review. Earlier versions of the legislation copied NEPA and made agency compliance with analytical procedures subject to independent judicial review. Later versions proposed two forms of nonindependent review. The most limited approach, patterned after the Executive Orders, precluded judicial enforcement of the analysis requirements themselves, although any analyses would become part of the rulemaking record that is subject to judicial review. Under a second approach, courts could review agencies' compliance with the rulemaking analysis procedural requirements. A court would be able to order an agency that had not adequately complied to do so, but it would not be able to enjoin the rule to which the analysis requirement pertained.

Timing

All of the judicial review provisions share one trait. They postpone any judicial review until there has been final agency action. In the case of NEPA, final agency action is a decision to proceed, or not to proceed, with some development project. In the case of regulatory impact analysis, final agency action is a decision to promulgate a regulation or a decision not to do so. There is a very good reason for conditioning the availability of judicial review on the presence of final agency action. If there were judicial review before an agency decided what action, if any, to take, the courts would be intervening in the middle of the agency's decision-making process. Such intervention would be highly disruptive of the agency process because an agency would be forced to defend a lawsuit even before it had reached a final decision on taking action. Judicial intervention at this early stage would also be inefficient, because the agency's ultimate decision might eliminate the need for review if it addresses the litigant's concerns.

Impact

The issue in designing a process of judicial review for risk regulation, therefore, is whether it should be an independent or nonindependent system. The fact that NEPA authorizes independent judicial review undoubtedly has made the statute more effective in promoting environmental consciousness in agencies and among the public. Because litigants can challenge the failure of agencies to undertake obligatory analysis, agencies must do more than pay lip service to these obligations. The same logic would appear to apply to regulatory impact analysis requirements. If compliance is not subject to judicial review, agencies might be tempted to treat the obligation in a pro forma manner. In fact, it appears that Congress amended the Regulatory Flexibility Act in 1996 to add independent review because legislators perceived that agencies tended to ignore their obligation to study the impact of proposed regulations on small businesses.

Independent review may increase agency compliance, but it might also significantly impede risk regulation. The reason is the difficulty of studying regulatory impacts, particularly the costs and benefits of proposed rules. As Chapter 5 discussed, substantial uncertainty pervades the effort to conduct risk analysis, monetize the benefits of risk regulation, and sometimes to estimate compliance costs. In light of this uncertainty, the critics of risk regulation will often be in a position to argue that an agency has not done a good enough job when it analyzed some potential impact of regulation. Thus agencies will be forced to defend lawsuits challenging their cost-benefit estimates even if they are reasonable in light of bounded rationality. The additional time and expense will be a drag on the agency's ability to carry out its substantive mission.

There is the additional risk that judges will misunderstand the degree of certainty of which an agency is capable, or that they will use review of agency compliance with impact requirements to further their own antiregulatory agenda. Because of the last two risks, agencies will be tempted to try to bulletproof their analyses, even in cases in which the additional effort is not necessary or appropriate for the regulatory decisions that they must make. Such efforts to perfect an analysis will also be a drag on the agency's capacity to carry out its substantive mission.

Finally, judicial review of the adequacy of regulatory impact analysis has the potential to result in a judicial reordering of the substantive policymaking standard chosen by Congress. In particular, the availability of judicial review of the adequacy of that analysis, separate from review of the entire rulemaking record, might elevate the role of efficiency considerations above other nonutilitarian values in the policy-making process by inviting judges to focus disproportionate attention on factors capable of precise and accurate quantification.[72]

These potential pitfalls of judicial review of the adequacy of cost-benefit analysis are illustrated by both the *Corrosion Proof Fittings* case,[73] discussed earlier, and similar examples of courts demanding a level of quantification greater than an agency is capable of producing. The *American Trucking Associations* case,[74] for example, involved judicial review of the merits of an agency's decision rather than of the adequacy of a procedural analytical rationality requirement. Nevertheless, it illustrates how even the most exhaustive agency analysis may not be sufficient to satisfy some judges. In *American Trucking*, the D.C. Circuit, in a decision later reversed by the Supreme Court, struck down EPA's 1997 revisions to the national ambient air quality standards for ozone and particulate matter under the Clean Air Act because EPA had failed to explain why it chose a certain level of contaminants as the one that resulted in an acceptable degree of risk, instead of a slightly lower or higher level of exposure. The court's basic objection was that EPA had not been able to offer a quantitative basis for choosing the level of regulation. The court in effect rejected EPA's extensive efforts to offer a qualitative explanation, as we will explain in more detail in Chapter 9.

Had the D.C. Circuit's opinion faulting EPA's explanation been upheld by the Supreme Court, that court's insistence that EPA do a better job of explaining why it had selected the "stopping point" that it did would likely have created difficulties for the agency in light of the scientific uncertainty that surrounds the question of whether there is a safe threshold level of exposure to the pollutants involved. As a result of the decision, "EPA [would have had to] decide how much risk it is willing to accept in a situation in which the Agency cannot accurately gauge the size of the risk."[75] Similar uncertainty exists about the beneficial health effects of incremental reductions in exposure. As the Clean Air Scientific Advisory Committee indicated, "there is no 'bright line' which distinguishes any of the proposed standards . . . as being significantly more protective of public health."[76]

The potential that judicial review will disrupt an agency and inappropriately slow its decision-making also exists in the context of NEPA. Indeed, this is the claim of NEPA's critics, as reported earlier. The argument for independent review, however, is stronger in the NEPA context than it is in the context of regulatory impact statements. If an agency makes a mistake regarding its NEPA analysis, the environmental destruction that may result is often irreversible. By comparison, if an agency makes a mistake regarding regulatory impact analysis, the mistake can usually be rectified. If, for example, an agency underestimates the impact of a proposed regulation on small business, it can amend its regulation, grant a waiver, delay implementation, or engage in other adjustments. In Chapter 8 we argue for a more incremental regulatory decision-making process that would increase reliance on these and other methods of correcting mistakes and adjusting regulations in light of new information and knowledge.

There is another difference between NEPA and other impact analysis requirements. A court can consider the information that an agency produces in regulatory impact analyses even if there is no independent review. As mentioned, this information becomes part of the rulemaking record, and it is subject to judicial review as part of a court's assessment of whether a regulation meets applicable substantive legal standards. If information is missing or incomplete, a court can take this oversight into account in determining whether an agency has adequately defended its regulation as consistent with legislative directives.

Several examples can illustrate this point. If the substantive mandate under which the agency is promulgating a rule is an open-ended balancing standard, the agency will be authorized to consider in some fashion the costs of regulation in relation to its benefits. If any cost-benefit analysis performed by the agency and placed in the record reveals serious deficiencies in the agency's reasoning process that do not appear to have been remedied in other parts of the record, the court is authorized to remand to the agency on the ground that the agency did not engage in reasoned decision-making: it failed to consider one or more relevant factors adequately.[77] If the substantive mandate under which the agency is promulgating a rule is a feasibility-based standard, the agency's failure to perform a conscientious cost-benefit analysis ought not to be relevant to the validity of the resulting rule because Congress has implicitly performed a cost-benefit analysis in mandating the most stringent feasible level of control. Even in such a context, however, if the agency's analysis suggests that it failed to adopt the least-cost way of protecting humans or the environment, even though it was as protective as more expensive options, a court might deem the agency's decision to be "arbitrary and capricious."

By comparison, the courts generally would lack the opportunity to address any deficiencies of environmental assessment if they were to review the legality of agency action under substantive enabling legislation. If a litigant challenges an agency decision to build a highway, for example, the results of the NEPA study are normally not relevant to the agency's legal justification for the highway (such as the need to improve safety or speed up traffic flow). The irrelevance of environmental factors to the agency's decision-making process is why Congress passed NEPA in the first place.

In short, although independent judicial review will enhance agency compliance with analytical obligations, it is also likely to provide opportunities for strategic delay in implementing risk regulation and open the door for judges to establish unrealistic analytical burdens on agencies. Further, unlike in the NEPA context, independent review is not essential to ensuring that agencies make rational decisions by taking into account important potential impacts of their actions. The information generated by impact studies is available to a court when it reviews the legality of an agency's decision to regulate.

Conclusion

This chapter considers what the role of regulatory impact analysis, particularly cost-benefit analysis, should be in the context of a regulatory system that uses constrained or open-ended balancing to establish the level of regulation. In light of bounded rationality, we favor pragmatic use of regulatory impact studies. NEPA offers a model of how such analysis might occur.

A pragmatic version of rationality review would be limited both in scope and function. Impact analysis requirements should be confined, as they are under most current statutes and Executive Orders, to major rules.[78] As NEPA provides, agencies should be afforded flexibility in defining the form of the analysis rather than being subject to a rigid and prescriptive step-by-step series of requirements.[79] Analytical requirements that micromanage how the agencies engage in risk assessment and factor cost and other matters into the decision-making equation are inadvisable, because they create the risk that agencies will focus on minutiae and that agency processes will grind to a halt as agencies struggle to comply with the myriad details of analysis procedure. They also may freeze current scientific techniques into law, preventing policy-makers from adapting assessment methodologies in response to scientific advances.[80]

The number of analytical endeavors with which agencies must comply should be reduced, by combining elements of more than one requirement instead of adding layer upon layer of analytical requirements, piecemeal. There is no reason why a risk regulatory agency should have to run the gauntlet of the 120 separate steps reflected in Table 7.1. Moreover, it is crucial that sufficient staff and funding be provided so that agencies can perform the required analyses in a timely and complete manner and so that the quest for analytical rationality does not become a poorly disguised attempt to reduce regulatory output, regardless of its merit.

Agencies should be required to maximize opportunities to foster meaningful public participation and promote debates among agencies and interested parties over proposed regulations. In particular, as CEQ regulations provide concerning NEPA, an agency should make clear when there is inadequate information to complete an analysis because the information is not available or because it is too costly to obtain it. For example, agencies should avoid end point estimates of regulatory costs and benefits when estimates are uncertain. Instead, agencies should provide upper and lower bound estimates of regulatory costs and benefits because a range would be more informative concerning the agency's lack of knowledge. Further, agencies should be required to disclose assumptions upon which their analyses are based so that these assumptions can be understood and contested. It would be helpful, for example, for an agency seeking to adopt life-protecting regulations to compare the impact of regulation if it discounts the value of a life and if it does not. Since, as Chapter 6 discussed, there are important policy implications in using discounted estimates, agencies should disclose the impact of discounting.

A pragmatic approach to regulatory impact analysis would emphasize qualitative analysis in addition to quantification. As discussed in Chapters 5 and 6, it is often impossible to identify the single "optimal" regulatory approach. Similarly, it is impossible to assign weights to factors such as federalism and protection of private property rights with any kind of mathematical precision. Any attempt to require quantification of factors that are inherently unquantifiable or difficult to quantify will inevitably promote guesswork as well as efforts to mask value judgments behind a facade of objective evaluation.[81]

A pragmatic approach to analytical rationality will also foster an interdisciplinary approach to decision-making. Pragmatism favors this approach because it is more likely to give nonquantifiable factors appropriate weight, which will enable and encourage noneconomists to contribute to the debate over risk regulation. Economists, and the narrow perspective they tend to reflect, should not be permitted to co-opt or dominate the policy-making process. As Professor McGarity has indicated, "In practice, comprehensive analytical rationality has been dominated by the paradigms of neoclassical microeconomics."[82]

A pragmatic approach would judge the adequacy of agency attempts to study potential impacts by whether they have received due consideration. This standard of review is, to use Professor McGarity's words again, "in a sense, a 'second best' rationality that recognizes the limitations that inadequate data, unquantifiable values, mixed societal goals, and political realities place on the capacity of structured rational thinking, and it does the best that it can with what it has."[83] It thus mirrors the way in which NEPA has come to be interpreted in the courts. As indicated above, both CEQ and the courts have by and large settled for a pragmatically rational approach to environmental impact assessment rather than a "comprehensively rational" approach, precisely because of their recognition of the inherent limitations on the cognitive capabilities of agency analysts and policy-makers. Under this "due consideration" approach, cost-benefit analysis would not provide the decision-making criterion for determining the appropriate levels of risk regulation, but would instead provide information for the agency to consider to the extent that the enabling legislation permits.

Finally, a pragmatic approach would not assign to agencies so many analytical burdens that they erase the tilt that Congress built into the statutes that protect humans and the environment. As Chapters 2 and 4 discuss, risk regulation statutes adopt a realistic burden of proof in light of bounded rationality. This tilt makes it possible to regulate in light of the uncertainties that pervade our knowledge of risks. It recognizes the intrinsic value of life and of the environment and seeks, within reason, to protect both. Thus the assignment of unreasonable obligations to study regulation, rather than actually regulate, can eliminate the pragmatism that is built into risk regulation.

We recognize that more limited impact analysis might miss problems with risk regulation that more elaborate analysis might reveal. We prefer to address such problems through incremental decision-making. In the next chapter, we discuss the potential for more flexible risk regulation by adjustments at the back end of the regulatory process, such as through the issuance of waivers, exceptions, and extensions and through the exercise of enforcement discretion. This approach can avoid the ossification and rigidity that results at the front end of the regulatory process because of elaborate analytical requirements. Moreover, information about the relationship of regulatory costs and benefits will tend to be better at the back than at the front end of the process.

8

Pragmatic Methods of Regulation

An approach to risk regulation based on pragmatism seeks to accommodate widely shared but potentially conflicting values by striving to achieve the maximum level of protection consistent with reasonable cost. Despite the advantages of this system, there are bound to be particular situations that yield regulation with which particular regulated entities cannot afford to comply, regulation whose application in a specific instance will impose costs of a magnitude that appears to be excessive, regulation whose application to a particular entity or economic sector may result in unacceptable dislocation, or regulation that has unintended adverse social consequences. This kind of regulatory output is inevitable because the bounded rationality problem discussed in Chapters 5 and 6 will preclude risk regulatory agencies from fully understanding all aspects of a problem before they take steps to address it. Risk regulation is necessarily based on the application of heuristics, whether they take the form of cost-benefit analysis or the more pragmatic approach to regulation we prefer. In short, even a pragmatic approach can yield regulation that reflects an unsuccessful effort to accommodate economic and noneconomic considerations.

One way to try to minimize instances of "excessive" or wrong-headed regulation would be to adjust the general statutory standards. One could weaken the standards, for example, so that few if any members of the regulated community lack the economic capacity to comply with them, or one could mandate more rigorous attention to and comparison of predicted regulatory costs and benefits in a futile attempt to overcome bounded rationality. The first option threatens to reduce the levels of protection against risk below those regarded as effective by most citizens. The second is likely to yield the kind of "paralysis by analysis" that we have criticized in Chapter 7, which, in turn, will also decrease the output of risk regulatory protection to levels that may be deemed unacceptable. Moreover, the very bounded rationality responsible for unintended regulatory consequences is likely to prevent the newly elaborate process from yielding more "rational" regulation.

In this chapter, we explore two alternative and, we think, preferable mechanisms for adjusting regulatory programs to eliminate unintended or counterproductive results. In his book on eco-pragmatism, Daniel Farber argues that experience with risk regulation during the past thirty years has demonstrated "the centrality of learning to the enterprise of environmental protection." According to Farber, this experience supports efforts to "raise our regulatory IQ," or, more colorfully, to "teach the elephant to waltz." We believe that the two mechanisms we will discuss in this chapter already make the current system of risk regulation to a considerable degree "responsive to additional information."[1] The first mechanism is to permit regulated entities to choose the method by which they comply with risk regulations. The second is to make greater use of incremental regulation in which regulators adjust general regulatory commitments in light of the specific circumstances of some regulated entities or the availability of new information. These two avenues for mitigating the unintended adverse economic and social consequences of risk regulation reflect a pragmatic approach to the implementation of that body of regulation.

Each of the flexibility devices we describe in this chapter has been tried, some with better effects than others. All are subject to abuse, but we believe that, on balance, they represent a more pragmatic method of accommodating divergent factors such as efficiency and fairness or other nonutilitarian values than does an attempt to incorporate in a rigid fashion all relevant factors into the risk reduction standard itself. To address the potential for abuse, we support the adoption of procedures that, on the one hand, enable agencies to dispense incremental relief in a relatively streamlined fashion but that, on the other hand, enhance accountability by requiring agencies to provide opportunities for public input and disclosing when and why they have afforded such relief. The adoption of such procedures is consistent with pragmatism's preference for methods of accountability that promote public participation.

A regulatory process that includes and relies upon the flexibility devices discussed in this chapter may enable an agency to avoid committing so many resources to perfecting regulation at the front end of the process that it is precluded from effectively assessing the practical effect of regulations once they have gone into effect. Critics of current risk regulation approaches claim that these approaches often result in misallocation of regulatory expenditures when agencies pursue relatively small risks while leaving larger risks unaddressed. But a regulatory approach based on a quest for comprehensive rationality may have an additional unintended adverse effect if it diverts agencies from the kind of planning that is capable of avoiding such misallocations. The final section of this chapter therefore addresses how a pragmatic system of risk regulation can use planning to minimize misallocation of regulatory expenditures.

Regulatory Methods

One method of reducing regulatory costs is to choose the least-cost method of achieving a regulatory goal. This goal is consistent with the risk reduction framework that Congress adopted, although critics of risk regulation sometimes claim otherwise. Risk regulation generally employs "performance" standards that allow regulated entities to choose the method by which they comply with the risk reduction the government has ordered. In other circumstances, Congress has authorized the use of "incentive-based" instruments, which give regulated entities even greater flexibility to select cost-effective compliance options. Some critics of risk regulation are so enamored with the use of "incentive-based" methods that they would create a presumption in favor of their use. Although incentive-based methods may be a less expensive way to regulate, the evidence does not support the conclusion that they are usually a better way.

This section starts with the failure of the critics of risk regulation to recognize that existing regulatory goals are consistent with cost-effective methods of regulation. We then consider the role of performance standards and incentive-based regulatory methods, and the potential of each to lower regulatory costs and achieve other regulatory values.

Options

The critics have charged that command-and-control regulation of the kind that has dominated federal risk regulation for the last thirty years is incapable of producing efficient regulation because, among other things, it bypasses opportunities for regulated entities to select the most cost-effective means of regulation available. According to the critics, command-and-control regulation tends to take the form of uniform standards applicable across the board to entire classes of risk-creating activities. The difficulty with such uniform controls is that they fail to recognize that the cost of control may vary significantly within a class of risk-creating activities. One polluter may have the capability of reducing its discharges at a fraction of the cost of another polluter discharging the same material. A rational approach to controlling pollution would be to impose stringent controls on the polluter whose costs of control are low, while imposing lenient controls on those with high control costs. In that manner, the desirable level of pollution control can be achieved at the least cost.

The complaint that traditional risk regulation forfeits opportunities for achieving cost-effective solutions to environmental problems is often misleading, because those making it generally fail to distinguish carefully between the adoption of environmental standards and the selection of techniques (or tools or instruments) for achieving those standards. The two inquiries need not be—and often are not—governed by the same analytical frameworks.

The formulation of environmental policy requires that policy-makers address two "central questions: (1) what is the desired level of environmental protection?; and (2) what policy instruments should be used to achieve this level of protection?"[2] The literature on environmental policy, however, does not always carefully distinguish between these two issues. This blurring of conceptually distinct questions tends to mask the possibility that an environmental policy goal might be set using criteria other than economic efficiency, but that, once the goal has been established, regulators may select the policy instrument likely to achieve that goal at the least cost. There is no reason why, for example, a regulatory system whose goal is set without reference to cost—such as an ambient quality-based regulatory scheme—could not be coupled with incentive-based policy instruments, such as marketable permits or pollution taxes.[3] Indeed, the Environmental Protection Agency (EPA) has long taken the position that although cost considerations play no legitimate role in the adoption of the Clean Air Act's national ambient air quality standards, those considerations are critically important when policy-makers are designing appropriate means of achieving the standards.[4]

Design versus Performance Standards

The failure to distinguish clearly between regulatory standards and instruments is exacerbated when the critics of risk regulation attack "command-and-control" regulation without acknowledging that the term encompasses both "design" standards and "performance" standards. Both types of standards typically specify a goal that the agency defines, such as a numerical limit on permissible emissions. The difference is that under a design standard the agency defines the method by which regulated entities are required to achieve the goal—such as by installing and operating a particular kind of pollution control technology or work practice—whereas under a performance standard, regulated entities are free to achieve the goal in any way they want. In the case of a technology-based standard, regulated firms may use the model technology or work practice identified by the agency as the one that makes compliance with the standard possible, or they can devise alternative means of meeting the standard. Thus regulated entities subject to a performance standard have an incentive to discover or develop such alternatives if they provide a more efficient means of achieving the regulatory standard. While this incentive may not be as significant as under other regulatory instruments in certain circumstances,[5] performance standards do promote cost-effective regulation.

Despite what some criticisms of risk regulation imply when they disparage it as an example of "a system of Soviet style centralized command and control,"[6] performance standards, not design standards, are the norm in risk regulation. The Clean Water Act, for example, requires that point sources comply with a series of technology-based effluent limitations (numerical goals),[7] but it allows those sources discretion to choose the means of compliance. The nationally uniform, technology-based emission standards under the Clean Air Act by and large follow the same pattern.[8] The statutes on occasion even explicitly bar EPA from specifying the means of compliance.[9] Even where they do not do so, however, it is clear that, as a general proposition, "the Administrator is not to prescribe the technology which must be used, but is rather to set discharge levels which can be met if indicated technology is used. The choice of technology at each plant is left to the operator."[10]

Incentive-Based Instruments

Further, many risk regulation statutes (or the regulations adopted to implement them) afford even greater freedom to regulated firms to select cost-effective compliance options by permitting the use of instruments that range well beyond those characteristic of a traditional command-and-control approach. EPA in particular has become increasingly enamored of incentive-based techniques such as marketable permits and emissions trading as a cost-effective mechanism for achieving various Clean Air Act standards that are not based on the application of cost-benefit analysis.[11] The best-known example of a marketable allowance scheme is the one reflected in the acid rain control program adopted in the 1990 Clean Air Act amendments. Under that program, regulated coal-burning electric utilities may not emit sulfur dioxide in excess of the number of allowances they hold for emissions of that pollutant. A regulated unit need not necessarily reduce its own emissions in order to meet the emissions cap by which it must abide. Instead, it may purchase allowances from other regulated units that have "overcontrolled" and therefore have excess allowances to sell.[12] Because those who sell allowances are likely to have lower control costs than those who buy them,[13] the aggregate level of control may be achieved at lower cost than if the statute simply imposed an emissions cap on each unit and required it to control its own emissions as the exclusive means of achieving compliance with that cap. State environmental agencies have provided further opportunities for the use of incentive-based instruments as a means of achieving the levels of emission reductions necessary to comply with national ambient air quality standards.[14]

Although incentive-based techniques of this sort to date have been most fully developed under the Clean Air Act's emission control scheme, there is no reason why the techniques may not be just as useful in appropriate contexts under other statutory schemes. Thus marketable permits and related incentive-based instruments promise to play a larger role in the future under the Clean Water Act. For example, EPA has considered authorizing trades between point and nonpoint sources as a means of generating efficiencies in discharge reductions and reaching sources that to date have not been regulated to any meaningful degree.

Evaluation

The potential for incentive-based techniques to promote cost-effective means of compliance with regulatory standards is widely acknowledged, as well it should be. If incentive-based techniques such as emissions trading can achieve regulatory standards at lower costs than other regulatory instruments, it would be irrational not at least to consider their use. Allowing regulated firms to resort to emissions trading as a means of complying with their regulatory obligations undoubtedly creates the possibility that those firms will manipulate the system by engaging in "paper trades" that do little if anything to improve environmental quality.[15] The fact that regulated entities may abuse the discretion to use emissions trading as a means of regulatory compliance is not a sufficient basis for condemning the entire technique, however. Rather, the criticism argues in favor of more careful creation of prerequisites for trading and more rigorous agency oversight.

Environmentalists also have objected to the symbolism of emission trading. Some view public resources such as clean air "as a basic inalienable right which is not for sale at any price. . . . Allowing firms to trade emission rights sends a message that decisions about tradeoffs between economics and environmental quality can be left to the polluters."[16] In light of the intrinsic value of the environment, this objection is not easily answered. Pragmatism, however, eschews essentialism, which argues against investing resource protection with the status of an inalienable right. Further, the negative symbolic aspects of an endorsement of trading may be an acceptable tradeoff for the efficiency gains that are available in some situations through resort to the practice. As indicated in Chapter 3, a pragmatic approach to risk regulation attempts the difficult task of finding solutions that accommodate conflicting values to the greatest extent possible. In particular, pragmatism favors mechanisms that reduce the cost of regulation because such approaches reduce opposition to nonutilitarian standards of risk reduction that pragmatism strongly supports.

Default Rules versus Case-by-Case Determinations

Even among those, including some of the major national environmental groups, which endorse incentive-based techniques such as emissions trading as a valuable method of regulatory compliance, the appropriate mix of more traditional regulatory devices (such as performance standards) and incentive-based techniques nevertheless remains a matter of ongoing debate. Cass Sunstein has recommended the adoption of economic incentives "as a presumptive substitute for command-and-control" regulation.[17] Under this modified approach to instrument selection, EPA would be *required*, "wherever feasible, to use economic incentives rather than a 'command-and control' approach."[18]

Although we agree that incentive-based instruments have a useful role to play in the implementation of risk regulation standards, we cannot agree that such a presumptive approach is desirable or consistent with pragmatic regulation. A pragmatist would argue that, before displacing traditional regulatory instruments with incentive-based techniques on a much larger scale, the proponents of such a change should bear the burden of demonstrating that practical experience with incentive-based instruments justifies such a shift. Although Professor Sunstein is convinced that "significant cost savings can be achieved by using more flexible, market-oriented instruments, such as tradable pollution permits rather than uniform national requirements,"[19] and that such cost savings support adoption of a presumption in favor of requiring a market-based approach, empirical support for his belief simply does not exist.[20] According to Daniel Cole and Peter Grossman, "the existing 'empirical' studies do not demonstrate either that command-and-control regulations are inherently inefficient or that they are invariably less efficient than market-based alternatives." Indeed, they assert further that in certain cases, command-and-control regulation can be and has been more efficient than alternative, incentive-based approaches.[21] Similarly, Daniel Farber has warned:

> Although these incentive systems are intriguing, we should not be too confident about translating [their theoretical advantages] into practice. There are good reasons for caution. Real-world implementation may raise significant enforcement problems, create barriers to entry by new firms, unduly favor some firms in the initial allocation of permits, or conflict with other goals like equity. Moreover, the actual legal entitlements are likely to differ considerably from the elegant theoreti-

cal models, if only for political reasons. . . . The only way to see if these market so-lutions will work is to try them provisionally and carefully monitor the results.[22]

Given the difficulty of ascertaining the costs of control that we describe in Chapter 6, a neutral baseline, in which policy-makers choose from available traditional performance standards and incentive-based instruments on a case-by-case basis with no preconceived bias, is preferable to any presumption. A second reason for rejecting a presumption is that the relative desirability of market incentive instruments is likely to be context-specific. As Professor Kenneth Richards recognizes, the "optimal choice of policy instrument to implement a particular pollution abatement goal depends on the nature of the pollutant, the kind of harm the pollutant causes, the available control technologies, the number and type of polluting entities, and the type of market failure."[23] Similarly, Daniel Cole and Peter Grossman have argued:

> There are institutional settings in which markets are not only less efficient than command-and-control regulations but are in fact completely ineffective in reducing pollution. In the real world, the relative efficiency with which a particular regulatory regime maximizes a social welfare function depends on institutional and technological circumstances. . . .[T]here may be important practical reasons for favouring [one among alternative] planning instruments. These reasons might involve ideological, political, legal, social, historical, administrative, motivational, informational, monitoring, enforcing, or other considerations.

Moreover, these considerations are not static, because "efficiencies can shift in response to institutional and technological evolution."[24]

As Professor Richards has pointed out, the total cost of applying a particular tool for achieving a specific risk regulation standard is composed of the sum of different kinds of costs, including "production" costs (such as capital, training, and operation and maintenance costs), "implementation costs" (such as measurement and enforcement costs), and "public finance" impacts. Although incentive-based regulation can have lower "production" costs than traditional regulation, higher "implementation" costs can offset any cost advantage that incentive-based regulation might have when only "production" costs are considered.[25]

The process of examining the degree to which emissions trading and marketable permits are capable of achieving risk reduction goals more cost effectively than command-and-control instruments has begun. Further experi-

ence with the use of such incentive-based instruments may in the future reveal that they are more cost-effective in most cases, or that they are more
cost-effective in particular contexts. A pragmatic approach to risk regulation
would encourage the proponents of incentive-based instruments to continue
trying to convince the relevant "critical communities" that such is the case.
To date, the available evidence does not seem to warrant a wholesale shift to
these kinds of instruments of the nature that would result from adoption of a
presumption in favor of incentive-based techniques. The evidence is weaker
still for instruments such as pollution taxes, which have not been applied to
any significant degree to federal risk reduction programs.

Effectiveness and Equity

Even if one assumes that incentive-based regulatory instruments by and
large yield more efficient efforts to comply with regulatory standards, it is not
necessarily the case that those instruments will be as effective at achieving the
desired levels of environmental protection as traditional regulatory instruments are. Similarly, compliance with a regulatory standard through a market-based mechanism will not necessarily yield the same distributional consequences as will compliance through traditional instruments.[26]

Regulatory instruments vary in terms of how well stakeholders will be as-
sured that environmental goals will be met. In a study that compared regulatory instruments, the federal Office of Technology Assessment (OTA) used
"assurance" as a criterion for comparative evaluation of regulatory instruments because it is a "bottom line criteri[on] for many stakeholders, especially when the environmental problem poses serious risks to human health."
When OTA compared instruments, it found that "command-and-control"
instruments are "the most effective at assuring stakeholders that environmental goals will be met." By comparison, OTA rated tradable emissions as
less reliable according to this criterion because of the "potential difficulty
with monitoring." Similarly, "pollution charges . . . have the potential to
move things in the right direction," but the "action-forcing component
is weakened since sources are given an option to pay rather than to reduce
their discharges."[27] Information disclosure strategies appear to be an effective
means of inducing firms engaged in risk-creating activities to reduce the lev-

els of the risks they create to avoid adverse publicity. Disclosure will also generate information that may be useful in measuring and monitoring environmental performance and in the implementation of more traditional regulatory regimes.[28] There is reason to suspect, however, that an information disclosure strategy that is cut off from a command-and-control program will tend to yield lower levels of protection against risk than a pure command-and-control system will.[29]

The OTA report also considered how instruments may differ in terms of the "equality of environmental outcomes, full participation by affected communities in decision-making, and freedom from bias in policy implementation." Consider, for example, environmental justice, which recognizes that "environmental policies have discriminated against racial minorities and low-income communities in both direct and indirect ways." OTA warns that market-based incentives, particularly tradable emissions and pollution charges, "may create serious problems if equity is a major concern." Tradable emissions, for example, may be a problem because firms or industries have a "choice which facilities will make improvements in performance and in which order improvements will be made." As a result, "individuals in one area or region could be comparatively worse off even though others are much better off" and "even though the overall environmental performance for the industries or firms involved is improved."[30] The phenomenon of "hot spots" that develop because purchasers of emissions allowances are more concentrated geographically than their sellers is a well-known pitfall of an emissions trading scheme.[31] The problem is likely to be less serious if the particular kind of risk-creating activity being regulated tends to have an undifferentiated impact on the environment in a large area than if the impact is more localized. Thus the use of an emissions trading regime as part of an effort to control carbon-based emissions that contribute to global warming is unlikely to produce these kinds of equitable concerns.[32] Pollution charges can cause the same kinds of problems because firms in an area or region may decide to pay the charges rather than reduce pollution, while firms in another area or region may reduce pollution.[33]

The kind of case-by-case comparison of regulatory instruments that we favor should therefore assess not only the relative cost-effectiveness of the various available alternative instruments but also their relative efficacy in achieving statutory standards and the distributional impact they are likely to have. A presumptive preference for market-based techniques is likely to hinder rather than enhance such a neutral comparative effort.

Adjustments

The context-specific focus of pragmatic risk regulation also supports a second approach to mitigating unintended and potentially counterproductive regulatory consequences. As Chapter 3 indicates, pragmatists like Dewey valued the scientific method as a means of testing ideas to determine their practical worth. Ideas that fail to withstand the public scrutiny that accompanies such a testing process are ripe for replacement by other approaches, which can then be tested.

In the context of risk regulation, this kind of incremental approach to decision-making takes the form of agency adjustments on a case-by-case basis to broader policy-based actions such as new or amended regulations. The bounded rationality that inevitably faces policy-makers responsible for designing a program of risk regulation ensures that those policy-makers will make mistakes when they fail to consider relevant information because it is not available to them or they do not yet understand its implications. Other "mistakes" will result when the circumstances that initially justified a particular regulatory application have changed. Default rules are useful precisely because bounded rationality precludes the formulation of comprehensive solutions to situations characterized by uncertainty. When the application of such rules to a particular situation produces an unacceptable result—a result, for example, that is inconsistent with the purposes of the rule, that is unnecessarily inefficient, or that is unfair—a pragmatic approach to risk regulation supports taking steps to change that result so that it conforms to prevailing values.

Options

The current system of risk regulation is characterized by a multitude of devices for making back-end adjustments to regulatory decisions that have already been made but that have not turned out as policy-makers anticipated they would. These include deadline extensions; waivers; negotiated adjustments to regulatory requirements; experimental regulatory programs and related administrative reforms; enforcement discretion; and periodic regulation review. Each of these devices has the potential to infuse risk regulation with the flexibility needed to avoid or mitigate unintended adverse consequences. Each has either already played a significant role in federal risk regulation or has the potential to do so in the future.

Deadline Extensions

A persistent criticism of command-and-control regulation is that it irrationally demands uniform levels of control even though circumstances such as differential levels of pollution or differences in compliance costs cry out for the creation of more nuanced, individuated control mechanisms. But even when a regulatory standard appears to require uniform controls in a variety of contexts, back-end adjustments such as deadline extensions often serve to create a de facto set of differential standards. According to Robert Percival:

> When health-based regulation has not succeeded in forcing the development of necessary technology within the time frame required for compliance, public policy inevitably permits deadline extensions or the relaxation of standards. . . . Thus, even laws that appear to require nationally uniform, health-based standards have been implemented in a manner that tolerates considerable regional variation in the severity of compliance timetables.[34]

The same point applies in the context of technology-based and technology-forcing standards as well.

These deadline extensions have differed in their magnitude. Sometimes, Congress has extended the deadlines for large geographic areas. The deadlines in the 1970 version of the Clean Air Act required compliance with the primary national ambient air quality standards by the mid-1970s.[35] When it became clear that many areas of the country would not be able to achieve the standards by the applicable deadlines, Congress amended the statute in 1977 to extend the deadlines to either 1982 or 1987, depending on the particular criteria pollutant involved.[36] Persistent noncompliance, particularly in urban areas, induced Congress in 1990 to extend the deadlines yet again. This time Congress allowed the most problematic areas to take more time than less

polluted areas to achieve the standards.[37] Thus, faced with the practical difficulty of achieving the standards along the time line originally envisioned,
Congress not only abandoned the original set of deadlines (twice) but also
crafted a series of substitute deadlines more attuned to the problems of particular kinds of nonattainment areas.

In some cases, Congress has extended regulatory deadlines for large classes
of regulated entities.[38] The 1970 version of the Clean Air Act required automobile manufacturers to reduce emissions of a variety of mobile source pollutants to an extent sufficient to comply with the standards by 1975 or 1976.
The auto manufacturers had claimed right from the start that the necessary
technology would not be available in time to meet the deadline. Congress required compliance by the mid-1970s anyway, in the hopes that the looming
deadlines would spur the development of more effective control technologies. When those hopes evaporated, both Congress and EPA issued a series of
deadline extensions for pollutants that included hydrocarbons and carbon
monoxide.[39] For oxides of nitrogen, Congress adopted a less stringent standard in addition to extending the deadline.

A similar story has played out in the context of the Clean Water Act. The
1972 Federal Water Pollution Control Act (whose name was later changed to
the Clean Water Act) required point sources to comply with one set of technology-based effluent limitations by 1977 and another by 1983.[40] When Congress amended the statute in 1977, it extended the deadline for the second
phase of these controls to a time between 1984 and 1987.[41] As the latter deadline approached, both industry and EPA acknowledged the impossibility of
compliance by some categories of point sources, in part because EPA had not
yet even issued regulations for some of those categories. The 1987 amendments extended the deadline again, to 1989 and beyond.[42]

Deadline extensions are sometimes available to individual regulated entities as well. The Clean Water Act, for example, includes provisions authorizing the issuance of deadline extensions to municipalities unable to complete construction of sewage treatment works in time to comply with their
regulatory obligations,[43] and to point sources proposing to replace existing
production capacity with innovative processes that achieve higher levels of
pollution reduction or that achieve equivalent levels at lower cost.[44] The latter provision is obviously designed to encourage regulated firms to engage in

research and development of better and more efficient pollution control technology. The Resource Conservation and Recovery Act authorizes EPA to adjust the deadlines by which those who manage hazardous waste must conform to a prohibition on the land disposal of specified hazardous wastes, such as dioxin.[45]

Waivers, Exceptions, and Exemptions

A related form of regulatory adjustment mechanism—the waiver, exception, or exemption—subjects a regulated entity to more lenient treatment or exempts it completely from regulatory obligations instead of extending the time for compliance. This "option can . . . be viewed as a recognition that formal rules are unlikely to capture the infinite varieties of empirical reality and that increased flexibility in the rulemaking process is necessary."[46] The issuance of a waiver or an exception is typically based on equitable grounds or on the grounds that insistence on compliance with a generic rule by the particular entity involved would be inconsistent with underlying regulatory objectives.[47] Had the agency adopting a rule been aware of the unique circumstances that make its application to a particular entity unfair or counterproductive, it presumably would (or could) have carved out an exception in the rule itself.[48] Having failed to do so, the issuance of a waiver or an exception simply represents an alternative procedural mechanism for accomplishing the same result—essentially, promulgation of a rule applicable to a category of one entity.[49]

Several different kinds of individualized adjustment mechanisms have been made available to entities subject to risk regulation statutes.[50] First, "hardship exceptions" represent adjustments based on the adverse economic impact of regulation on an individual firm or on the absence of available technology to comply with regulatory controls. According to Alfred Aman:

> Though Congress may have decided that industries should internalize certain environmental costs . . . , Congress's broad legislative objectives do not automatically outweigh the continued survival of regulated firms. The regulatory cures for environmental pollution . . . should not necessarily cripple the industries to which they apply. Stability and preservation of economic order go hand in hand with environmental or economic reforms. The regulatory preference for individual firm survival does not necessarily mean that shutdowns must always be avoided, but

such extreme consequences should be the result of a considered process, not the unintended or unconscious fallout of an overbroad statute or rule.[51]

Many of the federal risk regulation statutes provide explicitly for hardship exceptions.[52] In other cases, the courts have interpreted general statutory standards in a way that minimized economic disruption which would result from strict application of the standard.[53] State agencies operating under authority delegated to them by federal statutes have created analogous individual adjustment mechanisms.[54]

Adjustments also may be based on a demonstration that a particular regulated activity will not create the kinds of risks the regulatory scheme was designed to control. The Clean Water Act, for example, allows EPA to modify the technology-based effluent limitations applicable to point sources discharging certain kinds of pollutants if an individual point source can show that less onerous limitations will neither result in the imposition of additional effluent restrictions on other sources nor interfere with attainment or maintenance of fishable/swimmable water quality.[55] The Occupational Safety and Health Act allows the Occupational Safety and Health Administration (OSHA) to issue variances from occupational safety or health standards to an employer able to demonstrate that the alternative practices it proposes to use will provide places of employment as safe and healthful as those that would have resulted through compliance with the standard.[56] Under the Clean Air Act, EPA may waive the requirement that states containing areas not in attainment with the national ambient air quality standard for carbon monoxide require the sale of gasoline with a higher than normal oxygen content. To qualify for such a waiver, the state must show that mobile sources of carbon monoxide do not contribute significantly to excessive concentrations of that pollutant.[57] And the Resource Conservation and Recovery Act establishes a petition process pursuant to which generators may procure delisting of hazardous wastes at particular facilities.[58]

Third, individual adjustments may be available on equitable grounds. A regulated entity may qualify for one of these "fairness exceptions" if it can show that the costs it would incur if it complied with the regulations would be disproportionately higher than those incurred by similarly situated firms, that the regulation inadvertently punishes the entity for good-faith activities, or that the costs imposed on the firm are not justified by the resulting social benefits. "In other words, though the costs involved do not jeopardize the economic viability of the firm, and therefore do not justify an economic-hardship exception, the rule as applied to the petitioner is nevertheless unreasonable."[59]

Perhaps the best known example of a fairness exception is the fundamentally different factor (FDF) variance from the Clean Water Act's technology-based effluent limitations. Although the statute did not originally authorize EPA to issue such FDF variances, the Supreme Court conditioned EPA's authority to regulate point sources through categorywide regulations rather than on a point source-by-point source basis on the availability of individual variances from regulatory standards.[60] EPA fleshed out the conditions under which these variances would be available, and the Supreme Court interpreted the statute to authorize their issuance even for toxic pollutants, which are subject to the act's most stringent controls.[61] In 1987, Congress endorsed these developments by codifying the FDF variance mechanism for a point source able to convince EPA that its activities are fundamentally different with respect to a factor such as non–water quality environmental impact than the sources the agency considered when issuing the regulations otherwise applicable to the applicant for a variance.[62]

Fourth, individualized adjustments have been authorized when environmental protection objectives clash with other important social values. Provisions that authorize EPA to exempt activities whose pursuit is important to the national security from compliance with regulatory obligations are commonplace.[63] Similarly, the Clean Air Act has authorized the suspension of controls for fuel burning stationary sources in the event of a national or regional energy emergency.[64] The Clean Air Act also delegates to EPA the power to authorize the production of ozone-depleting substances that are otherwise banned to ensure aviation safety and sanitary food supplies and for use in medical devices, critical agricultural uses, and fire and explosion prevention.[65]

The risk regulation statutes have also acknowledged and accommodated important social values by affording preferential treatment to small business entities.[66] Some of these accommodations take the form of regulatory exemptions or deadline extensions,[67] while others are reflected in direct and indirect subsidies. Agencies such as EPA have supplemented these accommodations

by choosing not to rigorously enforce some obligations against small entities.[68] Such accommodations may be based on the premise, which has been
vigorously contested,[69] that the adverse environmental impacts generated by
small businesses are sufficiently small that allowing them to avoid regulations
applicable to larger concerns will not cause unacceptable setbacks to environmental protection goals. Alternatively, they may be based on a desire to
protect small businesses because of the vital role they have traditionally
played in providing for a diverse economy.[70]

The foregoing survey indicates that back-end adjustments can prevent
command and control regulations from producing needlessly inefficient and
otherwise perverse results. These types of back-end adjustments also reduce
the necessity for a comprehensive assessment of potential regulatory impacts
before a regulation is promulgated. Indeed, after-the-fact adjustments of the
sort involved in issuance of variances and exceptions will often provide a
better forum for policy-makers to fine-tune regulation, because experience
with operation of the regulations may reduce uncertainties and resulting
bounded rationality. Likewise, the smaller scope of the exercise may make it
easier for a decision-maker to understand the implications for relevant values
of a decision to grant or deny relief in a particular case than it would be to
predict such consequences on a larger scale.

Negotiated Adjustments

As Daniel Farber has recognized, regulatory standards sometimes function merely as "starting points in the lengthy interactions between agencies
and regulated parties, rather than as end points of compliance. . . . In effect,
the standards may merely be the government's opening demand in negotiations, and the final bargain is likely to be more favorable to the other side."[71]
Jody Freeman, a forceful advocate of what she calls "collaborative governance," contends that

> the goals of efficacy and legitimacy are better served by a model that views the ad-
> ministrative process as a problem-solving exercise in which parties share responsi-
> bility for all stages of the rule-making process, in which solutions are provisional,
> and in which the state plays an active, if varied, role. . . . [C]ollaboration requires
> us to focus on adaptive problem solving.

Freeman cites as an example negotiated rulemaking, which is a consensus-based process involving stakeholder negotiation of the substance of a rule.[72]

The federal risk regulation and natural resource protection statutes have authorized this kind of negotiation in some cases, and agencies such as EPA have created additional opportunities for agency-private negotiation. The incidental take permit process under the Endangered Species Act (ESA) provides one statutory example.[73] The Interior Department has created other opportunities for negotiated adjustments to regulatory obligations under the ESA through its related candidate conservation agreements, safe harbor policy, and no surprises policy.[74] According to J. B. Ruhl, these programs indicate that the Interior Department has realized "that economics do matter in the ESA and that economic interests are not necessarily the enemy of endangered species.... [T]hey provide economic incentives for businesses and landowners to participate in proactive species conservation and thereby help avoid the larger economic dislocation associated with species listings."[75]

EPA's Project XL (for excellence and leadership) is a better-known example of an agency-initiated negotiation mechanism. EPA created Project XL in 1985 as a means of trading off relatively insignificant regulatory violations for agreements by industry to exceed regulatory requirements in other instances.[76] EPA's goal was to reduce the net adverse environmental impact below what more straightforward application of regulatory standards is capable of achieving.[77] Because industry initiates the process by proffering site-specific plans that commit to achieving environmental benefits in exchange for exemptions from regulatory requirements that would otherwise apply, it can include in them the regulatory instruments that it finds optimal, instead of having to employ more costly or otherwise less acceptable techniques. Accordingly, Project XL plans have taken advantage of emissions trading among pollutants and environmental media.[78] Further, the process is iterative and "embraces provisionalism," in that participants predict the environmental impact of their plans but update plan provisions if testing reveals that the predictions were erroneous.[79] In short, Project XL seeks "to replace means-oriented requirements with means-oriented rewards. It is therefore a significant step towards implementing performance regulation in that it offers the company flexibility in determining how it can best meet required environmental benchmarks."[80]

While Project XL has been the most touted example of programs that depend on agency-stakeholder negotiation as a source of regulatory substance, it has not been the only one.[81] Together, these programs amount, at least in theory, to "a form of 'responsive regulation' where the regulators work creatively with individual corporations (or plant sites) to achieve an individuated level of compliance."[82]

Administrative Reforms

Agencies such as EPA have engaged in unilateral as well as negotiated adjustments to traditional regulatory programs to increase their efficiency or enhance their performance. Of the pollution control programs administered by EPA, none has been the subject of more sustained and virulent criticism than the hazardous substance cleanup program authorized by the Comprehensive Environmental Response, Compensation, and Liability Act.[83] In response to those criticisms, and perhaps as a means of staving off legislative reforms to which the agency would have objected, EPA adopted a series of administrative reforms during the Clinton administration that were designed to increase enforcement fairness, cleanup effectiveness, and consistency, as well as state and public participation, while reducing transaction costs. The agency's Brownfields Economic Redevelopment Initiative, for example, was meant to empower

> states, local governments, communities, and other stakeholders interested in economic redevelopment to work together to prevent, assess, safely clean up, and sustainably reuse brownfields. . . . One of the major enforcement activities under this initiative is to remove liability barriers to the cleanup and redevelopment of these contaminated properties, thereby giving prospective purchasers, lenders, and property owners more assurances of a safe investment.[84]

EPA also took steps to mitigate the difficulties experienced by owners of property containing contaminated aquifers in selling their properties or obtaining financing for development because of the risk of incurring cleanup liability.[85] If statutory delegations are sufficiently flexible to allow for the exercise of agency discretion and initiative, similar efforts to adjust ongoing regulatory programs could yield the same kinds of beneficial consequences as the issuance of deadline extensions and exceptions.

Adaptive Management

A form of back-end adjustment mechanism that has received consider-able attention in the field of public natural resource management is adaptive management. Originally conceived of by researchers at the Institute of Animal Resource Ecology at the University of British Columbia,[86] and later popularized by political scientist Kai Lee, adaptive management has been described by its proponents as "learning by doing."[87] It involves a willingness to act in the absence of complete information, coupled with a commitment to evaluate systematically the results of that action as it occurs. New actions are then formulated in light of the information derived from previous experience. This approach is designed to reflect a bias toward action rather than study without "losing sight of the perils of scientific uncertainty."[88] It is based on the recognition that the complexity and unpredictability of natural systems necessarily renders management efforts experimental.[89] Thus, adaptive management

> presumes ongoing institutional transformation; entities should develop their philosophies and strategies in an evolutionary way through continuous adaptation and assessment. These changes should be driven by a constant flow of information gathered from purposeful experiments. Adaptive management may be thought of as a research strategy designed to generate feedback.[90]

Adaptive management has been used for years to assist in ecosystem management,[91] such as the preservation of fish and wildlife resources in the Pacific Northwest and of endangered species more generally,[92] but it has not been widely used in other areas of environmental policy.[93] Recently, however, it has been described as the basis for regulatory reform efforts at EPA, such as the Project XL program, and it has filtered into a variety of other government environmental policy proposals and programs.[94]

Enforcement Discretion

The agencies that implement federal risk regulation also can mitigate the unfairness and unintended adverse consequences of particular regulatory applications by exercising their enforcement discretion.[95] Refusals to enforce violations regarded by an agency as *de minimis* or technical provide obvious examples. Occasionally, however, risk regulation agencies embark on more creative endeavors. EPA, for example, has negotiated supplemental environmental projects (SEPs) in which regulated entities that admit or are found to have committed violations agree to implement affirmative environmental protection measures, such as pollution prevention programs, in the future in lieu of paying civil or criminal penalties for which they would otherwise be responsible.[96] "[In] a sense, a corporation could receive some form of 'credit' for undertaking environmentally beneficial activities."[97]

Periodic Review

Yet another form of back-end adjustment is periodic review of regulations by the agencies responsible for issuing and enforcing them. Because periodic review of existing regulations necessarily takes place after the reviewing agency has had an opportunity to apply the regulations, the bounded rationality problems that surround the initial promulgation of risk regulations may be less pronounced at the regulation review stage.

Periodic review of existing regulations has been required both by statute and presidential decree. The Regulatory Flexibility Act requires that agencies review once every ten years existing regulations with a significant economic impact on a substantial number of small entities to determine whether to amend or repeal those regulations, or leave them in effect as is.[98] President Carter required "periodic" review of existing regulations under an Executive Order that expired in 1981.[99] President Bush imposed a 90-day moratorium in 1992 on the issuance of new regulations, during which agencies were supposed to evaluate existing regulations and take steps to eliminate unnecessary regulatory burdens.[100] President Clinton issued another Executive Order that requires agencies to submit to the Office of Information and Regulatory Affairs in the Office of Management and Budget a program establishing periodic review of significant regulations.[101]

A practical problem of requiring agencies to engage in periodic review of existing regulations is the lack of resources available to commit to the task. One recent study of periodic regulation review found that agencies almost universally complained that "time and resources are too limited to allow for regular, systematic reviews."[102] Requiring agencies to review existing regulations may require that they divert resources from consideration of regulations that address new problems. Indeed, when the Republican proponents of the

Contract with America proposed not only periodic review of existing regulations but also the imposition of sunset provisions that would terminate rules not reviewed in accordance with the statutory timetable, critics claimed that the exercise was a thinly veiled effort to reduce the volume of federal risk regulation rather than improve the substantive content of that regulation.[103]

But periodic review of existing regulations could be structured in such a way as to minimize such concerns. To begin with, if agencies are not expected to engage in comprehensive rationality of the sort required by rigorous cost-benefit analysis in initially issuing regulations, they may not need to devote as many resources at the front end of the regulatory process as they would if statutory delegations ignored the constraints of bounded rationality in defining the duties of agencies engaged in risk regulation. Some of the money saved at the front end could be committed to back-end adjustment in the form of periodic regulation review. Agencies may choose not to reduce the efforts they devote to the promulgation of risk regulations, however, even if the statutory standards under which they issue those regulations take full cognizance of bounded rationality. They may fear that courts will not be as sympathetic to the realities of bounded rationality as the legislature has been, and that reduced time and effort spent on issuing regulations will increase the risk of judicial invalidation. If so, the anticipated cost savings may not materialize. In that event, the best solution (though not necessarily a realistic one)[104] may be for Congress to appropriate more money for the agencies so that they can engage in conscientious periodic review of existing regulations. At some point, as the consequences of chronic underfunding for the agencies' ability to protect the public against risk become apparent, public pressure to do so may become impossible to ignore.

The American Bar Association's Section of Administrative Law and Regulatory Practice has made some other attractive suggestions to maximize the usefulness of periodic regulation review while minimizing the risk that it will unduly disrupt agency priority-setting and agency development of new regulations. Although the Section endorsed periodic review, it favored allowing agencies to fashion the details of their own review programs, taking into account the unique characteristics of each agency and its regulatory output. The agency should be able to select the pace at which it reviews existing regulations and the order in which it reviews them in light of other competing demands on its resources. Each agency should be required to establish a set of criteria against which it can measure the success or failure of that output.[105] The legislation requiring periodic review would commit agencies to good faith efforts to engage in periodic review that is consistent with requirements such as solicitation of public input.

Impact

The availability of back-end adjustments to regulation in the form of exceptions, waivers, and the like provides a forum in which an agency can take steps to mitigate regulatory inequities while preserving the efficiency gains of policy-making by rulemaking. At some point, however, the issuance of an excessive number of back-end adjustments may threaten to sacrifice the efficiency of policy-making by rule. Worse, it may threaten the integrity of the policy-making process or the ability to achieve the policy goals set by legislation or developed in the rulemaking process. According to Professor Mark Seidenfeld: "Giving unchecked discretion to regulators ultimately increases flexibility, but it also allows ad hoc decision-making to undermine the mission of the regulatory program." Accordingly, Seidenfeld continues, "society must strike some balance between granting administrators discretion to ignore substantive limits on their actions and constraining their exercises of discretion."[106] This section explores some of these tradeoffs in an attempt to define an appropriate role for back-end adjustments in the context of a pragmatic approach to federal risk regulation.

Advantages

Back-end adjustments serve as a means of shifting to the regulated entity the burden of proving that the particular application of a regulatory risk reduction standard is irrational or unjustified. This allocation is more consistent with the precautionary thrust of modern risk regulation than is a system in which agencies are subject to the task of justifying the propriety of a regulatory proposal in a manner that fails to reflect the reality of uncertainty and bounded rationality. It avoids delay in the issuance of a rule of widespread applicability because an agency can issue a regulation and rely on the members of regulated industry to alert it to implementation problems through the filing of a request for individualized relief. The creation of back-end adjustment mechanisms also serves to impose the burden of proving that an individualized adjustment is warranted on the entity most likely to possess information bearing on the unique aspects of the situation that arguably justify the adjustment. To the extent that risk regulation statutes or the Administrative Procedure Act does not currently allow such a shift in the burden of proof, they should be amended to do so.[107]

Back-end adjustments to previously issued regulations also represent a pragmatic means of preventing regulatory standards from inducing irrational or counterproductive results. Colin Diver has explained the appeal of supplementing broad-based policy-making with incremental adjustments instead of trying to get everything "right" at the front end of the regulatory process:

> The singular advantage of incrementalism is its ability to accommodate uncertainty and diversity. Where comprehensive rationality tortures fundamental value conflicts into an uncomfortable and often illusory truce, incrementalism creates a quasi-market for their serial reconciliation. While non-incrementalist policies are doomed to rigidity by the very political overselling needed to launch them, the modesty of incremental undertakings enables them more readily to adapt to novel circumstances. Where the synoptic method erects a flimsy bulwark of false certainty against the tide of technical and social change, incrementalism deals only with the present, leaving tomorrow to tomorrow.[108]

Similarly, Peter Schuck has contended that, "[in] principle, agency adjudication [through a back-end adjustment process] limits the scope of factual inquiry, demanding fewer analytical resources than rulemaking and consuming less time."[109]

Back-end adjustments allow agencies to accommodate unique or anomalous situations without sacrificing regulatory objectives.[110] They provide a means for agencies to preserve relatively stringent baseline risk reduction standards while accommodating concerns that the application of these stringent rules will cause irrational or unfair results in particular cases.[111] Instead of watering down the standards, policy-makers make case-by-case adjustments pursuant to a process that entails a fine-tuned balancing that would amount to a difficult if not impossible administrative task on a larger scale. Alfred Aman has asserted that adjustments like waivers and exceptions "can produce a healthy flexibility by infusing with a sense of reality what could otherwise have become a rigid regulatory regime."[112] "Administrative equity," according to Jim Rossi, "eschews the ability of rules to provide universal justice. ... [E]quitable adjustments in the implementation of regulations promulgated by rule provide an important 'safety valve' in the administrative process."[113] Exceptions processes also can head off challenges to regulations and reduce the need to use enforcement proceedings to interpret rules and make policy.[114]

Finally, as the preceding section on periodic regulation review has indicated, back-end adjustments can serve as a check on the rationality of a rule by convincing agency decision-makers faced with a plethora of meritorious applications for back-end adjustments that the underlying regulatory standard may be flawed and needs to be revisited.[115] Back-end adjustments are therefore fully consistent with pragmatism's emphasis on adaptation, practical problem-solving, and the ongoing process of testing ideas to determine the consistency of the results they produce with relevant values.

Pitfalls

While back-end adjustments are capable of infusing a regulatory program with much-needed flexibility and the ability to accommodate equitable concerns, they have the potential to frustrate the objectives of risk regulation or otherwise produce unacceptable results. If not appropriately structured and constrained, these adjustments can threaten the integrity of the regulatory program by watering down regulatory protections, creating uncertainty on the part of regulators and regulated firms alike, providing opportunities for favoritism, and allowing agencies to make decisions in the absence of meaningful public participation. A plethora of adjustments can even render regulatory policy incoherent.

One risk presented by the availability of back-end adjustments is that a raft of exceptions can swallow the rule from which they depart. Jim Rossi warns that excessive resort to exceptions can undermine the rules "on the books," resulting in "one set of rules for public consumption and oversight and another for the regulated industry."[116] The threat to the integrity of the regulatory standard is perhaps most acute if agencies fail to consider the cumulative impacts of adjustments. Thus, Daniel Farber, among others, has criticized the

Endangered Species Act's incidental take permit process on the grounds that the Interior Department has interpreted its authority to issue those permits "so broadly that it now threatens to eclipse the rest of the statute."[117] Rena Steinzor has attacked EPA's Project XL as "a regulatory free-for-all, with companies requesting lengthy lists of exemptions in their initial applications that bear little if any relationship to the environmental improvements they pledged to achieve."[118]

Back-end adjustments also create a risk of agency capture. Adjustments provide a means of affording favorable treatment to favored political interests in a way that may be less visible than preferential treatment in the regulations themselves, even if that treatment is inconsistent with underlying regulatory objectives. Jody Freeman, a strong supporter of the kind of "collaborative governance" reflected in negotiated regulatory solutions, nevertheless concedes "the real risks of factionalism and agency capture" posed by negotiated rulemaking and programs such as EPA's Project XL.[119] Similarly, back-end adjustments have the potential to adversely affect persons that are not directly involved in the adjustment-issuance process or that lack the political clout to have an impact in that process.[120]

These risks are increased if the adjustment process takes the form of closed door deal-making from which the public is excluded. According to Daniel Farber, back-end adjustment mechanisms do not always afford the same opportunities for public participation as do rulemaking proceedings governed by the federal Administrative Procedure Act (APA). To that extent, they take place "in the shadow of the law" instead of "in the light of public deliberation."[121] Critics of Project XL charge that barriers to public participation attributable to lack of funding and technical support for community and public interest groups have been one of its most controversial problems.[122] Indeed, there is a risk that the use of back-end adjustments may weaken the ability of national public interest groups and other interested members of the public to affect public policy by diluting their resources.[123] One type of back-end adjustment—contractual negotiation of regulatory requirements—is also subject to criticism on the grounds that this type of adjustment may amount to a questionable delegation of lawmaking power to private parties.[124] Contract-based regulatory commitments may also prove difficult for the government to adjust, even in the face of new information or other changed circumstances.[125] Finally, back-end adjustments for particular firms may afford them unfair advantages by reducing their compliance costs in comparison to those incurred by their competitors.[126]

Minimizing the Pitfalls

In light of the potential advantages of allowing agencies to dispense back-end adjustments to risk protection standards, it makes sense to consider ways that minimize the potential problems of this kind of incremental decision-making. We believe that various forms of oversight, by increasing accountability, can make at least some forms of back-end adjustments, on balance, a useful component of a pragmatic risk regulation program.

One way to protect against a de facto weakening of regulatory standards through excessive issuance of back-end adjustments such as exceptions is to specify by statute what the criteria are for making such adjustments available.[127] Congress, however, should not make the criteria too detailed. An effort to adopt criteria that account for all possibilities would not only reduce the flexibility that make back-end adjustments useful; it would also confront the same bounded rationality that makes it so difficult to adopt comprehensive rules in the first place. But general standards are not the same thing as no standards. Prior to its demise, the Administrative Conference of the United States endorsed "explicit congressional prescription of the equitable or other criteria that shall govern an exceptions process."[128] Alternatively, Congress could order the agencies to develop their own criteria for the making of incremental adjustments.[129] While agencies would have broad discretion to develop the criteria, once they did so the criteria would serve as benchmarks to assess agency performance and provide some measure of consistency and coherence in the dispensation of individual relief and related adjustments. An agency should be required to issue a written explanation of any back-end adjustment decision it makes, so that affected interests and reviewing courts can scrutinize the agency's analysis of why the adjustment is consistent with relevant statutory policies.

The Superfund cleanup program provides an example of how the process of formulating and applying the criteria for back-end adjustments might work. The statute requires that actions selected by EPA for the remediation of facilities contaminated by hazardous substances comply with certain applicable or appropriate requirements, but the law also authorizes EPA to select remedial actions that do not meet these requirements if it finds that certain circumstances exist, such as evidence that compliance with the requirements will result in greater risk to human health and the environment than alternative options, or that compliance with the requirements is technically impracticable.[130] Any decision to issue a waiver must be accompanied by an explanation of why one or more of the waiver criteria are satisfied.

If agencies were required by statute to report to Congress on the development and implementation of adjustment criteria, the legislature could provide an additional layer of oversight. In the event of abuse, Congress could jawbone agency officials or adopt statutory correctives to protect the substantive integrity of the regulatory program.[131] Requiring (either by legislation or agency regulation) that exceptions, waivers, and the like be confined to unique circumstances also provides a means of combating agency efforts to use back-end adjustments to dispense unjustified favors. Finally, legislative specification of the criteria for adjustments (or statutory delegation to the agency of the authority to set such criteria) can assuage concerns that the agency is acting beyond the scope of its power and thereby minimize the uncertainties that sometimes accompany novel or creative agency reform initiatives.

There is no way to eliminate the possibility of agency capture. One way to protect against it, however, is to mandate that agencies provide opportunities for meaningful public participation in any adjustment processes they undertake. As Kenneth Culp Davis recognized long ago, "discretion can be cabined through the use of structural procedures."[132] Accordingly, requiring public participation may provide an additional safeguard against excessive dispensation of adjustments. We support the use of back-end adjustments only if the opportunities for participation afforded interested persons are essentially equivalent to those that govern adoption of regulatory standards in the first place.[133] If an agency such as EPA decides to issue a waiver from a technology-based pollution control standard, for example, it should have to publish notice of its intended action in the Federal Register and solicit public comment.[134] Mandating public participation of this sort will undoubtedly sacrifice some of the speed and flexibility that makes these back-end devices attractive to agencies and regulated parties alike.[135] The price in reduced agency accountability and process legitimacy that would result from not requiring opportunities for public input, however, would be too high.

Finally, to provide yet another level of accountability, Congress should make judicial review of the issuance of back-end adjustments available to private individuals and organizations and to public interest groups that satisfy constitutional standing requirements if that authority does not already exist.[136] Judicial review of individualized adjustments should be available for both compliance with procedural requirements and compliance with substantive statutory mandates under an arbitrary and capricious standard.

Prospects

In the end, we believe that, while expansion of the availability of back-end adjustments poses a danger that risk reduction regulation will be watered down on a piecemeal basis, such a danger is less worrisome than a wholesale adoption of comprehensive, economic rationality as the governing substantive criterion. The risk always exists that administrators who are not committed to achieving the agency's statutory mandate can undermine that mandate through excessive grants of back-end adjustments. But judicial review and congressional oversight can discover and correct many such abuses, as they did during the first Reagan administration when EPA officials took actions inconsistent with the statutes they were charged with administering.

Conclusion

Pragmatism recognizes that institutional arrangements are context-specific. Instead of assessing the value of risk regulation mechanisms against an ideal standard, a pragmatic approach demands evidence that proposed reforms to such arrangements will yield superior results in practice. We endorse efforts by policy-makers to take steps to reduce the need for the kind of information that bounded rationality is likely to make difficult to obtain. Because of the uncertainty that tends to limit our ability to understand (and certainly to quantify) regulatory costs and benefits, any attempt to fashion a general regulatory standard that universally avoids irrational results is doomed to failure. Regulated entities often have access to more information about the cost of regulation than the regulatory agency does. To the extent that regulators must rely on cost estimates supplied by the regulated community in developing regulatory standards, they are to a certain extent at the mercy of that community. As we noted in Chapter 4, regulated entities have a built-in incentive to behave opportunistically by overestimating the cost of compliance. Affording regulated entities flexibility in the choice of the means of compliance with regulatory standards turns a potential negative factor at the standard development stage into a positive one at the stage of regulatory implementation. It takes advantage of the superior knowledge of regulated entities by affording them incentives to select the most cost-effective means of compliance possible.

Another component of pragmatism is its commitment to incremental decision-making as a means of addressing bounded rationality problems. In the context of risk regulation, such a commitment entails testing regulatory approaches on an ongoing basis to determine which ones fail to provide useful solutions, so that they can be adjusted or replaced. We therefore endorse commitment by regulatory agencies to incremental change in the implementation of risk regulation through resort to a series of mechanisms by which they may adjust the application or enforcement of general risk regulation standards in particular cases. Pragmatic regulatory implementation of the sort we describe in this chapter allows agencies to take advantage of knowledge of the impacts of regulation—beneficial and adverse—yielded through real world regulatory applications. The current risk regulation statutes provide many opportunities for this kind of "back-end" flexibility, and agencies have invented others even where they are not explicitly authorized. To the extent that flexibility of this sort is not currently available, we favor steps to make it so.

9

Promoting Accountable Risk Regulation

One of the enduring problems of American administrative law has been ascertaining how federal administrative agencies fit into a tripartite form of government that does not on its face accommodate them. Given the breadth of the scope of risk regulation, it is not surprising that the delegation to agencies such as the Environmental Protection Agency (EPA) and the Occupational Safety and Health Administration (OSHA) of the power to make regulatory decisions with profound social and economic consequences has given rise to questions about the wisdom of such delegations and about the legitimacy of the exercise of delegated regulatory authority.[1] This chapter proceeds by assessing the appropriate role of the executive, legislative, and judicial branches of the federal government in promoting accountable risk regulation by administrative agencies. In each instance, the chapter provides a framework for a pragmatic approach to such oversight.

An important early-twentieth-century justification for the creation of administrative agencies was grounded in the Progressive notion of expertise. Agencies were conceived of as "role-specific, problem-solving institutions" whose neutrality and empirical approach to analysis of public policy problems could restrain special interest politics in the adoption of solutions to those problems.[2] A pragmatic approach rejects both of those premises. As the preceding chapters of this book have indicated, agencies responsible for implementing the federal risk regulation statutes typically engage in a process of decision-making that is complex, multifactored, and multidisciplinary. Moreover, regulators engaged in this process are subject to bounded rationality. Thus "neutral" agency decision-makers are not capable in most instances of ascertaining "correct" solutions through the application of empirical evaluation.

A pragmatic approach to risk regulation nevertheless draws on the Progressive tradition in the sense that it endorses deference to the exercise of agency discretion. Because of the conditions of bounded rationality that often surround questions about risk regulation policy, regulatory decision-making inevitably requires the exercise of judgment. Regulators by and large are in a better position to exercise the necessary judgment than are the public at large or other government decision-makers, such as the President's staff or members of Congress.[3] As Chapter 3 explains, that is because regulators (within the career bureaucracy, at least) operate within a critical community of inquiry that specializes in the scientific and policy details of risk regulation science in a way that those other decision-makers can not and do not.

This comparative advantage, however, does not justify ignoring the role of democratic accountability as a cherished tradition in this country. An essential task of a pragmatic system of risk regulation, therefore, is to strike a balance between the desire to reap the benefits that will accrue from affording flexibility and discretion to agencies in the exercise of informed judgment and the need to ensure the accountability of agency decision-makers.

Executive Oversight

The purpose of political oversight is not only to ensure consistency of the agency's judgments with governing legislative and administrative standards, but also to provide the political branches an opportunity to alter the result settled upon by the agency. If conducted appropriately, political oversight should not only provide a check on unauthorized or arbitrary decision-making but also enhance the legitimacy of the agency's endeavors by putting upon them the stamp of democratic accountability.

The potential for abuse of the political oversight process, however, should not be overlooked. Political oversight can subvert the benefits of reliance on agency expertise and judgment if the overseeing entity overrides agency technical judgments. Such subversion can occur, for example, when overseers alter agency decisions without an appropriate empirical basis for doing so, or when overseers ignore the extent to which the agency is capable of choosing "optimal" solutions because of considerations of bounded rationality. Any such abuse is likely to be exacerbated if the oversight is conducted in a manner that is designed to obscure rather than reveal the true substantive basis for the overseer's objections, or if it is immune from the same kind of public scrutiny to which the agency's deliberations were subject.

Degree of Proof

The first problem is the possibility that those engaged in oversight will insist upon a degree of "proof" for agency regulatory policy decisions that is inconsistent with the degree to which risk regulation policy questions are subject to bounded rationality. One of the principal tasks of the Office of Information and Regulatory Affairs (OIRA) since the 1980s has been to assess agency compliance with presidential Executive Orders requiring agencies to conduct cost-benefit analyses for major rules. As we have indicated in Chapter 7, the advocates of cost-benefit analysis have sometimes pressed for the adoption of a version of that analytical tool that is based on a model of comprehensive rationality that agencies engaged in risk regulation are unlikely to be able to follow. At least to date, the literature does not support the claim that an approach to regulation based on comprehensive analytical rationality is likely to yield better regulatory policy than the more flexible standards reflected in most current risk regulation statutes. A more pragmatic form of executive oversight would assess agency performance against a relatively flexible version of cost-benefit analysis that acknowledges bounded rationality. To the extent that the statutory standard governing agency efforts to establish appropriate levels of risk is designed to accommodate bounded rationality, executive oversight that demands of the agency proof that it is incapable of providing is also inconsistent with applicable law.[4]

Unidimensional Analysis

The second related problem is the possibility that the overseers will place undue emphasis on one factor among the many that the agency considered in reaching its decision. Office of Management and Budget (OMB) overseers are usually economists, who may be inclined to consider a narrower array of factors than agency personnel charged with the responsibility of taking into account a broad range of values.[5] Some of OMB's critics have charged that "in performing its review function, OIRA has focused almost exclusively on the cost of regulation and its economic impact."[6] One critic of OMB review during the Reagan era described that process as one characterized by "a myopic vision of the regulatory process which place[d] the elimination of cost to industry above all other considerations."[7] If these perceptions are accurate, then executive branch oversight has the potential to conflict with pragmatism's commitment to accommodating a wide range of social values instead of allowing one—such as wealth maximization—to predominate. To the extent that executive branch oversight insists upon determining the appropriate level of protection against risk exclusively through a utilitarian calculus, it displaces other forms of accommodating economic concerns and other factors that, as we have argued in previous chapters, are more consistent with widely shared social values.

Delay

The third problem relates to the potential for executive branch review to cause inordinate delays in formulation and implementation of risk regulation. In Chapter 7, we described how the pursuit of comprehensive analytical rationality mandated by statute or Executive Order can paralyze efforts to implement risk regulation. That kind of regulatory impact analysis can significantly increase the level of resources agencies must commit to regulatory assessments and provide incentives for regulated entities to procrastinate in submitting relevant data to the agencies. The same kind of delay can result from executive branch oversight of agency rulemaking initiatives, both directly and indirectly. Direct delays can result when an overseer such as OIRA precludes an agency from issuing regulations pending executive branch review.[8] OMB's critics charged that during the Reagan administration, OMB engaged in a "war of attrition,"[9] holding up regulations so that it could extract substantive concessions from the promulgating agency in return for releasing the rules.[10] This practice at times afforded OMB "a de facto veto power" over the regulations of agencies such as EPA.[11] Indirect delays can result when the targeted agencies seek to build a record that can stand up to the test of comprehensive analytical rationality, even if applicable statutes or Executive Orders do not require them to do so, so that the resulting regulatory output can pass muster with the overseeing entity.[12]

Secret Oversight

The process of executive branch review of agency rules in the 1980s was beset by another characteristic that is inconsistent with the standards of pragmatic risk regulation described in Chapter 2. Executive branch review during this period, particularly during the Reagan administration, was conducted largely in secret. President Reagan's Executive Order 12,291 required that OMB conduct its review before the issuance of proposed regulations, thereby "depriv[ing] the public of an opportunity to learn the unfiltered views of the agency." OMB's reviews of agency rules were not included in the public record, sometimes in violation of congressional directives requiring inclusion.[13] "The Reagan orders contained no provisions governing disclosure or regulation of communications between private parties and OIRA, or within the executive branch itself."[14] Considerable evidence supports the charge that OMB "serve[d] as a conduit for relaying information and arguments ex parte from the regulated industries to the agencies."[15] According to one critic, "Secrecy pervade[d] virtually all of OMB review, and undisclosed industry lobbying of OMB in some cases appear[ed] to influence OMB's positions on EPA rules under review."[16] Another critic charged that "the entire process operate[d] in an atmosphere of secrecy and insulation from public debate that [made] a mockery of the system of open participation embodied in the Administrative Procedure Act."[17] The process, in short, was the antithesis of one that formulates risk regulation policy by allowing citizens to form an effective community of inquiry through public participation and open debate.

President Clinton, by issuing Executive Order 12,866,[18] took some steps to redress some of the most glaring defects in past executive oversight regimes.[19] The Order, for example, established deadlines for completion of OIRA's review of regulations as a means of minimizing regulatory delay and ossification. It restricted ex parte communications by allowing only the OIRA Administrator to receive oral communications from people outside the executive branch and by requiring the presence of agency personnel whenever OIRA personnel speak with those outsiders. OIRA was required to disclose written communications it received from outsiders as well as written communications between OIRA and the agency. As Professors Richard Pildes and Cass Sunstein have indicated, these procedures opened up internal executive branch communications to public scrutiny and thereby "safeguard[ed] the appearance and the reality of independence from private interests."[20] They also reduced the risk that an agency would base its decisions on erroneous or unreliable information.[21]

Intrusiveness

Finally, OMB review, particularly if it operates in secret, can engage in oversight that is overly intrusive and beyond the capabilities of the overseers. OMB's review of OSHA's formaldehyde rule during the Reagan administration illustrates this potential.[22] A panel of the D.C. Court of Appeals remanded the rule back to OSHA because it had failed to explain why it had not adopted a more protective regulation in light of the evidence in the record that formaldehyde poses a risk of cancer to workers below the exposure limitation established by the agency.[23] After the remand, OSHA did adopt a more restrictive regulation.[24] OSHA was pressured by OMB to adopt the weaker standard after OMB economists did their own risk assessment for formaldehyde, which OMB concluded posed a *de minimis* risk.[25] This conclusion was at odds with the conclusions of EPA; the American Conference of Government Industrial Hygienists, a professional association composed largely of hygienists employed by industry; and the International Agency for Research on Cancer. Indeed, although the Formaldehyde Institute sought judicial review of OSHA's original standard, it did not challenge OSHA's conclusion that formaldehyde poses a significant risk of cancer to workers.

OMB's attempt to pressure OSHA to adopt a less stringent formaldehyde regulation illustrates how executive oversight can displace agency judgment with uninformed, or relatively less informed, judgments by entities such as OMB. It would hardly be appropriate to assume that all individuals engaged in executive branch oversight are sufficiently ignorant that they are incapable of engaging in good faith review of agency risk regulation policy decisions. Pragmatism, however, suggests a wariness toward a system of executive oversight that empowers entities like OMB to override an agency's judgment calls, particularly concerning matters outside of OMB's expertise, such as risk assessment.

Pragmatic Oversight

Executive oversight ought to be designed so that the focus is on the matters most likely to fall within the competence of those assisting or reviewing agency regulatory policy decisions. As one of us has previously argued, "[p]residential oversight should have as its first priority the establishment of a regulatory agenda, as its second priority the coordination of regulation, and as its last priority the review of individual regulations."[26] The President and his advisors are likely to provide the most valuable insights into the "big picture" issues that fall into the first two categories. They are less likely to have the expertise to provide meaningful input on the details of individual regulations, and the dangers of the executive overseers falling prey to special interests can be expected to be greater in the context of individual regulations. Thus OIRA review should focus on matters such as whether an agency's regulatory agenda is consistent with the administration's general policy goals and whether the agencies are performing their regulatory responsibilities in a timely manner.[27] The latter function would enable the White House to acquire the information it needs to assess whether an agency has sufficient resources to implement its statutory responsibilities, formulate agency budget requests in light of such an assessment, and seek additional funding or necessary corrective legislation.[28]

To the extent that executive oversight involves the review of individual regulations, it should not be designed to force agencies to displace multifaceted risk regulation standards (such as constrained or open-ended balancing) with a unilateral focus on utilitarian criteria. A pragmatic version of executive oversight would avoid insisting upon a level of analytical precision by the agencies that is inconsistent with the inherent uncertainties that surround much of risk regulation policy-making. Insistence upon comprehensive analytical rationality can serve to mask the reviewing entity's own substantive biases.[29] A pragmatic form of oversight would vest in agency decision-makers flexibility concerning the means by which the agency chooses to accomplish regulatory objectives established by statute or ordained by the President, and afford deference to the factual and policy findings upon which regulatory choices have been made.

Finally, the process by which the executive branch reviews the output of risk regulation agencies should be one that operates in the light of day in order to minimize the threat of capture by special interests. In addition to the reforms implemented by President Clinton, White House overseers should be required to provide a written justification whenever they block an agency's issuance of a proposed or final rule, and agencies should be required to include in regulatory preambles a description of any significant changes that resulted from executive branch oversight.[30] And the White House should be required to publish regularly a list of all proposed or final rules in the process of executive review and when those rules were submitted for review.[31]

Legislative Oversight

Broad delegations by Congress to administrative agencies of the authority to adopt regulations and take other actions to minimize health, safety, and environmental risks have been commonplace since the adoption of the Clean Air Act in 1970. Even when Congress engages in broad assignments of policy-making responsibility to agencies, however, it retains the ability to supervise the exercise of that authority through a variety of oversight mechanisms. These include control over the appointment of top agency officials, legislative hearings to study the performance of agencies at which agency officials may be subjected to extensive questioning,[32] the allocation of funds to agencies through the appropriations process, and statutory amendments.[33]

Like executive oversight, this form of political oversight has the capacity to improve the work product of agencies engaged in risk regulation at the same time as it promotes the legitimacy of that product by subjecting it to the control of a democratically elected institution. Also like executive oversight, however, legislative oversight has the capacity to thwart a pragmatically designed system of risk regulation. It is likely to do so if it proceeds without an adequate informational foundation, ignores the bounded rationality that pervades efforts to adopt and implement risk regulation, divests agencies of the flexibility they need to adjust to changes in circumstances and the acquisition of new information, or precludes public participation in and opportunities for public assessments of legislative policy-making through the use of non-deliberative and secretive processes.

Nonpragmatic Oversight

This section begins by providing examples of legislative oversight techniques that have fostered or hindered the operation of a pragmatic risk regulation system in recent years. It ends by setting forth a framework for a pragmatic approach to legislative oversight that complements the framework for executive oversight sketched out in the previous section.

Superfund Reform

As discussed earlier, the most common and persistent criticism of risk regulation has been that it is inefficient in the sense that it fails to ensure that the benefits of regulation exceed its costs. The Superfund program, created by the Comprehensive Environmental Response, Compensation and Liability Act (CERCLA), has been the poster child for the argument that federal risk regulation is irrational.[34] For years, the critics of CERCLA have complained that it takes too long to accomplish a site cleanup and that the remedies for contaminated facilities selected by EPA are unnecessarily expensive.[35] The Clinton administration responded to these criticisms in 1994 by proposing reform of CERCLA to speed up the pace and lower the cost of cleanup.[36] After extensive congressional hearings, a consensus bill modeled largely on the administration's proposal emerged, but the bill died shortly before the adjournment of the 103rd Congress.[37]

The bill's failure did not dampen widespread, bipartisan enthusiasm for it. Senator Baucus, the chairman of the Senate Environment and Public Works Committee, praised the progress made on the bill before adjournment, noting particularly that negotiators on both sides of the aisle had "ended the 'religious wars' that divided the business and environmental communities, and produced a bill they support." Similarly, Michael Oxley, the ranking Republican on the House Energy and Commerce Subcommittee on Transportation and Hazardous Materials, expressed disappointment over the failure to adopt "a good bill" and blamed the minimum wage dispute for the bill's demise. Senator Baucus's characterization of the breadth of support for the bill was borne out when both the Environmental Defense Fund and the Chemical Manufacturers Association (CMA) praised the defunct bill as one that would increase consistency among cleanups, cut cleanup costs, and accelerate the pace of cleanups. A CMA spokesperson urged the yet-to-be-elected Congress to "act as soon as possible to make Superfund reform a reality." EPA Administrator Carol Browner noted the establishment of a "broad-based coalition for reform" and expressed the administration's commitment to building a consensus as the best way to achieve Superfund reform.[38]

The chances for serious consideration of a consensus approach such as the one nearly adopted in 1994 declined at the beginning of the 104th Congress when Republican legislators proposed radical reforms of CERCLA. Just months before, Michael Oxley had bemoaned the fate of the 1994 bill, which he had characterized as a "good one." Now he pledged himself to a complete overhaul of CERCLA, claiming that "[if] we do our job right this year, the product we come up with will be totally alien to what we now have."[39] The political defections emboldened industry as well. Previous supporters of the consensus bill, such as the CMA, now took the position that the 1994 bill could be significantly improved by decreasing the cost of the remedies selected on the basis of "hypothetical risk."[40] A spokesperson for the American Insurance Association stated that the debate over CERCLA reform was "no longer limited by fundamental philosophical assumptions." The question was no longer how to pay for the program, but instead "whether there is a superfund program."

Despite the enthusiasm for gutting CERCLA, the federal affairs environmental director for Chrysler Corporation warned that Congress needed to "strike a middle ground" because "[if] you go too far one way or another, you are not going to be successful."[41] The prediction proved to be accurate. The change in the political environment made compromise impossible, and the reform effort collapsed entirely. To this day, CERCLA's remedy selection provisions have not been amended, leaving in place the provisions that had been roundly criticized before 1994.[42]

It is probably not fair to attribute the failure to amend CERCLA in the mid-1990s to any one cause. Nevertheless, the shift from a pragmatic approach that had garnered substantial support from politicians in both parties, environmental groups, and important segments of affected industry to one that was decidedly unpragmatic is certainly an important part of the story. The consensus bill was the result of a lengthy information-gathering process that included congressional hearings at which environmental, industry, and community-based groups all provided input. The resulting bill sought to strike a balance between the goal of effectuating hazardous substance cleanups that reduce health and environmental risks to acceptable levels, and the desire to avoid cleanup requirements that were infeasible or unnecessarily costly. By comparison, the proposals introduced during the 104th Congress would have skewed the cleanup process toward cost minimization at the expense of remedial adequacy in a manner that was inconsistent with the prevailing approach to risk regulation. The same legislative proposals would have subjected EPA's decisions about environmental remedies to judicial review at multiple points in the process.[43] Pragmatism favors accountability, but not through a process that in practice is so laden with check points that it risks making it practically impossible for agencies to carry out their responsibilities.

Appropriation Riders

The supporters of the Contract with America proposed a series of reforms concerning CERCLA and other environmental protection that would have radically altered the landscape of environmental law in the United States.[44] Majority Whip Tom Delay, for example, proposed to repeal in their entirety the 1990 amendments to the Clean Air Act.[45] The upshot of this alteration almost certainly would have been a significant weakening of the protections afforded to the public health and safety and the environment through implementation of federal risk regulation. Aside from the Unfunded Mandates Reform Act,[46] none of the major components of the Contract's environmental program were adopted. At bottom, the explanation for this result was the inconsistency between the goals of the would-be reformers and the American public's continued support for the environmental protection endeavor that was then about twenty-five years old.

The response of the legislative critics of the existing system of risk regulation represents legislative oversight at its worst. Unable to push through weakening reforms after consideration and debate over the substantive merits of their proposals, the critics went underground. They turned increasingly to appropriations riders as a means of enacting reforms they were incapable of adopting in the form of substantive legislation.

Environmental policy-making by appropriations rider was certainly not the invention of the supporters of the Contract with America.[47] For example,

Congress used riders throughout the 1980s to restrict judicial review of timber harvest plans adopted by the Forest Service and the Bureau of Land Management (BLM) that, according to environmental groups, contravened a series of environmental laws. A rider adopted in 1989, for example, provided that the management of thirteen national forests known to contain northern spotted owls would satisfy requirements under statutes such as the National Environmental Policy Act (NEPA) and the Endangered Species Act as long as management met the standards set forth in the rider.[48] The rider also provided that compliance with the guidelines for timber management it contained would not be subject to judicial review.[49] After the rider expired in 1990, the federal Court of Appeals for the Ninth Circuit affirmed a series of lower court decisions whose practical effect was to shut down the timber industry in the old growth forests of the Pacific Northwest based on the Forest Service's and the BLM's noncompliance with environmental statutes.[50]

Congress responded to the court's decision by passing what was probably the most notorious of the Contract-era appropriation bills with environmental implications. In a 1995 supplemental appropriation bill, Congress again restricted judicial review of the legality of timber sales with potentially serious environmental impacts. The bill authorized the land management agencies to award salvage timber sales, notwithstanding any other provision of law, and precluded any court from enjoining certain categories of salvage timber sales. Finally, it provided that timber sales conducted in accordance with specified procedures would "be deemed to satisfy" all applicable federal environmental and natural resources laws."[51] Riders were introduced in a variety of other contexts, including attempts to bar the Fish and Wildlife Service from listing additional species or making critical habitat designations under the Endangered Species Act.[52]

Not all of the riders have been sponsored by Republican legislators. When a federal district court declared the practice of mountaintop mining to be a violation of the Clean Water Act and the Surface Mining Control and Reclamation Act,[53] Democratic Senator Robert Byrd attached riders to pending appropriations bills that, if enacted, would have reversed the decision.[54] Nor have all of the riders been designed to narrow the scope of environmental protection and other risk regulation measures. In 1994, Congress passed a bill that included a rider imposing a moratorium on the issuance of patents for federal lands containing hardrock minerals.[55] The moratorium was subsequently extended several times.[56]

Policy-making by appropriations rider is inconsistent with the promotion of accountable government. Appropriations riders are often tacked onto substantive legislation at the last minute, leaving little or no time for legislators to inform themselves or the public about the substance of the riders, much less debate their merits. Often the appropriations bill and the rider attached to it are completely unrelated in subject matter. The 1995 salvage timber sale rider was attached to a bill called the Emergency Supplemental Appropriations for Additional Disasters, for Anti-Terrorism Initiatives, for Assistance in the Recovery from the Tragedy that Occurred at Oklahoma City, and Rescissions Act, 1995.[57] The riders are also often placed in legislation that totals hundreds of pages, making the riders difficult, if not impossible, for the public to spot.

Further, policy-making by appropriations rider detracts from the role of the President in the policy-making process. The practice of attaching unrelated riders to initiatives that are otherwise so popular as to be veto-proof in effect prevents the President from weighing in on the substantive merit of the rider. The Oklahoma City emergency relief bill is again illustrative. President Clinton would have had a difficult time justifying a veto of a measure adopted in the wake of the country's outrage about the bombing of the federal building in Oklahoma City on the basis of an obscure and unrelated rider dealing with sales of salvage timber. Finally, appropriations riders that limit judicial review of administrative decisions reduce the efficacy of that oversight technique.

It was perhaps for those reasons that William Reilly, who served as EPA Administrator under the first President Bush, characterized the use of appropriations bills to limit EPA's discretion to enforce environmental laws within its jurisdiction as "a guaranteed recipe for disillusionment on the part of the public." Instead of confronting environmental policy issues in "the honest way," legislators chose to engage in the charade of leaving the substantive laws unaffected but using riders such as the salvage timber sale rider to preclude their enforcement.[58] If pragmatism supports the development of public policy through a process of open debate, inquiry, and participation by all appropriate communities of inquiry, including the general public, then policy-making by appropriations rider is the antithesis of pragmatic policy-making on risk regulation matters.

Pragmatic Oversight

A pragmatic system of legislative oversight of risk regulation begins, then, by eschewing policy-making by appropriations rider. Such a system conflicts with fundamental standards of pragmatic governance because, in effect if not by design, it blocks communication on the policy issues at stake and makes open debate on the merits difficult if not impossible. Policy-making by appropriations rider therefore undermines democratic account-ability.[59]

Several other components of pragmatic legislative oversight more or less track the components of executive oversight discussed above. Part of the rationale for imposing on agencies regulatory impact analysis requirements is to assist Congress in overseeing agency implementation of statutory mandates. Legislative oversight, however, should acknowledge the bounded rationality that is virtually ubiquitous when risk regulation policy matters are at issue. Congressional ignorance of, or unwillingness to acknowledge, bounded rationality may lead the legislature to fail to provide sufficient resources for agencies to fulfill their responsibilities, as legislators underestimate the difficulty of the tasks they have imposed on the agencies.[60]

Next, a pragmatic system of oversight seeks to fix specific, narrow problems that have been identified through experience with the implementation of legislation. A pragmatic system of legislative oversight would be characterized by some of the same reliance on incremental change that we endorsed in Chapter 8, in our discussion of back-end adjustments by the agencies. Congress has demonstrated convincingly that it is capable of identifying and responding effectively to discrete practical problems in the implementation of risk regulation (even though such change is not always readily achievable). Several examples should be sufficient to make the point.

Pollution Control

When Congress adopted its first wave of pollution control legislation in the early 1970s, it established a statutory standard for toxic water pollutants and hazardous air pollutants that required EPA to protect the public health with an ample margin of safety.[61] Most of the substances that qualified as toxic or hazardous, however, turned out to be known or potential carcinogens. At the time, the consensus of scientific opinion was that it was impossible to identify a safe threshold level of exposure to a carcinogenic substance. As a result, EPA's choices were to promulgate zero-level emission standards or forgo regulation under the relevant provisions of these two statutes. Unwilling to impose regulations with potentially dramatic negative economic consequences, EPA chose to virtually abandon regulation under the two provisions.[62] Eventually, Congress responded by altering the approach to the regulation of both toxic water pollutants and hazardous air pollutants. In 1977 it authorized EPA to shift to a technology-based approach to the regulation of toxic water pollutants.[63] In 1990, Congress amended the Clean Air Act to shift from a health-based to a technology-based approach to the regulation of hazardous air pollutants.[64]

Safe Drinking Water

Another example of a focused congressional response to a risk regulatory statute arguably gone awry arose in the context of the Safe Drinking Water Act. When Congress amended the statute in 1986, it established a series of deadlines for EPA's promulgation of national drinking water regulations for eighty-nine contaminants identified by Congress itself. The new scheme, unfortunately, produced unintended consequences. Because some of the contaminants listed in the statute occurred so infrequently in public water systems, the statute precluded EPA "from concentrating its resources on regulating contaminants that pose the highest health risks."[65] In the Safe Drinking Water Act Amendments of 1996,[66] Congress responded by restoring EPA's flexibility to regulate drinking water contaminants that EPA perceives as the ones that pose the highest health risks.[67] Thus, faced with criticism that the existing regulatory regime required EPA to regulate insignificant risks, Congress in 1996 inserted a significant risk threshold into the statute.

The pre-1996 version of the Safe Drinking Water Act also spurred criticism on the basis of its statutory standard. The statute required that EPA establish enforceable maximum contaminant levels as close as was feasible to the level at which no known or anticipated adverse effects on public health occurred, allowing an adequate margin of safety. Congressional hearings convinced legislators that this approach in some circumstances imposed large costs in exchange for small gains in public health protection. This was particularly true for low-potency carcinogens that occurred at low concentrations.[68] Congress responded in the 1996 amendments by authorizing EPA to issue a maximum contaminant level at less than the maximum feasible level if it concludes that feasibility-based regulation is not cost-justified.[69]

Other Examples

Further examples of the adoption by Congress of amendments in response to criticisms of the operation of risk regulation statutes include the 1990 amendments to the Clean Air Act. That statute included a new program that responded to the arguments that market-based regulatory tools have the potential to achieve pollution reduction goals more efficiently than traditional command-and-control regulation. The acid deposition control provisions of the statute authorize the trading of SO_2 emission allowances.[70] Congress has also reacted to charges that CERCLA's liability scheme impaired the extension of credit by institutional lenders and frustrated environmentally beneficial recycling activities when it adopted the Asset Conservation, Lender Liability, and Deposit Insurance Protection Act[71] and the Superfund Recycling Equity Act,[72] respectively.

These statutory changes illustrate the potential for Congress to adopt incremental changes as practical experience with risk regulation statutes reveals flawed approaches, or as new information and ideas provide the potential for regulatory improvements.[73] The availability of this mechanism for eliminating ineffective or counterproductive regulatory approaches ought to reduce the pressure for Congress to pin down every statutory detail at the outset and should enhance the legislature's willingness to afford discretion to the agencies to adopt the approaches they deem best suited to resolving particular risk regulation problems.[74]

Judicial Oversight

The final piece of the oversight puzzle is judicial review of agency risk regulation decisions. Congress usually accompanies broad delegations of discretionary authority to an administrative agency, with a delegation to the courts

of the authority to review the propriety of the agency's exercise of that authority.[75] Judicial review of agency decisions has the potential to enhance the
accountability of agency decision-makers through invalidation of agency decisions that are inconsistent with the terms of the authorizing statute, thereby
preserving the integrity of the policy decision reflected in the statute adopted
by an elected branch of government. Judicial review, for example, was viewed
by social activists in the 1960s and 1970s (including environmental public interest groups) as a means of mitigating agency capture.[76] The judges during
this period themselves sometimes articulated their role in these terms. Judge
James Oakes, for one, remarked that "a substantive judicial role is absolutely
essential if judges are to meet their serious constitutional obligation to check
abuses of agency discretion."[77] Similarly, Judge Skelly Wright, in the landmark *Calvert Cliffs'* case, explained that the court's duty was "to see that important legislative purposes, heralded in the halls of Congress, are not lost or
misdirected in the vast hallways of the federal bureaucracy."[78]

The courts themselves, however, are not a politically accountable institution. Judicial activism, such as invalidation of an agency decision that is consistent with statutory authorization but inconsistent with a judge's individual
policy preferences, has the potential to infringe upon the policy-making
functions of the political branches of the government.[79] Thus, Richard Pierce
has criticized a decision of the Court of Appeals for the District of Columbia
Circuit in which the court struck down EPA regulations that increased the
stringency of the national ambient air quality standards for ozone and particulate matter under the Clean Air Act:

> Two unelected, life-tenured judges have decided that the United States should
> forego the opportunity to save about 10,000 lives per year in order to save about
> fifty billion dollars per year. Judges are the *least* politically accountable officials.
> They are the worst possible choice of officials to make such fundamental policy
> decisions in our system of constitutional democracy.[80]

One of the standards we have identified as a hallmark of a pragmatic policy-making regime is its effectiveness in enabling relevant critical communities of inquiry to participate in the process of open debate, inquiry, and
evaluation that promote good public policy. Agencies constitute one such
community of inquiry, while political and judicial oversight provide others.
The question, then, in evaluating the role of judicial review as a means of en-

hancing democratic accountability, is whether the courts are likely to provide assistance in that critical inquiry process and, if so, whether that assistance is likely to be outweighed by any adverse consequences of judicial review.

At the inception of the environmental era, the judges tended to harbor few doubts that they could provide a valuable function. Judge Harold Leventhal spoke of "a unique three-way partnership between the legislature, executive and judiciary" that was contemplated by Congress and reflected in the provisions of statutes such as the Clean Air Act.[81] According to Leventhal, the agencies and the courts together constituted "a 'partnership' in furtherance of the public interest."[82] Similarly, Judge Bazelon praised "the long and fruitful collaboration of administrative agencies and reviewing courts" on environmental regulatory matters.[83]

After more than two decades of experience with this collaboration, Judge Patricia Wald continued to speak of a partnership between courts and agencies, but she acknowledged that it was an "uneasy" one. The source of the uneasiness, she claimed, was "the unavoidable and irreducible tension" between the desire to establish through judicial review "a check on agency absolutism or arrogance [as] a means of insuring that laws are actually carried out as intended" by Congress, and "a deep-seated conviction, rooted in our constitutional format of separation of powers, that the courts should not take control of public policy from the two political branches." Judge Wald seemed optimistic that the courts were capable of drawing an appropriate line "between obsequious deference and intensive scrutiny." Although she conceded that the dilemma would inevitably persist, she suggested that "an emphasis on pragmatic flexibility over formalistic and abstract principle is particularly appropriate."[84] If judges paid attention to the likely impact of their decisions on agency functioning, judicial review could fulfill its promise as a means of enhancing the accountability of administrative government.[85] Similarly, Mark Seidenfeld has expressed a preference for discrete "operational modifications" to stringent judicial review as opposed to adoption of deferential review as the best way to suffuse agency policy-making endeavors with flexibility "without encouraging sloppy or nondeliberative agency decisionmaking."[86]

Other observers have not been nearly as sanguine about the impact of judicial review on the implementation of legislation authorizing risk regulation. Tom McGarity has postulated that stringent judicial review has contributed to an "ossification" of the agency rulemaking process through the imposition on agencies of burdensome analytical requirements. McGarity asserts that judges need to exercise caution in performing substantive review functions because of the "clear limits to judicial competence in the area of highly scientific and technical rulemaking," the potential for stringent substantive review to frustrate the achievement of congressionally articulated policies, and the risk that rigorous review would hamper innovation and experimentation. Adopting the metaphor of the "pass-fail prof," McGarity urged courts engaged in substantive review to view their role as "screening out bad decisions, rather than ensuring that agencies reach the 'best' decisions."[87] More recently, Frank Cross has argued in favor of an even more limited judicial role in reviewing administrative policy-making. Cross identified "five discrete pathological effects of judicial review":

> The first effect is ossification, whereby unpredictable judicial requirements considerably complicate and delay the promulgation of individual regulations. The second effect is agenda disruption, through which judicial demands for agency action undermine other actions that otherwise could have been taken through a more coherent and effective planning process. Third, judicial review compels inefficient and ineffective agency allocation of resources, as agencies become more concerned with surviving judicial review than with advancing their commissioned agendas. Fourth, judicial review commonly fails to understand the political and pragmatic limitations that agencies face, instead demanding an unachievable "best" that is the enemy of an achievable "good" outcome. Fifth and finally, judicial review results in poorer quality rules.

Cross thus denied any "pragmatic" justification for judicial review of administrative rulemaking.[88]

Our aim in this concluding section is to provide just such a pragmatic justification for at least a limited judicial oversight role in the implementation of risk regulation, although the role we carve out for the courts is probably closer to Professor McGarity's "pass-fail prof" than it is to Judge Leventhal's notion of "partnership." Pragmatism, as we have defined it, is committed to the accommodation to the greatest extent possible of widely shared values in the protection of the public health and the environment. Given the distrust of government that forms an important part of the American experience, the democratic accountability of government and a commitment to the rule of law are both values that are "part of 'the nature and theory' of American government."[89]

The problem of designing a system for judicial oversight of agency risk regulation decisions is that techniques that enable the courts to perform oversight functions that enhance the accountability of bureaucrats may frustrate the achievement of risk regulation's goals, as both Professors McGarity and Cross have charged. Neither a system in which judicial oversight is eliminated nor one in which the courts are permitted to engage in rigorous review of agency decisions in a manner that hamstrings agencies in the pursuit of their missions provides an acceptable accommodation of the relevant values. Neither, therefore, is pragmatic. Indeed, "the unavoidable and irreducible tension" referred to by Judge Wald makes the search for a system of oversight that ensures fidelity to statutory commands while eliminating the risk of judicial overreaching a quixotic one.

Instead of insisting upon the development of such an unrealistic ideal, pragmatism dictates that judges take cognizance of the limits of their own ability to understand risk regulation choices and defer to agency solutions when the competence of agency decision-makers exceeds their own. It also dictates judicial acknowledgment of the impact of bounded rationality on the ability of agencies to justify their regulatory choices, and it compels that judges refrain from imposing on agencies analytical burdens of proof that agencies are not practically capable of sustaining. In such cases, the courts should exercise deferential review that preserves the flexibility of agency decision-makers to exercise informed judgment. Finally, a pragmatic system of judicial oversight should seek to enhance public participation in agency policy-making endeavors, consistent with congressionally imposed procedures. As the following discussion illustrates, these components of a pragmatic system of judicial oversight support a more or less intrusive judicial role depending upon the context.

Policy Decisions

Perhaps the most difficult task of defining a pragmatic system of judicial oversight concerns review of substantive policy decisions, such as those reflected in agency regulations. We have previously described how the imposition of prescriptive regulatory impact analysis requirements by Executive

Order or legislation has tended to ossify the rulemaking process. Judicial review can have similar effects. Professor McGarity has explained the phenomenon in the following terms:

> Fully aware of the consequences of a judicial remand, the agencies are constantly "looking over their shoulders" at the reviewing courts in preparing supporting documents, in writing preambles, in responding to public comments, and in assembling the rulemaking "record." Because they never know what issues dissatisfied litigants will raise on appeal, they must attempt to prepare responses to all contentions that may prove credible to an appellate court, no matter how ridiculous they may appear to agency staff. . . .
>
> The predictable result of stringent "hard look" judicial review of complex rulemaking is ossification. Because the agencies perceive that the reviewing courts are inconsistent in the degree to which they are deferential, they are constrained to prepare for the worst-case scenario on judicial review. This can be extremely resource-intensive and time-consuming.[90]

Similarly, Cass Sunstein has argued that aggressive judicial review can contribute to delay and even discourage agencies from engaging in rulemaking altogether.[91]

Judicial fly-specking of agency decision-making rationales thus poses a risk that agencies straining to build impregnable support for their decisions despite limited resources will become unable to fulfill their statutory missions. The problem is exacerbated if the courts insist upon a level of empirical justification that agencies are incapable of providing because of the nature of the issues involved. What Adrian Vermeule has said about the judiciary's approach to the review of questions of statutory interpretation is also relevant to review of the policy choices made by agencies in the implementation of risk regulation statutes. "The critical questions are in many instances transscientific (meaning that they are empirical but intractable), and even where the questions are tractable courts lack the capacity to answer them."[92] If the courts insist that agencies provide answers to these unanswerable questions, the result is likely to be that agencies responsible for taking action to provide protection of the public health and safety and the environment against risk-creating activities will effectively be unable to do so, even if the authorizing statutes take a form (such as constrained or open-ended balancing) that Congress meant to accommodate bounded rationality.

Corrosion Proof Fittings

Two oft-cited examples of this kind of unrealistic judicial expectation are the decisions of the Court of Appeals for the Fifth Circuit in *Corrosion Proof Fittings*[93] and the Court of Appeals for the District of Columbia Circuit, later reversed by the Supreme Court, in *American Trucking*.[94] As discussed in Chapter 7, the first case involved an EPA regulation under the Toxic Substances Control Act (TSCA) phasing out the use of asbestos-containing products. The court found EPA's cost-benefit analysis to be insufficient because, among other things, it relied too heavily on the unquantified benefits that would accrue from the rule. The court also chastised EPA for its failure to consider adequately the fact that some industries lacked substitute products for asbestos, even though EPA did in fact consider that lack, concluded that substitutes would be available before the ban took effect, and provided a waiver provision in the event that the prediction turned out to be wrong. Finally, the court decided that EPA failed to demonstrate that the adverse effects of commercial substitutes for the banned products would not exceed those attributable to continued use of the banned products, even though EPA explicitly indicated that, given the known dangers of asbestos exposure, it was unwilling to defer the ban pending the availability of more information about the risks of exposure to likely substitutes.

Shortly after the case was decided, officials in EPA's Office of Pollution Prevention and Toxics predicted that the agency would most likely abandon efforts to use its authority under TSCA to impose comprehensive chemical or product bans.[95] The prediction came to fruition as "EPA seems to have abandoned enforcement of [TSCA], largely as a result of intense judicial scrutiny of EPA activity" in *Corrosion Proof Fittings*.[96]

American Trucking

American Trucking was a case in which a coalition of small businesses challenged EPA's issuance in 1997 of revised national ambient air quality standards under the Clean Air Act for ozone and fine particulate matter.[97] The provision of the Clean Air Act relied on by EPA in issuing the revised standards gives EPA the authority to issue air quality standards that are "requisite to protect the public health," allowing an adequate margin of safety.[98] The appellate court held that EPA had failed to justify how the exposure levels it chose met this statutory requirement.

According to the court, the problem was that EPA did not offer "any determinate criterion for drawing lines." EPA chose the regulatory levels by considering the nature and severity of the health effects involved, the size of the sensitive populations at risk, the types of health information available, and the kinds and degrees of uncertainties that had to be addressed. The court regarded the agency's position, however, as nothing more than the "intuitive proposition" that a more stringent standard than the pre-existing standard for ozone would result in less harm to the public health. In other words, the agency failed to indicate why it stopped where it did instead of at a higher or lower concentration level.

The court recognized that the question was one of degree, but it found that EPA offered "no intelligible principle by which to identify a stopping point."[99] In searching for a possible intelligible principle for EPA to supply on remand, the court suggested that EPA consider the adoption of clinical criteria for the definition of adverse health effects or an approach analogous to one used by one state to determine eligibility criteria for Medicaid benefits, which involved a ranking of treatments based on calculating the value of improvements in "quality-adjusted life years" divided by the cost of treatment. As Professor Richard Pierce recognizes, however, there is little apparent benefit to efforts by EPA to translate each health effect into a common unit of measurement: "It is simply another symptom of the science charade—requiring the illusion of objectivity and quantitative precision in a context in which science is incapable of providing either."[100] The Supreme Court agreed, and it reversed the Court of Appeals decision, finding that EPA's exercise of authority "fits comfortably within the scope of discretion permitted by our precedent."[101]

Zone of Reasonableness

Judicial oversight that serves the function of promoting agency accountability need not be so heavy-handed. In other cases, including some decided by the D.C. Circuit concerning implementation of the Clean Air Act, the courts have recognized that "an appropriate margin of safety on a pollution control standard need not 'spring from a bounty of definitive research as the clear and sole appropriate standard.' . . . Where the administrative record is inconclusive as to the ideal level at which to establish a standard, and suggests a range of values, EPA acts within its discretion to select the appropriate" level.[102]

This more deferential approach is more consistent with several related components of a pragmatic approach to the implementation of risk regulation. It acknowledges the bounded rationality that often faces policy-makers in this field. It adopts a deferential posture toward the exercise of agency judgment and the application of technical expertise, thereby leaving agency decision-makers greater flexibility than one requiring agencies to justify each choice as the single most optimal solution. And it takes account of the relative competencies of courts and agencies in addressing the implications of bounded rationality.

A system of judicial oversight that affords agencies relatively broad discretion is bound to result in some slippage. "Pass-fail" review may not detect some instances of agency departures from legislative mandate. Pragmatism, however, is satisfied with adjustments to existing institutional arrangements that improve their performance, even if they do not measure up against some theoretical but impractical ideal. Judicial review of the sort exercised by the courts in *Corrosion Proof Fittings* and *American Trucking* seems more likely to derail legislative initiatives, while more deferential review retains the potential for holding agencies accountable to the electorate by identifying and reversing decisions that are inconsistent with legislative directives, or that reflect serious gaps in reasoning. Even deferential review, moreover, preserves an oversight role for the courts in overturning an agency's statutory interpretation when it conflicts with the terms of the agency's enabling authority.

Political Realities

Another facet of a pragmatic approach to judicial oversight involves judicial recognition of the political constraints to which risk regulation agencies are subject. Frank Cross insists that judicial review "consistently ignores the external political and practical factors that must lie at the heart of effective administrative action." Because "[p]olitical realities critically constrain and direct agency decisionmaking,"[103] an agency operating under a statutory regime that appears to vest in it relatively boundless authority may in reality have a relatively narrow range of policy choices at its disposal.

Whether or not Cross is correct that the courts "consistently" ignore political realities, there is no doubt that they do so in some cases. Political constraints were largely responsible for putting a halt to the efforts of both EPA
during the early 1980s and Congress during the mid-1990s to weaken environmental protection standards. The presence of political constraints, including the kinds of executive and legislative oversight techniques endorsed
earlier in this chapter, do not justify elimination of substantive judicial review
of the output of risk regulation agencies. The function of substantive review,
however, is not to provide an opportunity for individual judges to impose
their own political views on agencies that, though not composed of elected
officials, can nevertheless be made accountable through a mix of executive,
legislative, and judicial oversight techniques.

Unreasonable Delay

Other facets of judicial review involve tasks to which the courts tend to
be better suited. One way in which courts can enhance agency accountability
with relatively little risk that the courts will exceed the bounds of judicial
competence is to authorize the courts to require agencies to comply with clear
statutory duties that they have violated. We think, therefore, that a pragmatic
system of judicial oversight should include, as most risk regulation statutes
currently do, provisions authorizing action-forcing citizen suits to enforce
nondiscretionary duties or to otherwise prompt delinquent agency action.

A perfect example of the appropriate use of the judicial power to force
administrative agencies to take action that has been unjustifiably delayed is
the OSHA farm workers case.[104] Representatives of farm workers petitioned
OSHA to adopt safety and health standards that would require employers to
provide toilets and drinking water facilities in the fields to prevent the spread
of contagious disease and to minimize the risk of exposure to pesticides on
the workers' hands. Fourteen years after the filing of the petition, OSHA still
had not acted. Judge Wald regarded OSHA's refusal to issue standards as intractable. The court ordered OSHA to issue standards within thirty days to
"bring an end to this disgraceful chapter of legal neglect."[105]

Similarly, the federal courts in the late 1990s responded to citizen suits
filed by environmental groups by ordering EPA to take steps to implement
the Clean Water Act's state water quality standards program that were years

overdue.[106] One court, noting EPA's thirteen-year delay in complying with its statutory mandate to issue total maximum daily loads for water bodies not in compliance with state water quality standards, concluded that "[w]hen such dereliction occurs, it is up to the courts in their traditional, equitable, and interstitial role to fashion the remedy."[107] The court upheld a lower court's order requiring EPA to prepare a report on water quality monitoring. In another case, the court ordered EPA to take steps to implement the water quality standards program for a state that would have taken more than one hundred years to fulfill its obligations if it continued to act at its current pace.[108]

These cases illustrate the salutary nature of action-forcing litigation as an accountability-enhancing technique. Congress can establish a comprehensive program to protect the public health and safety or the environment, but if the agency fails to implement the program, the desired levels of protection will not materialize. If an agency has failed to regulate because of neglect or hostility to achievement of the mission that Congress has conferred upon it, a judicial order in response to a citizen petition is capable of preventing the agency from subverting the statutory mandate by omission.

Empowering the courts to order agencies to comply with statutory duties is certainly not without its costs. A court may contribute to resource misallocation if it establishes a deadline for an agency to perform a task that the agency has delayed because it regards the matter as a low priority. Compliance with the court's order may require the agency to shift resources away from what the agency regards as more pressing tasks. The courts are often solicitous, however, to such agency explanations in fashioning timetables for compliance.[109] Because the focus of an action-forcing suit is on whether the agency has justified its failure to act, the courts will generally be required to steep themselves in technical, scientific, and policy questions to a lesser degree than they must when they review the validity of the merits of an agency action such as issuance of a rule.

Violation of Clear Statutory Duties

Another category of cases in which the issue of judicial competence is a relatively unimportant one is citizen suits against regulated entities alleged to be in violation of their statutory or regulatory obligations. In many cases, the issue will be simply whether the defendant has exceeded the numerical limitations set forth in a discharge permit. Discharge reports filed by the defendant may provide a definitive answer. Even where the issue is not that straightforward, the courts will face the same task in determining whether a violation has occurred (and if so, what the appropriate penalty should be) as they do in enforcement actions brought by the government. Fashioning an equitable remedy, moreover, is likely to require judgments similar to those that courts have long been comfortable making in common law tort actions such as nuisance suits.

Citizen suits of this sort serve a beneficial function because they supplement government enforcement efforts in circumstances in which resource shortages or lack of will to enforce make government enforcement inadequate to redress statutory or regulatory violations. Justice Scalia, among others, has raised concerns that citizen enforcement of environmental statutes has the capacity to infringe on the core power of the President to "take Care that the Laws be faithfully executed."[110] The Supreme Court has not yet addressed the issue in any depth.[111] Most of the environmental statutes require those who anticipate the filing of citizen suits to provide prior notice to federal and state regulators and preclude such suits if a governmental entity initiates and diligently pursues enforcement action of its own.[112] In such cases, the argument that citizen suits improperly intrude on executive prerogatives appears to turn largely on whether the executive branch has a right to block prosecution of an alleged violation that it had the opportunity but chose not to pursue.

Public Participation

One final role for the courts in a pragmatic system of judicial oversight is to ensure the availability of legislatively created procedures that are designed to enhance public participation in the risk regulation process. The courts further pragmatism's commitment to allowing citizens to form an effective community of critical inquiry when they force agencies to adhere to the procedural requirements of statutes like NEPA. That statute, as Chapter 7 explains, was adopted not only to require agencies to consider the environmental effects of their proposals before committing to them but also to require agencies to reveal the substance of their deliberations to the public. The statute itself promotes public participation by requiring agencies to solicit the input of state and local agencies and make environmental impact statements available to the general public.[113] The Council on Environmental Quality's implementing regulations require agencies to circulate impact statements to any person or organization that requests the information.[114] The courts can play a useful role by ensuring that agencies make these required opportunities for public participation available. Moreover, review for procedural compliance poses none of the risks of institutional incompetence that attach to review of the substance of agency decisions.

The public cannot seek the assistance of the courts in enforcing statutory procedures (or, for that matter, in reviewing the substance of agency decisions) unless it has access to a judicial forum. The most controversial means by which the courts have deprived private citizens of access to the courts in environmental litigation has been the doctrine of standing to sue. During the 1990s, the Supreme Court made it increasingly difficult for private citizens and entities such as public interest groups to demonstrate their standing to sue. The Court's grudging approach to standing was reflected in its interpretation of relevant constitutional[115] and statutory[116] provisions. The Court seemed more accommodating in its approach to standing in cases initiated by regulated entities.[117] In two recent cases, however, the Supreme Court has allowed more access to the federal courts.[118] It is unclear whether these latest cases indicate that the Supreme Court intends to reverse its prior, more restrictive trend.

By itself, a set of standing principles that limit citizen input into the implementation and enforcement of risk regulation conflicts with pragmatism's commitment to the availability of methods of holding agencies accountable that promote public participation. The adverse effects of narrowed standing for intended regulatory beneficiaries become exacerbated when coupled with a broader set of standing rules for regulated entities such that the latter have preferential access to the courts as an overseeing entity. Pragmatism favors readily available access to the courts by regulatory beneficiaries and regulated entities alike, within the fairly interpreted limits set forth in the Constitution and by statute.

Conclusion

The framework for pragmatic oversight of risk regulators described in this chapter is designed to promote the basic standards of pragmatic policy-making described in Chapter 3 and referred to in subsequent chapters of this book. The essential underpinnings of that framework can be applied equally to all three branches of the federal government. All three sources of oversight should perform their review functions in a manner that takes account of the bounded rationality to which risk regulation agencies tend to be subject. Oversight mechanisms for the executive, legislative, and judicial branches alike should be designed and applied in a way that takes advantage of the relative competence of the overseers and agency decision-makers. In areas that call for the application of agency technical expertise or policy judgment, a deferential oversight posture that preserves agency flexibility is generally appropriate. Finally, oversight should promote rather than hinder the creation of an effective critical community of inquiry among the general public. General though these principles are, they are capable of providing guidance in the development of an effective system of oversight that enhances the legitimacy of agency work product by fostering accountability.

APPENDIXES

APPENDIX 3

Nondiscounted Estimates: Methodology

1. Hazardous Waste Listing for Wood-Preserving Chemicals (EPA: 1990): EPA estimated that the rule would prevent three hundred cancer cases over three hundred years, or 1.0 cancer case per year. EPA's calculation equates cancer cases with premature deaths averted. EPA estimated that total national compliance costs were between $11 million and $14 million. Upper bound estimate: $14 million/1.0 death averted = $14 million/death averted. Lower bound: $11 million/1.0 death averted. See 55 Fed. Reg. 50,450 (1990). The benefit calculation excludes environmental protection.

2. Atrazine/Alachlor Drinking Water Standard (EPA: 1991): The regulation promulgated by EPA established maximum contaminant levels (MCLs) for thirty synthetic organic and seven inorganic chemicals, including Atrazine, Alachlor, and 1,2 Dichloropropane. EPA's cost and benefit estimates in the *Federal Register* were for all thirty-seven chemicals. EPA estimated that compliance with MCLs for the synthetic organic chemicals would prevent seventy cases of cancer per year. The estimate equates cases of cancer with cancer deaths. EPA estimated that the annualized cost was $88 million for water systems in compliance with a prior EPA regulation. There was a one-time cost of $39 million for unregulated contaminants. Estimate: $88 million + $39 million = $127 million/70 cancer deaths = $1.81 million per life saved. The cost for water systems that were not in compliance with the prior EPA regulation was considerably higher. EPA did not break out in the *Federal Register* costs attributable to the new regulation for such water systems. See 56 Fed. Reg. 3526, 3576 (1991).

3. 1,2 Dichloropropane Drinking Water Standard (EPA: 1991): See note 2.

4. Benzene NESHAP (Revised: Waste Operations) (EPA: 1990): EPA estimated that the regulation would reduce the residual incidence of leukemia from 0.6 case/year to 0.05 case/year, or that it would save 0.55 cancer case/year. EPA assumed that individuals would be exposed for seventy years. The estimate equates cancer cases with lives saved. Over seventy years, the regulation would save 38.5 lives (0.55×70). EPA estimated the capital cost to be $250 million and the annual cost to be $87 million. The cost estimate is $250 million + $6,090 million ($87 million x 70) = $6,340 million. The

cost per life saved is $6,340 million/38.5 lives = $164.68 million/life saved. See 55 Fed. Reg. 8292 (1990).

5. Asbestos Ban (EPA: 1989): The rule was remanded by the D.C. Circuit and never went into effect. See *Corrosion Proof Fittings v. EPA*, 947 F.2d 1201 (5th Cir. 1991). EPA estimated that the asbestos ban would result in the avoidance of at least 202 quantifiable cases of lung and gastrointestinal cancer and mesothelioma over a thirteen-year period when benefits are not discounted. The calculations equate a cancer case with a premature death averted. EPA estimated that the present value of the total costs at a discount rate of 3.0 percent would be between $458.89 million and $806.51 million for thirteen years. The future value of the costs in thirteen years at 3.0 percent compounded interest is $674.1 million and $1,184.8 million. Upper bound estimate: $1,184.8 million/202 lives saved = $5.87 million/life saved. Lower bound estimate: $674.1 million/202 lives saved = $3.34 million/life saved. See 54 Fed. Reg. 29,460, 29,484–85 (1989). Benefit and cost estimates are for the entire rule; estimates of the cost per life saved concerning the ban of specific products are higher. See 947 F.2d at 1222.

6. Lockout/Tagout (OSHA: 1989): OSHA estimated the cost per death averted was $1.2 million. After adjustment for additional benefits to employers (i.e., less lost production time, less cost in preparing insurance claims and accident reports, and less inefficiency, a result of replacing injured workers), OSHA estimated the cost per death averted fell to $0.19 million. See 54 Fed. Reg. 36,644 (1989).

7. Benzene NESHAP (Revised: Transfer Operations) (EPA: 1990): EPA estimated that the regulation would reduce the residual incidence of cancer from 1.0 case/year to 0.02 case per year, or that the regulation would prevent 0.98 case of cancer per year. The estimate equates cases of cancer with cancer deaths. EPA assumed that persons would be exposed for a seventy-year period. Over the seventy years, the regulation would prevent 68.6 deaths. EPA estimated that the annual cost was $30 million and the capital cost was $167 million. The total cost over seventy years is $167 million + $2,100 million (70 × $30 million) = $2,267 million. The cost per life saved is $2,267 million/68.6 deaths saved = $33.0 million/life saved. See 55 Fed. Reg. 8292 (1990).

8. EPA estimated that the rule would avoid 1–3 cancer cases per year. The estimate equates cancer cases with deaths avoided. EPA estimated that the present value of capital costs (annualized over a twenty-year lifetime at a discount rate of 3.0 percent) ranged between $42 million and $407 million for a select group of refineries. The agency estimated the total annualized costs for all refineries to be in the range of $57 million to $131 million per year. The estimate assumes that the annualized estimate includes capital costs. Upper bound estimate: $131 million/1 life saved = $131 million. Lower bound estimate: $57 million/3 lives saved = $19 million/life saved. See 55 Fed. Reg. 46,354 (1990).

9. Benzene Occupational Exposure Limit (OSHA: 1987): OSHA estimated that

over forty-five years the rule would cause a reduction of 230 leukemia deaths and 96 aplastic anemia deaths, or 326 deaths averted. OSHA estimated the total annualized cost to be $24.0 million or $1,080.0 million over forty-five years ($24.0 million x 45). The cost per death averted is $1080.0 million/326 = $3.31 million/death averted. See 52 Fed. Reg. 34,460, 34,511, 34,516 (1987). This estimate does not include some health benefits. OSHA's analysis does not account for decreases in health conditions other than leukemia and aplastic anemia and improved health for employees who were exposed to benzene in circumstances not analyzed in the rulemaking proceeding. See 52 Fed. Reg. 34,460, 34,511, 34,516 (1987).

Discounted Estimates: Methodology

1. Formaldehyde Occupational Exposure (EPA: 1991): OSHA estimated that the regulation would cost $64.2 million per year. For "illustrative purposes," the agency estimated that the regulation would save between 6.5 and 47.5 lives that would have been lost to cancer over a forty-five-year exposure period. Finally, OSHA determined that the regulation would produce monetary benefits of $41.2 million from cost savings resulting from avoided cases of respiratory irritation and dermatitis. The net annual cost = $64.2 (annual cost) – $41.2 million (nonfatality monetary benefits) = $23 million. See Lisa Heinzerling, "Regulatory Costs of Mythic Proportions," 107 *Yale Law Review* 1981, 2026, 2026 n. 285 (1998); 52 Fed. Reg. 46,168 (1987). The regulation would produce an annual reduction in lives saved per year of between 0.14 (6.5/45) and 1.06 (47.5/45). Assuming that the annual cost was $23 million per year and the annual benefit was 0.14 life saved, the present value of the cost of the lives saved equals $164 million/life saved ($23 million/0.14). Assuming that the annual cost was $23 million per year and the annual benefit was 1.06 lives saved/year, the present value of the cost of the lives saved equals $21.7 million per life saved ($23 million/1.06).

2. Benzene NESHAP (Revised: Waste Operations) (EPA: 1990): EPA estimated that the regulation would reduce the residual incidence of leukemia from 0.6 case/year to 0.05 case/year or that it would save 0.55 cancer case/year. EPA assumed individuals would be exposed for seventy years. The estimate equates cancer cases with lives saved. EPA estimated the capital cost to be $250 million and the annual cost to be $87 million. See 55 Fed. Reg. 8292 (1990). The present value of 0.55 life per year for seventy years is 20.62 lives. The present value of an annual cost of $87 million for seventy years is $3,262.4 million. The present value of costs is $3,262.4 million (annual costs) + $250 million (capital costs) = $3,512.4 million. The present value of cost per life saved = $3,512.4 million/20.62 = $170.3 million/life saved.

3. Asbestos Ban (EPA: 1989): EPA estimated that the asbestos ban would result in the avoidance of at least 148 quantifiable cases of lung and gastrointestinal cancer and mesothelioma over a thirteen-year period when benefits are discounted at 3 percent. The calculations equate a cancer case with a premature death averted. EPA estimated

that the present value of the total costs at a discount rate of 3.0 percent would be between $458.89 million and $806.51 million for thirteen years. Upper bound estimate: $806.51 million/148 = $5.45 million per life saved. Lower bound estimate: $458.89 million/148 = $3.1 million per life saved. See 54 Fed. Reg. 29,460 (1989). Benefit and cost estimates are for the entire rule; estimates of the cost per life saved concerning the ban of specific products are higher. See *Corrosion Proof Fittings,* 947 F.2d at 1222. EPA did not estimate the reduction in the number of asbestosis cases or cases of other diseases avoided. In addition, the benefits of the rule did not include losses resulting from lost work days or medical care costs. 54 Fed. Reg. at 29,468.

4. Lockout/Tagout (OSHA: 1989): OSHA estimated that 1,530 fatalities would occur over 10 years in the absence of regulation, 54 Fed. Reg. at 36,684, and that its rule would prevent 85 percent of the total number of injuries, or 1,300 total fatalities. The regulation therefore saves 130 fatalities per year over 10 years. The present value of 130 lives saved per year for 10 years is 1,167.8 lives saved. OSHA estimated that the capital costs were $214.30 million and the annual costs were $135.4 million. The present value of $135.4 million in annual costs for 10 years is $1216.30. The present value of the total costs is $214.30 million + $1216.30 million = $1430.60 million. The present value of the cost per life saved is $1430.60 / 1, 167.8 = $1.23 million. See 54 Fed. Reg. 36,644 (1989).

5. Benzene NESHAP (Revised: Transfer Operations) (EPA: 1990): EPA estimated that the regulation would reduce the residual incidence of cancer from 1.0 case/year to 0.02 case per year or that the regulation would prevent 0.98 case of cancer per year. The estimate equates cases of cancer with cancer deaths. EPA assumed that persons would be exposed for a seventy-year period. EPA estimated that the annual cost was $30 million and the capital cost was $167 million. See 55 Fed. Reg. 8292 (1990). The present value of 0.98 life saved per year over seventy years is 36.75 lives. The present value of an annual cost of $30 million over seventy years is $1,124.75 million. The present value of the costs is $1,124.75 million + 167 million (capital costs) = $1,291.75 million. The present value of the cost per life saved is $1,291.75 million/36.75 lives = $35.14 million per life saved.

6. Cover/Move Uranium Mill Tailings (Inactive Sites) (EPA: 1983): EPA estimated that the rule would prevent two hundred potential premature deaths over one hundred years or two lives per year. EPA estimated that the total cost of the rule was $314 million over seven years or $44.86 million per year. Heinzerling, "Regulatory Costs," 2031; see 48 Fed. Reg. 590, 596–97 (1983). The present value of two lives per year for one hundred years is 86.2 lives saved. The present value of $44.86 million over seven years is $290.32 million. The present value of the cost per life saved is $290.32 million/86.2 = $3.37 million.

7. Arsenic/Copper NESHAP (EPA: 1986): OSHA estimated that its regulation

would prevent 457–871 cancers over a fifty-year period. The estimate equates cancer cases with deaths avoided. A reduction of 457 premature deaths over fifty years is 9.14 deaths per year and a reduction of 871 deaths over fifty years is 17.42 deaths per year. OSHA estimated the total annualized cost to be $35.45 million. Heinzerling, "Regulatory Costs," 2036; see 49 Fed. Reg. 25,734, 25767–68 (1984). Assuming an annual cost per year for fifty years of $35.45 million and a reduction of 9.14 deaths per year, the present value of the cost of the lives saved is $3.88 million per life saved ($35.45 million/9.14). Assuming an annual cost for fifty years of $35.45 million and a reduction of 17.42 lives saved per year, the present value of the cost of the lives saved is $2.04 million per life saved ($35.45 million/17.42). Analysis does not account for reduction of "serious and significant" risks of health effects (including decreased risk of spontaneous abortion, neotoxicity, decreased fertility, decreased sperm count and motility, mutagenicity, and chromosomal aberrations). 49 Fed. Reg. at 27,768.

8. Ethylene Oxide Occupational Exposure Limit (OSHA: 1984): OSHA estimated that its regulation would prevent 457–871 cancers over a fifty-year period. The estimate equates cancer cases with deaths avoided. A reduction of 457 premature deaths over fifty years is 9.14 deaths per year, and a reduction of 871 deaths over fifty years is 17.42 deaths per year. OSHA estimated the total annualized cost to be $35.45 million. Heinzerling, "Regulatory Costs," 2036; see 49 Fed. Reg. 25,734, 25767–68 (1984). Assuming an annual cost per year for fifty years of $35.45 million and a reduction of 9.14 deaths per year, the present value of the cost of the lives saved is $3.88 million per life saved ($35.45 million/9.14). Assuming an annual cost for fifty years of $35.45 million and a reduction of 17.42 lives saved per year, the present value of the cost of the lives saved is $2.04 million per life saved ($35.45 million/17.42). Analysis does not account for reduction of "serious and significant" risks of health effects (including decreased risk of spontaneous abortion, neotoxicity, decreased fertility, decreased sperm count and motility, mutagenicity, and chromosomal aberrations). 49 Fed. Reg. at 27,768.

Notes

PREFACE

1. See, e.g., Symposium, "The Renaissance of Pragmatism in American Legal Thought," 63 *Southern California Law Review* 1569 (1992).

2. Daniel A. Farber, *Eco-Pragmatism: Making Sensible Environmental Decisions in an Uncertain World* (1999); see also *Environmental Pragmatism* (Andrew Light and Eric Katz, eds., 1996).

3. Charles W. Anderson, *Pragmatic Liberalism* ix (1990).

4. See, e.g., Louis Menand, *The Metaphysical Club: A Story of Ideas in America* (2001); Hillary Putnam, *Realism with a Human Face* (1990); Richard Rorty, *Consequences of Pragmatism* (1982).

CHAPTER 1

1. Marc Allen Eisner, *Regulatory Politics in Transition* 120 (1993); Michael Pertschuk, *Revolt against Regulation: The Rise and Fall of the Consumer Movement* 5 (1982); Murray Weidenbaum, *Business, Government, and the Public* 7–10 (2d ed., 1981).

2. See David M. Ricci, *The Transformation of American Politics: The New Washington and the Rise of the Think Tanks* (1993).

3. Milton Silverman and Phillip R. Lee, *Pills, Profits and Politics* 95–96 (1974).

4. Jerry L. Mashaw and David L. Harfst, *The Struggle for Auto Safety* 53–55 (1990).

5. Thomas O. McGarity and Sidney A. Shapiro, *Workers at Risk: The Failed Promise of the Occupational Safety and Health Administration* 34 (1993).

6. Samuel P. Huntington, "The United States," in *The Crisis of Democracy* 59–60 (Michael Crozer, Samuel P. Huntington, and Joji Watanuki, eds., 1975).

7. Michael W. McCann, *Taking Reform Seriously: Perspectives on Public Interest Liberalism* (1986).

8. Richard Andrews, "Cost-Benefit Analysis as Regulatory Reform," in *Cost-Benefit Analysis and Environmental Regulations, Politics, Ethics and Methods* 107, 112 (David Swartzman, Richard A. Liroff, and Kevin Croke, eds., 1982).

9. Talbot Page, "A Generic View of Toxic Chemicals and Similar Risks," 7 *Ecology Law Quarterly* 207, 208–9 (1978).

10. See Lisa Heinzerling, "Environmental Law and the Present Future," 87 *Georgetown Law Journal* 2025, 2049–50 (1999); Barton H. Thompson Jr. "People or Prairie Chickens: The Uncertain Search for Optimal Biodiversity," 51 *Stanford Law Review* 1127, 1157 (1999).

11. John S. Applegate, "The Perils of Unreasonable Risk: Information, Regulatory Policy, and Toxic Substances Control," 91 *Columbia Law Review* 261, 273 (1991).

12. *Ethyl Corp. v. EPA*, 541 F.2d 1 (D.C. Cir. 1976).

13. The statute has since been amended to afford EPA even broader authority to regulate risk. Under current law, EPA is authorized to regulate or prohibit the sale of fuel additives if, in the agency's judgment, "any emission product of such fuel or fuel additive causes, or contributes to, air pollution which *may reasonably be anticipated to endanger* the public health or welfare." 42 U.S.C. §7545(c)(1) (emphasis added).

14. McCann, *Taking Reform Seriously*, 44.

15. Sidney A. Shapiro, "A Delegation Theory of the APA," 10 *Administrative Law Journal* 89, 100 (1996).

16. Richard B. Stewart, "The Reformation of Administrative Law," 88 *Harvard Law Review* 1669 (1975).

17. See Frederick R. Anderson, Robert L. Glicksman, Daniel R. Mandelker, and A. Dan Tarlock, *Environmental Protection: Law and Policy* 372–73, 578–79, 886–87 (3d ed., 1999); Thomas O. McGarity and Sidney A. Shapiro, "OSHA's Critics and Regulatory Reform," 31 *Wake Forest Law Review* 587, 594–99 (1996); Robert Crandall, Howard K. Gruenspecht, Theodore E. Keeler, and Lester B. Lave, *Regulating the Automobile* 74–79 (1986).

18. Shapiro, "Delegation Theory," 703–6.

19. Paul H. Weaver, "Regulation, Social Policy, and Class Conflict," 50 *Public Interest* 45, 52 (1978).

20. Kristol is quoted in Barbara Ehrenreich, *Fear of Falling: The Inner Circle of the Middle Class* 159 (1989).

21. Edith Efron, *The Apocalyptics: How Environmental Politics Controls what We Know about Cancer* 9 (1984).

22. Mary Douglas and Aaron Wildavsky, *Risk and Culture* 7 (1982).

23. See, e.g., Bruce A. Ackerman and William T. Hassler, *Clean Coal, Dirty Air* (1981).

24. Cass R. Sunstein, *After the Rights Revolution: Reconceiving the Regulatory State* 86 (1990).

25. Stephen Breyer, *Breaking the Vicious Circle: Toward Effective Risk Regulation* (1993).

26. Cass R. Sunstein, "Cognition and Cost-Benefit Analysis," 29 *Journal of Legal Studies* 1059 (2000).

27. Deborah Stone, *Policy Paradox: The Art of Political Decision Making* 375 (1997).

28. Thomas O. McGarity, *Reinventing Rationality: The Role of Regulatory Analysis in the Federal Bureaucracy* 5 (1991).

29. Deborah A. Stone, "Clinical Authority in the Construction of Citizenship," in *Public Policy for Democracy* 45, 46 (Helen Ingram and Stephen Rathgeb Smith, eds., 1993).

30. 5 U.S.C.A. §601 et seq.

31. See 2 U.S.C.A. §1532 (a).

32. See Robert L. Glicksman and Stephen B. Chapman, "Regulatory Reform and (Breach) of the Contract with America," 5 *Kansas Journal of Law and Public Policy* 9, 17 (1996).

33. Thomas O. McGarity, "The Expanded Debate over the Future of the Regulatory State," 63 *University of Chicago Law Review* 1463 (1996); see also John S. Dryzek and James P. Lester, "Alternative Views of the Environmental Problematic," in *Environmental Politics and Policy* 329 (James P. Lester, ed., 2d ed., 1995).

CHAPTER 2

1. Morris Dickstein, "Introduction: Pragmatism Then and Now," in *The Revival of Pragmatism: New Essays on Thought, Law, and Culture* 1, 5 (Morris Dickstein, ed., 1998).

2. Richard Rorty, *Consequences of Pragmatism (Essays 1972–1980)* 162 (1982).

3. Daniel A. Farber, "Reinventing Brandeis: Legal Pragmatism for the Twentieth Century," 1995 *University of Illinois Law Review* 163, 168.

4. John Stick, "Can Nihilism Be Pragmatic?" 100 *Harvard Law Review* 332, 340 (1986).

5. Thomas C. Grey, *Holmes and Legal Pragmatism*, 41 *Stanford Law Review* 787, 796 (1989).

6. Ibid.

7. Ibid., 797.

8. James is quoted in Louis Menand, "An Introduction to Pragmatism," in *Pragmatism: A Reader* xiv (Louis Menand, ed., 1997).

9. Ibid.

10. Ibid.

11. Grey, *Holmes*, 798.

12. Ibid.

13. Dewey is quoted in Michael W. McCann, *Taking Reform Seriously: Perspectives on Public Interest Liberalism* 77 (1986).

14. Richard J. Bernstein, *The New Constellation: The Ethical-Political Horizons of Modernity/Postmodernity* 328 (1992).

15. See Lisa Heinzerling, "Book Review: Pragmatists and Environmentalists," 113 *Harvard Law Review* 1421, 1432 (2000).

16. Hilary Putnam, "A Reconsideration of Deweyan Democracy," 63 *Southern California Law Review* 1671, 1681 (1990).

17. James T. Kloppenberg, "Pragmatism: An Old Name for Some New Ways of Thinking," in *The Revival of Pragmatism*, 83, 101.

18. Charles W. Anderson, *Pragmatic Liberalism* 46 (1990).

19. Putnam, "Reconsideration," 1680.

20. Richard Bernstein, "Pragmatism, Pluralism, and the Healing of Wounds," in *Pragmatism: A Reader*, 382, 388.

21. Ibid., 389.

22. Gene Shreve, "Rhetoric, Pragmatism and the Interdisciplinary Turn in Legal Criticism—A Study of Altruistic Judicial Argument," 46 *American Journal of Comparative Law* 41, 58 (1998).

23. Peirce is quoted in Bernstein, "Pragmatism, Pluralism," 387.

24. Daniel Farber and Suzanna Sherry, "Telling Stories Out of School: An Essay on Legal Narratives," 45 *Stanford Law Review* 807, 820 (1993).

25. Hilary Putnam, "Are Moral and Legal Values Made or Discovered?" 1 *Legal Theory* 5, 8 (1995).

26. Ibid.

27. Ibid.

28. Frank Michelman, "Bringing Life to the Law: A Plea for Disenchantment," 74 *Cornell Law Review* 256, 258 (1989).

29. Anderson, *Pragmatic Liberalism*, 8–9.

30. Ibid., 12.

31. Menand, "Introduction to Pragmatism," xiv.

32. James March and Herbert Simon, *Organizations* (1958); Herbert Simon, *Models of Man* (1957); Herbert Simon, *Administrative Behavior: A Study of Decisionmaking Processes in Administrative Organizations* (3d ed., 1976); see also Richard Cyert and James March, *A Behavior Theory of the Firm* (1963).

33. Charles E. Lindblom, "The Science of 'Muddling' Through," 19 *Public Administrative Review* 79, 80 (1959).

34. Simon, *Administrative Behavior*, xxix–xxx.

35. Ibid., xxviii (emphasis in original).

36. Charles W. Anderson, "Political Philosophy, Practical Reason, and Policy

Analysis," in *Confronting Values in Policy Analysis: The Politics of Criteria* 26 (Frank Fischer and John Forester, eds., 1987).

37. Charles Lindblom, *The Policy Making Process* 24–27 (1968); Lindblom, "'Muddling' Through."

38. Anderson, "Political Philosophy," 26.

39. See Howard Latin, "Ideal Versus Real Regulatory Efficiency: Implementation of Uniform Standards and 'Fine-Tuning' Regulatory Reforms," 37 *Stanford Law Review* 1267, 1270 (1985).

40. See Jerry Mashaw, "Prodelegation: Why Administrators Should Make Political Decisions," 1 *Journal of Law, Economics, and Organization* 1 (1985).

41. Anderson, *Pragmatic Liberalism*, 46.

42. Dewey is quoted in Kloppenberg, "Pragmatism," 101.

43. Daniel A. Farber, *Eco-Pragmatism: Making Sensible Environmental Decisions in an Uncertain World* (1999).

44. E.g., David Roe, "Review: Green Scholarship," 3 *Green Bag* 97 (1999).

45. E.g., Richard A. Epstein, "Too Pragmatic by Half," 109 *Yale Law Journal* 1639 (2000).

46. J. B. Ruhl, "Working Both (Positivist) Ends toward a New (Pragmatist) Middle in Environmental Law," 68 *George Washington Law Review* 522, 546 (2000).

47. Heinzerling, "Pragmatists and Environmentalists," 1446–47.

CHAPTER 3

1. If the meaning of a statutory standard is not clear, administrative or judicial interpretation of the standard may assist in identifying its content. For that reason, it may not be clear that Congress has rejected a cost-benefit test until an agency or a court issues an interpretation of the statutory provision in question.

2. Professor Applegate labeled what we are calling the statutory trigger the "predicate," which he defined as "the set of circumstances that must exist before the agency takes action." John S. Applegate, "Worst Things First: Risk, Information, and Regulatory Structure in Toxic Substances Control," 9 *Yale Journal on Regulation* 277, 305 (1992).

3. 21 U.S.C. §§348(c)(3), 379e(b)(5)(B).

4. 42 U.S.C. §7411(b)(1)(A).

5. 29 U.S.C. §652(8).

6. *Industrial Union Dep't v. American Petroleum Inst.*, 448 U.S. 607, 642 (1980).

7. 7 U.S.C. §136a(c)(5)(C)–(D).

8. Ibid., §136d(b).

9. Professor Applegate has called this component of regulation the "target," which

he said "defines the extent to which a particular risk is to be reduced." Applegate, "Worst Things First," 306.

10. 21 U.S.C. §348(c)(3).

11. 21 U.S.C. §346a(b)(2)(A), (c)(2)(A).

12. See, e.g., *Lead Indus. Ass'n, Inc. v. EPA,* 647 F.2d 1130 (D.C. Cir. 1980). In that case, the court held that cost is irrelevant to the establishment of an ambient quality-based standard.

13. 42 U.S.C. §§7671c–e.

14. Ibid., §7671a(a)–(b).

15. Ibid., §7671(a), (c). For class II substances, a substance may be added if EPA finds that it is known or may reasonably be anticipated to cause or contribute to harmful effects on the ozone layer. Ibid., §7671(b), (c). EPA may extend the deadline for compliance with an applicable prohibition on production or use for a newly designated substance if compliance with the deadline is otherwise unattainable. Ibid., §7671(d).

16. 42 U.S.C. §7502(c)(1). Sources subject to this requirement may actually become subject to even more stringent controls under other provisions of the statute if controls on other kinds of sources do not bring an area into compliance with the CAA's national ambient air quality standards.

17. Safe Drinking Water Amendments of 1996, Pub. L. No. 104–182, 110 Stat. 1613.

18. 42 U.S.C. §300g-1(b)(4)(A)–(B). Feasible means "feasible with the use of the best technology, treatment techniques, and other means" that EPA finds are available. Ibid., §300g-1(b)(4)(D).

19. EPA can choose an alternative level if such a level minimizes the overall risk of adverse health effects by balancing the risk from the contaminant and from other contaminants whose concentrations would be affected by efforts to comply with the MCL. EPA can also choose an alternative level if cost-benefit analysis demonstrates that a feasibility-based MCL would not justify the costs of compliance. In the latter situation, EPA may issue a MCL that maximizes risk reduction benefits at a cost that is justified by the resulting benefits. Ibid., §300g-1(b)(5), (6)(A).

20. 29 U.S.C. §655(b)(5) (emphasis added).

21. *American Textile Mfrs. Inst. v. Donovan,* 452 U.S. 490, 509 (1981).

22. *Texas Oil and Gas Ass'n v. United States Environmental Protection Agency,* 161 F.3d 923, 936 (5th Cir. 1998).

23. 7 U.S.C. §136a(d)(1)(C).

24. Ibid., §136(bb).

25. 15 U.S.C. §§2051–84.

26. Ibid., §2058(f)(3)(E).

27. Ibid., §2058(f)(3)(F).

28. 49 U.S.C. §60102(b)(5).

29. 21 U.S.C. §348(c)(3).

30. See, e.g., Stephen Breyer, *Breaking the Vicious Circle: Toward Effective Risk Regulation* 41 (1993).

31. 21 U.S.C. §346a(b)(2)(A), (c)(2)(A). EPA may also permit pesticide residues in food if the elimination (or reduction) of such residues would create a greater risk to consumers than the risks caused by allowing continued dietary exposures. Ibid., §346a(b)(2)(B)(iii). Thus, the general statutory risk-based management standard is itself subject to exceptions based on comparative risk assessment. For threshold effects, the statute requires an additional tenfold margin of safety to protect infants and children, unless EPA determines, on the basis of reliable data, that a different margin will be safe for those particularly susceptible components of the population. Ibid., §346a(b)(2)(C).

32. We have denominated the CWA's water quality standards as open-ended balancing standards for the same reason.

33. 42 U.S.C. §7412(a)(1), (b)(1)(B) (1988).

34. Ibid., §7412(b)(1)(B) (1988).

35. 42 U.S.C. §7412(d)(2).

36. See U.S. Congress, Senate Committee on Environment and Public Works, *Clean Air Act Amendments of 1989*, 101st Cong., 1st Sess., 1989, S. Rpt. 101–228, 131.

37. 42 U.S.C. §§7671c(a)–(b), 7671d(b) phase out the production of chemicals harmful to the stratospheric ozone layer. 15 U.S.C. §2605(e)(2)(B) bans all PCB uses except those that do not present an unreasonable risk to the environment.

38. 42 U.S.C. §§7671c–7671e.

39. 15 U.S.C. §2605(e).

40. See, e.g., U.S. Congress, Senate Committee on Commerce, *Toxic Substances Control Act*, 94th Cong., 2d Sess., 1976, S. Rpt. 94–698, 4, reprinted in 1976 U.S. C.C.A.N. 4491, 4494, which determined that PCBs "have been found to cause liver cancer in rats and to have contaminated fish stocks throughout the United States."

41. 33 U.S.C. §§1311(b), 1316, 1317(b), 1342(a)–(b).

42. 42 U.S.C. §§7475(a)(1), (4), 7479(3). These provisions require permits for major emitting facilities to be constructed in areas that have air quality better than what is required by the NAAQS (so-called prevention of significant deterioration, or PSD, areas).

43. 42 U.S.C. §7502(c)(1) deals with existing stationary sources, while ibid., §§7503(a)(2), 7501(3), deal with new or modified stationary sources.

44. Ibid., §§7411(a)(1), (b)(1)(A), authorize the regulation of new stationary sources which, in the Administrator's judgment, may cause or contribute to "air pollution which may reasonably be anticipated to endanger public health or welfare."

45. E.g., ibid. §7521(a)(3)(A), which authorizes issuance of standards for heavy-duty vehicles or engines reflecting the greatest degree of emission reduction achievable through the application of available technology.

46. 42 U.S.C. §7412(d)(2).

47. 42 U.S.C. §§300g–1(b)(1)(A), (b)(4)(A)–(B).

48. 42 U.S.C. §§6924(m)(1)–(2).

49. 15 U.S.C. §§2605(a), 2605(c)(1).

50. 29 U.S.C. §§651–67.

51. 49 U.S.C. §§30101–169.

52. Ibid., §30102(a)(8), which authorizes regulation if it will prevent an "unreasonable risk" of an accident.

53. 15 U.S.C. §2605(c)(1) lists factors that EPA must consider to determine if an "unreasonable risk" exists. See *Corrosion Proof Fittings v. EPA,* 947 F.2d 1201 (5th Cir. 1991), in which the court interpreted the trigger for that provision as a "cost-benefit" test.

54. 42 U.S.C. §7412(b)(3)(B) lists pollutants that EPA must regulate as hazardous and delegates to EPA the authority to add a substance upon a showing that its emissions, ambient concentrations, or bioaccumulation are known to cause or may reasonably be anticipated to cause adverse health or environmental effects. Ibid., §7412(b)(3)(C) delegates to EPA the power to delete a substance from the initial congressional list upon a showing that the substance may not reasonably be anticipated to cause such effects.

55. See the discussion in the "Statutory Triggers" section, above, to the effect that OSHA must prove that a risk is "significant."

56. 42 U.S.C.A. §300g-1(b)(1)(A). That provision requires EPA to prove that a contaminant may have an adverse effect on health and that it is likely to occur in drinking water systems "with a frequency and at levels of public health concern."

57. 42 U.S.C. §6903(5) defines hazardous wastes as those that may cause or significantly contribute to increases in mortality or serious illness or pose a substantial hazard to health or the environment when improperly managed.

58. Although the statute on its face thus bars the unpermitted discharge of any pollutant, EPA policies have required permits for pollutant discharges only at levels reasonably anticipated to cause or contribute to pollutant concentrations in excess of those set by state water quality standards, described below. See, e.g., Memorandum from Director, Office of Wastewater Enforcement and Compliance to Water Management Division Directors, Regions I–X, at 2–3 (Aug. 14, 1992) (quoted in *Atlantic States Legal Found. v. Eastman Kodak Co.,* 12 F.3d 353, 358 [2d Cir. 1993]). This means that the permit-issuing agency (either EPA or a state with delegated authority to issue

permits) may apply a risk-based threshold in determining whether a permit is required for discharge of a particular pollutant.

59. 33 U.S.C. §1313(c)(2)(A).

60. 42 U.S.C. §7410(a).

61. See *Union Elec. Co. v. EPA,* 427 U.S. 246 (1976). For a description of why we placed both the CAA's NAAQS and the CWA's water quality standards programs under the rubric of open-ended balancing standards, see the discussion that appears under the heading of "Risk- or Ambient Quality–Based Standards" in the section entitled "Triggers and Standards."

62. Cleanups conducted under CERCLA must proceed in accordance with the National Contingency Plan (NCP), 42 U.S.C. §9604(a)(1), which must include standards that ensure cost-effective remedial measures. Ibid., §§9605(a)(7), 9621(a). Statutory guidance on cleanup standards added in 1986 requires that EPA select remedial alternatives that are protective of health and the environment, that are cost-effective, and that employ permanent solutions and alternative treatment technologies or resource recovery technologies to the maximum extent practicable. Ibid., §9621(b)(1). Alternative remedial actions may be selected even if they have not been achieved in practice at other facilities, although the agency may take into account the degree of support for such an action by interested parties. Ibid., §9621(b)(2). In evaluating the cost-effectiveness of remediation, EPA must evaluate the costs of operation and maintenance. Ibid., §9621(a).

63. See 7 U.S.C. §136a(d)(1)(C), which gives no indication of the weight EPA is to assign the various factors listed in the definition of unreasonable adverse effects.

64. See the discussion at the end of the material in this chapter on "Constrained Balancing" under the Heading "Triggers and Standards."

65. 7 U.S.C. §136a(c)(5)(C)–(D) mandates that EPA register a pesticide if it will perform its intended function without unreasonable adverse effects on the environment. Ibid., §136(bb) defines unreasonable adverse effects as unreasonable risks to man or the environment, "taking into account the economic, social, and environmental costs and benefits of the use of any pesticide." Ibid., §136d(b) authorizes EPA to cancel an existing registration if the pesticide generally causes such effects.

66. 42 U.S.C. §7408(a)(1)(A) authorizes EPA to issue NAAQS for pollutants whose emissions "may reasonably be anticipated to endanger public health or welfare."

67. EPA's statutory cleanup authority is invoked when there is a release or substantial threat of a release into the environment of hazardous substances or of pollutants or contaminants which may present an imminent and substantial danger to the public health or welfare. 42 U.S.C. §9604(a)(1). The act defines a hazardous substance through incorporation by reference of a series of other statutory definitions of haz-

ardous wastes and toxic pollutants; ibid., §9601(14), which are risk-based, such as the definition of a hazardous waste under RCRA, 42 U.S.C. §6903(5), or the delineation of hazardous air pollutants under the CAA. The other half of the statutory trigger is explicitly significant risk-based. EPA may exercise its response authority if the release of a pollutant or contaminant "may present an imminent and substantial danger" to health or welfare. 42 U.S.C. §9604(a)(1)(B).

68. 15 U.S.C. §§2056(a), 2058(f)(3)(A) requires that any standard be reasonably necessary to eliminate an unreasonable risk of injury associated with the targeted product. Under ibid., §2058(f)(3)(E), the CPSC must establish that the benefits expected from a standard bear a reasonable relationship to its costs. The CPSC must choose the standard that imposes the least burdensome requirement that prevents or adequately reduces the risk of injury for which the rule is being promulgated. Ibid., §2058(f)(3)(F). The statute also mandates that the CPSC rely on voluntary "standards" whenever compliance would eliminate or adequately reduce the risk of injury being addressed and it is likely that there will be substantial compliance with the voluntary standards. Ibid., §2056(b)(1).

69. 49 U.S.C. §60102(b)(2)(C)–(E) requires that the Secretary consider a series of factors, including the reasonableness of the standard, and, based on a risk assessment, the reasonably identifiable costs and benefits expected to result from implementation or compliance. Another provision, ibid., §60102(b)(5), bars the Secretary from proposing or issuing any standard except upon a "reasoned determination" that its benefits justify its costs.

70. The statute requires only that the Secretary of Transportation consider a standard's reasonableness and the extent to which it would contribute to public safety and environmental protection. 49 U.S.C. §60102(b)(3)–(4) (Supp. III 1997).

71. Pub. L. No. 104–304, 110 Stat. 3800 (1996) (codified at 49 U.S.C. §60102[b][5]).

CHAPTER 4

1. Ronald Coase, "The Problem of Social Cost," 3 *Journal Law and Economics* 1 (1960).

2. Ibid., 13, 27–28.

3. See Christopher H. Schroeder, "Rights against Risk," 86 *Columbia Law Review* 495, 508 (1986).

4. Ibid.

5. Aldo Leopold, *A Sand County Almanac and Sketches Here and There* 228 (1968).

6. We have borrowed this phrase from Professor Tom McGarity, who uses it to describe what we have called "constrained balancing." See Thomas O. McGarity, "Media Quality, Technology, and Cost-Benefit Balancing Strategies for Health and

Environmental Regulation," 46 *Law and Contemporary Problems* 159, 199 (summer 1983). As the text explains, we believe that it generally describes the commitment of risk regulation.

7. Ibid.

8. For a case describing the Clean Air Act as a technology-forcing statute, see *Union Elec. Co. v. EPA,* 427 U.S. 246, 257 (1976).

9. 29 U.S.C. §655(b)(5).

10. Margaret Jane Radin, *Contested Commodities: The Trouble with Trade in Sex, Children, Body Parts and Other Things* 2 (1996).

11. Ibid., 2, 13.

12. Ibid., 5.

13. Ibid., 87–88.

14. Ibid., 93.

15. Thomas C. Grey, "Holmes and Legal Pragmatism," 41 *Stanford Law Review* 787, 861 (1989).

16. Ibid.

17. Alan Marin and George Psacharopoulos, "The Reward for Risk in the Labor Market: Evidence from the United Kingdom and a Reconciliation with Other Studies," 90 *Journal of Political Economy* 827, 838 (1982).

18. Summers is quoted in "Let Them Eat Pollution," *Economist*, 8 Feb. 1992, at 66.

19. W. Kip Viscusi, "The Dangers of Unbounded Commitments to Regulate Risk," in *Risks, Costs and Lives Saved: Getting Better Results from Regulation* 148 (Robert W. Hahn, ed., 1996).

20. 21 U.S.C. §346a(b)(2)(C). EPA may set a different margin of safety if it determines that such a margin will be safe for these particularly susceptible components of the population. Ibid.

21. *American Lung Ass'n v. EPA,* 134 F.3d 388, 389 (D.C. Cir. 1998). See also *Lead Indus. Ass'n Inc. v. EPA,* 647 F.2d 1130, 1152 (D.C. Cir. 1980); *American Petroleum Inst. v. Costle,* 665 F.2d 1176, 1183 (D.C. Cir. 1980).

22. E.g., *Hazardous Waste Treatment Council v. EPA,* 886 F.2d 355, 362 (D.C. Cir. 1989) (RCRA); *NRDC, Inc. v. EPA,* 812 F.2d 721, 723 (D.C. Cir. 1987) (SDWA); *United States v. Vertac Chem. Corp.,* 33 F. Supp. 2d 769, 778 (1998) (CERCLA).

23. Steven Kelman, "Cost-Benefit Analysis—An Ethical Critique," 5 *Regulation* 38 (Jan./Feb. 1981).

24. Mark Sagoff, "At the Shrine of Our Lady of Fatima, or Why Political Questions Are Not All Economic," 23 *Arizona Law Review* 1283, 1286 (1981).

25. For a list of articles in the economic literature, see Karine Nyborg, "Homo Economicus and Homo Politicus: Interpretation and Aggregation of Environmental Values," 42 *Journal of Economics, Behavior and Organization* 305, 306 (2000).

26. Mark Seidenfeld, "A Civic Republican Justification for the Bureaucratic State," 105 *Harvard Law Review* 1512, 1514 (1992).

27. Mark Sagoff, "Economic Theory and Environmental Law," 79 *Michigan Law Review* 1393, 1411 (1981).

28. See, e.g., Bruce A. Ackerman and William T. Hassler, *Clean Coal/Dirty Air* 124–25 (1981).

29. Viscusi's comment is reported in Marin and Psacharopoulos, "Reward for Risk," 841.

30. Frank H. Knight, *Risk, Uncertainty and Profit* 301 (1921).

31. W. Kip Viscusi, *Risk by Choice: Regulating Health and Safety in the Workplace* 103 (1983).

32. James R. Robinson, *Toil and Toxics: Workplace Struggles and Political Strategies for Occupational Health* 94 (1991).

33. E.g., John Mendeloff, *The Dilemma of Toxic Substances Regulation: How Over-regulation Causes Underregulation* 42–43 (1988).

34. Arthur Oken, *Equality and Efficiency: The Big Trade-Off* (1975).

35. Peter Asch, *Consumer Safety Regulation: Putting a Price on Life and Limb* 59 (1988).

36. Mendeloff, *Dilemma of Toxic Substances*, 33.

37. E.g., Asch, *Consumer Safety Regulation*, 59.

38. Viscusi, *Risk by Choice*, 20.

39. Lisa Heinzerling, "The Rights of Statistical People," 28 *Harvard Environmental Law Review* 189, 206 (2000).

40. Ibid., 189.

41. Ibid.

42. Oliver E. Williamson, *The Economic Institutions of Capitalism* (1985).

43. Ibid., 46.

44. Ibid., 47.

45. Ibid., 18.

46. Douglas C. North, "Institutions and a Transaction-Cost Theory of Exchange," in *Perspectives on Positive Political Economy* 182, 191 (James E. Alt and Kenneth A. Shepsle, eds., 1990).

47. For an argument against per se rules, see Robert Bork, *The Antitrust Paradox* (1978).

48. For a discussion of the impact of decision rules on optimal level of deterrence, see C. Frederick Beckner III and Steven C. Salop, "Decision Theory and Antitrust Rules," 67 *Antitrust Law Journal* 41 (1999).

49. In light of *Corrosion Proof Fittings v. EPA*, 947 F.2d 1201 (5th Cir. 1991), EPA officials indicated that they would not seek to impose comprehensive chemical bans or

restrictions under TSCA. U.S. General Accounting Office, *Toxic Substances Control Act—Legislative Changes Could Make the Act More Effective*, GAO/RCED 94–103, 1994 WL 840961 (1994). The *Corrosion Proof Fittings* case is the focus of further discussion in Chapters 7 and 9.

50. See, e.g., Richard A. Merrill, "CPSC Regulation of Cancer Risks in Consumer Products: 1972–1981," 67 *Virginia Law Review* 1261 (1981).

CHAPTER 5

1. See Murray L. Weidenbaum, "On Estimating Regulatory Costs," 2 *Regulation* 17 (May/June 1978). Litan and Nordhaus describe the estimate as the "oft-heard" claim of the Reagan Administration. Robert E. Litan and William D. Nordhaus, *Reforming Federal Regulation* 20 (1983).

2. The Cato Institute, for example, cites Professor Hopkins's cost estimates in Yesim Yilmax, "Private Regulation: A Real Alternative for Regulatory Reform," 303 *Policy Analysis* 7–8 (Apr. 20, 1998). The Heritage Foundation cites the cost estimates in Angela Antonelli, "Regulation: Demanding Accountability and Common Sense," in *Issues '98: The Candidate's Briefing Book* (Stuart M. Butler and Kim R. Holmes, eds., 1998).

3. Thomas Hopkins, "Regulatory Costs in Profile," *Center for the Study of American Business Policy Study* 132 (Aug. 1996).

4. Murray L. Weidenbaum and Robert De Fina, "The Cost of Federal Regulation of Economic Activity," American Enterprise Institute Reprint No. 88, 1978.

5. For a description of Weidenbaum's methodology, see Litan and Nordhaus, *Reforming Federal Regulation*, 20. For an explanation of the methodology, see Weidenbaum, "On Estimating Regulatory Costs," 20.

6. Litan and Nordhaus, *Reforming Federal Regulation*, 20; George C. Eads and Michael Fix, *Relief or Reform: Reagan's Regulatory Dilemma* 30 (1984); see also U.S. Congress, House Subcomm. on Oversight and Investigations of the Comm. on Interstate and Foreign Commerce, *Cost-Benefit Analysis: Wonder Tool or Mirage?*, 96th Cong., 2d Sess. (1980).

7. Weidenbaum, "On Estimating Regulatory Costs," 17; see also Eads and Fix, *Relief or Reform*, 31.

8. Office of Management and Budget, *Draft Report to Congress on the Costs and Benefits of Federal Regulations*, 62 Fed. Reg. 39,352, 39,361 (1997).

9. Robert W. Hahn and John A. Hird, "The Costs and Benefits of Regulation: Review and Synthesis," 8 *Yale Journal on Regulation* 233, 253 (1991). An earlier, nonquantified estimate by Robert Litan and William Nordhaus concluded in 1984 that risk regulation had produced "significant" benefits for the country. Litan and Nordhaus, *Reforming Federal Regulation*, 18.

10. Office of Management and Budget, *Draft Report to Congress on the Costs and Benefits of Federal Regulations*, 63 Fed. Reg. 44,034, 44,039 (1998).

11. Robert W. Hahn, "Regulatory Reform: Assessing the Government's Numbers," AEI-Brookings Joint Center for Regulatory Studies Working Paper 99–96, July 1999. For an earlier version of Hahn's estimates, see Robert W. Hahn, "Regulatory Reform: What Do the Government's Numbers Tell Us?," in *Risks, Costs, and Lives Saved: Getting Better Results from Regulation* 208 (Robert W. Hahn, ed., 1996).

12. Hahn, " Regulatory Reform," 14 n. 34.

13. Hahn, "The Government's Numbers," 246 n. 27.

14. Communication with Jeneva A. Craig, program analyst, Office of Air and Radiation, Office of Policy Analysis and Review, EPA, Apr. 15, 1999.

15. U.S. Environmental Protection Agency, *The Benefits and Costs of the Clean Air Act (1970 to 1990)* ES-8 (1997).

16. For a criticism of EPA's upper bound estimate, see General Accounting Office, *Regulatory Accounting: Analysis of OMB's Reports on the Costs and Benefits of Regulation* 35 (1999).

17. Based on published studies and a few original calculations, one source estimates the current economic value of seventeen ecosystem services for sixteen biomes is in the range of $16–54 trillion per year, with an average of $33 trillion per year. Robert Costanza et al., "The Value of the World's Ecosystem Services and Natural Capital," 387 *Nature* 253 (1987).

18. SAB Council, Letter to EPA Administrator Carol Browner, July 8, 1997, at 1, quoted at 63 Fed. Reg. 44,042 (1998).

19. Office of Management and Budget, *Draft Report to Congress on the Costs and Benefits of Regulation* (2000). In 1998, OMB estimated that safety and environmental regulation produced net benefits between $34 billion and $3.38 trillion per year (in 1996 dollars), based on benefits of $258 billion to $3.551 trillion and costs of $170–224 billion. OMB, *1998 Draft Study*, 44,060. A less extensive 1997 OMB study estimated that risk regulation produced net benefits of approximately $100 billion, based on benefits of $298 billion and costs of $198 million. OMB, *1997 Draft Study*, 39,361.

20. OMB, *1998 Draft Report*, 44,059. The estimates of costs and benefits that OMB attributes to the EPA's CAA study do not correspond to the estimates cited earlier in this chapter. OMB does not explain how it derived this figure, although it appears that EPA's estimate was adjusted slightly to reflect 1988 benefits and then converted to 1996 dollars. See Randall W. Lutter, "An Analysis of the Use of EPA's Benefit Estimates," in AEI-Brookings Joint Center for Regulatory Studies Comment 98–92, *OMB's Draft Report on the Costs and Benefits of Regulation*, Oct. 1998, 3 n. 9.

21. EPA, *Benefits and Costs*, ES-8.

22. John F. Morrall III, "A Review of the Record," *Regulation* 25 (Nov./Dec. 1986).

23. Office of Management and Budget, *Regulatory Program of the United States (April 1, 1991–March 31, 1992)* xx (1991); Office of Management and Budget, *Regulatory Program of the United States (April 1, 1987–March 31, 1988)* xx (1987).

24. Lisa Heinzerling, "Regulatory Costs of Mythic Proportions," 107 *Yale Law Journal* 1981, 1994 (1998). For a listing of books, articles, and studies that have reprinted Morrall's table or the OMB revisions of it, see ibid., 1983 n. 2, 1995–96.

25. See, e.g., Richard L. Revesz, "Environmental Regulation, Cost-Benefit Analysis, and the Discounting of Human Lives," 99 *Columbia Law Review* 941, 972 (1999); Cass R. Sunstein, Daniel Kahneman, and David Schkade, "Assessing Punitive Damages (With Notes on Cognition and Valuation in Law)," 107 *Yale Law Journal* 1071, 2138 (1998); James K. Hammitt, "Improving Comparative Risk Analysis," 8 *Duke Environmental Law and Policy Forum* 81, 87 (1997); C. Boyden Gray, "Obstacles to Regulatory Reform," 1997 *University of Chicago Legal Forum* 1, 1 (1997).

26. Professor Viscusi, for example, identifies any regulation in Morrall's table that cost more than $2.8 million per life saved as failing a cost-benefit test. W. Kip Viscusi, *Fatal Tradeoffs: Public & Private Responsibilities for Risk* 264–65 (1992).

27. Stephen Breyer, *Breaking the Vicious Circle: Toward Effective Risk Regulation* 22 (1993).

28. Identification and Listing of Hazardous Waste: Wood Preserving, 55 Fed. Reg. 50,450, 50,453 (1990).

29. Ibid., 50,473, 50,476–77.

30. Heinzerling, "Regulatory Costs," 1984.

31. Ibid., 2000, 2017.

32. Ibid., 2017.

33. Ibid., 1985.

34. John J. Donohue III, "Why We Should Discount the Views of Those Who Discount Discounting," 108 *Yale Law Journal* 1901, 1902–3 (1999).

35. EPA concluded that there was a "high probability" that current practice concerning the disposal of sludge "degrades the environment." 55 Fed. Reg. at 46,387–88. The regulation would reduce "pollutant loadings to fresh and saline surfaces or other wetlands near refineries or near off-site sludge disposal areas." Ibid., 46,392. EPA did not quantify potential neurotoxicological risks or potential kidney or liver damage. Ibid., 46,391.

36. See Heinzerling, "Regulatory Costs," 2025–38.

37. A retrospective study has found that OSHA significantly overestimated the costs of the regulation. The actual cost appears to be one-half of OSHA's original estimate. Office of Technology Assessment, *Gauging Control Technology and Regulatory Impacts in Occupational Safety and Health: An Appraisal of OSHA's Analytical Approach* 60 (1995). Our estimate is based on the higher, erroneous estimate that OSHA

employed at the time the regulation was promulgated. In addition, our cost estimate for formaldehyde does not reflect additional health benefits that were not quantified by OSHA. In *International Union, UAW v. Pendergrass*, 878 F.2d 389, 393 (D.C. Cir. 1989), the court remanded the formaldehyde rule because OSHA underestimated the number of lives it would save.

38. Tammy O. Tengs et al., "Five-Hundred Life-Saving Interventions and Their Cost-Effectiveness," 15 *Risk Analysis* 369 (1995).

39. Tammy O. Tengs and John D. Graham, "The Opportunity Costs of Haphazard Social Investments in Life-Saving," in *Risks, Costs and Lives Saved*, 167.

40. See the written testimony of John Graham in U.S. House of Representatives, Committee On Science, *Risk Assessment and Cost Benefit Analysis*, 104th Cong., 1st Sess., 1995, 1124.

41. See Testimony of Professor Lisa Heinzerling Concerning the Nomination of John D. Graham to be Administrator of the Office of Information and Regulatory Affairs, Office of Management and Budget (Undated).

42. Ibid., 4.

43. Tengs et al., "Five Hundred Life-Saving Interventions," 377.

44. Ibid., 375–76.

45. See Hahn, "Assessing the Government's Numbers," 12, 17, 42.

46. Robert W. Crandall, Christopher Demuth, Robert W. Hahn, Robert E. Litan, Pietro S. Nivola, and Paul R. Portney, *An Agenda for Federal Regulatory Reform* (1997).

47. OMB, *2000 Draft Report*, 31.

48. We calculated the range of benefits in the following manner. For the lower bound estimate, we subtracted the highest bound estimate of costs from the lowest bound estimate of benefits. For the upper bound estimate, we subtracted the lowest bound estimate of costs from the highest bound estimate of benefits.

CHAPTER 6

1. National Research Council, *Risk Assessment in the Federal Government: Managing the Process* 3 (1983).

2. Thomas O. McGarity and Sidney A. Shapiro, *Workers at Risk: The Failed Promise of the Occupational Safety and Health Administration* 6, 269 (1993); Thomas O. McGarity, "A Cost-Benefit State," 50 *Administrative Law Review* 7, 24 (1998); Elinor P. Schroeder and Sidney A. Shapiro, "Responses to Occupational Disease: The Role of Markets, Regulation, and Information," 72 *Georgetown Law Review* 1231, 1232–36 (1984).

3. See Wendy E. Wagner, "The Science Charade in Toxic Risk Regulation," 95 *Columbia Law Review* 1613, 1685–86 (1995); David E. Burmaster and Jeanne W. Ap-

pling, "Introduction to Human Risk Assessment, with an Emphasis on Contaminated Properties," 25 *Environment Reporter (BNA)* 2431, 2437 (1995); Donald T. Hornstein, "Reclaiming Environmental Law: A Normative Critique of Comparative Risk Analysis," 92 *Columbia Law Review* 562, 592–94 (1992); John S. Applegate, "The Perils of Unreasonable Risk: Information, Regulatory Policy and Toxic Substances Control," 91 *Columbia Law Review* 261, 278 (1991); Mary L. Lyndon, "Information Economics and Chemical Toxicity: Designing Laws to Produce and Use Data," 87 *Michigan Law Review* 1795, 1797 (1989); Thomas O. McGarity, "Substantive and Procedural Discretion in Administrative Resolution of Science Policy Questions: Regulating Carcinogens at EPA and OSHA," 67 *Georgetown Law Review* 729 (1979).

4. McGarity, "Cost-Benefit State," 53; Carl F. Cranor, *Regulating Toxic Substances: A Philosophy of Science and the Law* 21 (1993).

5. C. Richard Cothern, William A. Coniglio, and William L. Marcus, "Estimating Risk to Human Health," 20 *Environment, Science and Technology* 111, 115 (1986).

6. McGarity, "Cost-Benefit State," 13.

7. Celia Cambell-Mohn and John S. Applegate, "Learning from NEPA: Guidelines for Responsible Risk Regulation," 23 *Harvard Environmental Law Review* 93, 102 (1999).

8. Environmental Protection Agency, Proposed Guidelines for Carcinogen Risk Assessment, 61 Fed. Reg. 17,960, 17,964 (1996).

9. John S. Applegate, "A Beginning and Not an End in Itself: The Role of Risk Assessment in Environmental Decision-Making," 63 *University of Cincinnati Law Review* 1643, 1656 (1995); see also Lisa Heinzerling, "Regulatory Costs of Mythic Proportions," 107 *Yale Law Journal* 1981, 2057 (1998).

10. Adam Finkel, "A Second Opinion on an Environmental Misdiagnosis: The Risky Prescriptions of *Breaking the Vicious Circle*," 3 *New York University Environmental Law Journal* 295, 348–52 (1995).

11. John Mendeloff, *The Dilemma of Toxic Substances Regulation: How Overregulation Causes Underregulation at OSHA* 248 (1988). For a discussion of Mendeloff's adjustments, see Sidney A. Shapiro and Thomas O. McGarity, "Not So Paradoxical: The Rationale for Technology-Based Regulation," 1991 *Duke Law Journal* 729, 732.

12. John F. Morall III, "A Review of the Record," *Regulation* 29 (Nov./Dec. 1986).

13. OMB's adjustments are discussed in Heinzerling, "Regulatory Costs," 2025–38.

14. See Chapter 5.

15. John D. Graham et al., *In Search of Safety: Chemicals and Cancer Risk* 177 (1988); see also Alan Rosenthal et al., "Legislating Acceptance of Cancer Risk from Exposure to Toxic Chemicals," 19 *Ecology Law Quarterly* 269, 360 (1992).

16. McGarity, "Cost-Benefit State," 28; Applegate, "Beginning and Not an End," 1655.

17. Silbergeld is quoted in McGarity, "Cost-Benefit State," 28.

18. Thomas O. McGarity and Sidney A. Shapiro, "OSHA's Critics and Regulatory Reform," 31 *Wake Forest Law Review* 587, 613 (1996).

19. See, e.g., W. Kip Viscusi, *Fatal Tradeoffs: Public and Private Responsibilities for Risk* 34–74 (1992).

20. Peter Asch, *Consumer Safety Regulation: Putting a Price on Life and Limb* (1988).

21. See, e.g., Douglas R. Williams, "Valuing Natural Environments: Compensation, Market Norms, and the Idea of Public Goods," 27 *Connecticut Law Review* 365, 402 (1995); Frank B. Cross, "National Resource Damage Valuation," 42 *Vanderbilt Law Review* 269, 310 (1989).

22. See Sidney A. Shapiro and Joseph P. Tomain, *Regulatory Law and Policy* 24 (2d ed., 1998).

23. See Peter Dorman, *Markets and Morality: Economics, Dangerous Work, and the Value of Human Life* 35–36 (1996).

24. For a description of representative studies, see ibid., 74–79; Viscusi, *Fatal Tradeoffs*, 40–41, 61–63.

25. Viscusi, *Fatal Tradeoffs*, 40.

26. Ibid., 51–74; see also Stephen Breyer, *Breaking the Vicious Circle: Toward Effective Risk Regulation* 99–100 n. 122 (1993).

27. Peter Dorman and Paul Hagstron, "Wage Compensation for Dangerous Work Revisited," 52 *Industry and Labor Relations Review* 116, 133 (1998). For an explanation why this measure lacks plausibility, see ibid., 121.

28. Professor Viscusi, for example, cautions that his calculations do not indicate the size of the wage premium that workers would demand if they were fully informed of workplace risks. Viscusi, *Fatal Tradeoffs*, 41.

29. James Robinson, *Toil and Toxics: Workplace Struggles and Political Strategies for Occupational Health* 21–24 (1991).

30. McGarity and Shapiro, *Workers at Risk*, 20.

31. For citation of studies that find existing statistics to understate workplace risks, see McGarity and Shapiro, "OSHA's Critics," 591–92.

32. See Daniel Kahneman and Amos Tversky, "Prospect Theory: An Analysis of Decision under Risk," 47 *Econometrica* 263 (1979); Daniel Kahneman and Amos Tversky, "Choices, Values, and Frames," 39 *American Psychologist* 341, 342–44 (1984); Amos Tversky and Daniel Kahneman, "The Framing of Decisions and the Psychology of Choice," 211 *Science* 453 (1981).

33. Dorman and Hagstron, "Wage Compensation," 133.

34. Robinson, *Toil and Toxics*, 93.

35. Dorman and Hagstron, "Wage Compensation," 133.

36. McGarity and Shapiro, *Workers at Risk*, 271.

37. Richard L. Revesz, "Environmental Regulation, Cost-Benefit Analysis and the Discounting of Human Lives," 99 *Columbia Law Review* 941, 971–72 (1999).

38. Richard H. Pildes and Cass R. Sunstein, "Reinventing the Regulatory State," 62 *University of Chicago Law Review* 1, 78 (1995).

39. Ibid., 79.

40. Ibid.

41. Revesz, "Environmental Regulation," 972; Shapiro and McGarity, "Not So Paradoxical," 734 n. 29.

42. Cass R. Sunstein, "Bad Deaths," 14 *Journal of Risk and Uncertainty* 259 (1997).

43. George Tolley, Donald Kenkel, and Robert Fabian, "State-of-the-Art Health Values," in *Valuing Health for Policy: An Economic Approach* 323 (George Tolley, Donald Kenkel, and Robert Fabian, eds., 1994); see also Ian Savage, "An Empirical Investigation into the Effect of Psychological Perceptions on the Willingness-to-Pay to Reduce Risk," 6 *Journal of Risk and Uncertainty* 75 (1993).

44. See Paul Slovic, "Perception of Risk," 236 *Science* 280 (1987).

45. Revesz, "Environmental Regulation," 970. It might be argued that some environmental risks are voluntary, since a person could move to a safer location, although this argument assumes that individuals can easily assess the risks they assume by not moving, which is unlikely. Ibid., 968 n. 129.

46. See Sunstein, "Bad Deaths," 272.

47. Revesz, "Environmental Regulation," 971. Revesz cites Maureen L. Cropper and Uma Subramanian, *Public Choice between Life Saving Programs* (1995) (World Bank Policy Research Working Paper 197).

48. For a review of the literature, see Slovic, "Perception of Risk." For a study using regression techniques to identify major explanatory variables for risk perceptions in addition to mortality, see Robin Gregory and Robert Mendelson, "Perceived Risk, Dread and Benefits," 13 *Risk Analysis* 259 (1993). For a report recommending multidimensional ranking of risks, see Carnegie Commission on Science, Technology, and Government, *Risk and the Environment: Improving Regulatory Decision Making* 88–89 (1993).

49. Revesz, "Environmental Regulation," 982.

50. See Laurence Tribe, "Policy Science: Analysis or Ideology?" 2 *Philosophy and Public Affairs* 66, 96 (1972); Laurence Tribe, "Trial by Mathematics: Precision and Ritual in Legal Process," 84 *Harvard Law Review* 1329, 1361–63 (1971).

51. See Chapter 5.

52. Tribe, "Trial by Mathematics," 1361.

53. Frederick R. Anderson, Robert L. Glicksman, Daniel R. Mandelker, and A. Dan Tarlock, *Environmental Protection: Law and Policy* 1045–47 (3d ed., 1999).

54. Anthony E. Boardman, David H. Greenberg, Aidan R. Vining, and David L. Weimer, *Cost-Benefit Analysis: Concepts and Practice* 238 (1996).

55. Cropper and Subramanian, *Public Choice.*

56. For a description of survey studies of nonfatal risk, see Viscusi, *Fatal Tradeoffs*, 70–73.

57. Pildes and Sunstein, "Reinventing the Regulatory State," 81.

58. Williams, "Valuing Natural Environments," 470.

59. McGarity, "Cost-Benefit State," at 65; see also Williams, "Valuing Natural Environments," 401.

60. McGarity, "Cost-Benefit State," 65.

61. See Brian R. Binger et al., "The Use of Contingent Valuation Methodology in Natural Resource Damage Assessments: Legal Fact and Economic Fiction," 89 *Northwestern University Law Review* 1029 (1995).

62. McGarity, "Cost-Benefit State," 53.

63. Frank Arnold, "It's *Not* the Economy," 15 *Environmental Forum* 30, 32 (Sept./Oct. 1998).

64. Eban Goodstein and Hart Hodges, "Polluted Data: Overestimating Environmental Costs," 8 *American Prospect* 64 (Nov./Dec. 1997).

65. Adam M. Finkel, "A Return to Alchemy," 13 *Environmental Forum* 15 (Sept./Oct. 1996). Electric utility officials predicted during congressional debate on the 1990 Clean Air Act amendments that curbing sulfur dioxide emissions would cost $10,000 per ton, but reductions were subsequently made for as little as $100 per ton. Margaret Kriz, "Heavy Breathing," *National Journal* 8, 11 (Jan. 4, 1997). Aggregate annual compliance costs with acid rain control provisions were $1.2–2.5 billion, not the $4 billion predicted. Dallas Burtraw and Byron Swift, "A New Standard of Performance: An Analysis of the Clean Air Act's Acid Rain Program," 26 *Environmental Law Reporter* 10411, 10423 (1996). Utility projections of rate increases that would result from adoption of proposed 1982 sulfur dioxide emission reduction requirements were far too high. Curtis Moore, "The Impracticality and Immorality of Cost-Benefit Analysis in Setting Health-Related Standards," 11 *Tulane Environmental Law Journal* 187, 199 n. 55 (1998).

66. Goodstein and Hodges, "Polluted Data," 66.

67. Shapiro and McGarity, "Not So Paradoxical," 731, 731 n. 14. The costs of controlling acid deposition under the 1990 CAA amendments also turned out to be substantially lower than before-the-fact estimates. Anderson et al., *Environmental Protection*, 540.

68. Office of Technology Assessment, *Gauging Control Technology and Regulatory Impacts in Occupational Safety and Health: An Appraisal of OSHA's Analytical Approach* 58 (1995).

69. Ibid., 59.

70. Alan S. Miller, "Environmental Policy in the New World Economy," 3 *Widener Law Symposium Journal* 287, 296 (fall 1998).

71. For support, see Michael E. Porter, "America's Green Strategy," 265 *Scientific American* 168 (1991); Michael E. Porter and Claas van der Linde, "Toward a New Conception of the Environmental-Competitiveness Relationship," 9 *Journal of Economic Perspectives* 97 (1995). For a counter view, see Adam B. Jaffee, Steven R. Peterson, Paul R. Portney, and Robert N. Stavins, "Environmental Regulations and the Competitiveness of U.S. Manufacturing: What Does the Evidence Tell Us?" 23 *Journal of Economic Literature* 132 (1995); Karen Palmer, Wallace Oates, and Paul Portney, "Tightening Environmental Standards: The Benefit Cost or the No-Cost Paradigm," 9 *Journal of Economic Perspectives* 119 (1995).

72. Goodstein and Hodges, "Polluted Data," 68. See also Arnold, "Its *Not* the Economy," 31; Finkel, "A Second Opinion," 369, 372.

73. Winston Harrington, Richard D. Morgenstern, and Peter Nelson, "On the Accuracy of Regulatory Cost Estimates," *Resources for the Future Discussion Paper 99–18*, Jan. 1999, 14–15.

74. Office of Technology Assessment, *Gauging Control Technology*, 59.

75. Harrington, Morgenstern, and Nelson, "On the Accuracy," 14–15.

76. Ibid., 9.

77. Office of Technology Assessment, *Gauging Control Technology*, 60.

78. Ibid.

79. McGarity, "Cost-Benefit State," 48.

80. John S. Applegate and Steven M. Wesloh, "Short Changing Short-term Risk: A Study of Superfund Remedy Selection," 15 *Yale Journal on Regulation* 269 (1998).

81. Cass R. Sunstein, "Forward," in *Risk vs. Risk: Tradeoffs in Protecting Health and the Environment* viii (John D. Graham and Jonathan Baert Wiener, eds., 1995).

82. Aaron Wildavsky, *Searching for Safety* 61 (1988).

83. Ibid., 60.

84. *International Union, UAW v. OSHA*, 938 F.2d 1310, 1326 (D.C. Cir. 1991) (Williams, J., concurring).

85. W. Kip Viscusi, "The Dangers of Unbounded Commitments to Regulate Risk," in *Risks, Costs, and Lives Saved: Getting Better Results from Regulation* 160 (Robert W. Hahn, ed., 1996).

86. Randall Lutter and John F. Morrall III, "Health-Health Analysis: A New Way to Evaluate Health and Safety Regulation," 8 *Journal of Risk and Uncertainty* 43 (1993); Ralph L. Keeney, "Mortality Risks Induced by Economic Expenditures," 10 *Risk Analysis* 147 (1990).

87. For a list of the studies, see Cass Sunstein, *Free Markets and Social Justice* 303, Table 12.1 (1993); Viscusi, *Fatal Tradeoffs*, 161, Table 7–5.

88. McGarity, "Cost-Benefit State," 46–49.

89. The General Accounting Office contended that the proponents of "richer is safer" analysis, including OMB, have failed to recognize that a correlation between wealth and health may not be causal in nature. U.S. General Accounting Office, *Risk-Risk Analysis: OMB's Review of a Proposed OSHA Rule* (1992).

90. Eban B. Goodstein, *Jobs and the Environment: The Myth of a National Trade-off* (1994); Kirsten H. Engel, "State Environmental Standard-Setting: Is There a 'Race' and Is It 'To the Bottom'?," 48 *Hastings Law Journal* 271, 330–31 (1997). For a list of relevant studies, see John R. E. Bliese, "Conservative Principles and Environmental Policies," 7 *Kansas Journal of Law and Public Policy* 1, 28 n. 160 (spring 1998).

91. Finkel, "A Second Opinion," 326.

92. McGarity, "Cost-Benefit State," 49.

93. For a description of discounting as a form of reverse compound interest, see Environmental Law Institute, *Law of Environmental Protection* §5A.02 (Sheldon M. Novick et al., eds., 1987).

94. Lisa Heinzerling, "Discounting Life," 108 *Yale Law Journal* 1911, 1914–15 (1999).

95. Testimony of Lisa Heinzerling Concerning the Nomination of John D. Graham to be Administrator of the Office of Information and Regulatory Affairs, Office of Management and Budget (Undated), 18.

96. Ibid.

97. For a description of the available evidence, see Lisa Heinzerling, "Discounting Our Future," 34 *University of Wyoming Land and Water Review* 39, 57–59 (1999).

98. Michael J. Moore and W. Kip Viscusi, "Discounting Environmental Health Risks: New Evidence and Policy Implications," 18 *Journal of Environmental Economics and Management* S-51, S-61 (1990).

99. Heinzerling, "Discounting Our Future," 60.

100. Heinzerling, "Testimony," 18.

101. For a description of the available evidence, see Heinzerling, "Discounting Our Future," 59.

102. For a description of the studies, see ibid., 62.

103. Ibid., 43; Revesz, "Environmental Regulation," 986.

104. Peter S. Menell and Richard B. Stewart, *Environmental Law and Policy* 91 (1994).

105. Heinzerling, "Discounting Our Future," 47; Revesz, "Environmental Regulation, 946.

106. Revesz, "Environmental Regulation," 979–80, 1017; see also Daneil A. Farber and Paul A. Hemmersbaugh, "The Shadow of the Future: Discount Rates, Later Generations, and the Environment," 46 *Vanderbilt Law Review* 267, 284 (1993).

107. Heinzerling, "Regulatory Costs," 2054.

108. Ibid.

109. See, e.g., Revesz, "Environmental Regulation," 1015; Daniel A. Farber, *Eco-Pragmatism: Making Sustainable Environmental Decisions in an Uncertain World* 155 (1999).

CHAPTER 7

1. Celia Campbell-Mohn and John S. Applegate, "Learning from NEPA: Guidelines for Responsible Risk Legislation," 23 *Harvard Environmental Law Review* 93 (1999).

2. Nicholas C. Yost and James W. Rubin, "The National Environmental Policy Act," in *Environmental Law Inst., Law of Environmental Protection* §9.01[1][b][i] (Sheldon M. Novick et al., eds., 1987).

3. Michael B. Gerrard, "The Dynamics of Secrecy in the Environmental Impact Statement Process," 2 *New York University Environmental Law Journal* 279 (1993).

4. 42 U.S.C. §4332(2)(C).

5. Thomas O. McGarity, *Reinventing Rationality: The Role of Regulatory Supervision in the Federal Bureaucracy* 161 (1991).

6. Paul J. Culhane, "NEPA's Impacts on Federal Agencies, Anticipated and Unanticipated," 20 *Environmental Law* 681, 685 (1990). Compare Michael Herz, "Parallel Universes: NEPA Lessons for the New Property," 93 *Columbia Law Review* 1668, 1693 (1993). Professor Herz characterizes NEPA as an example of "reflexive informal legal rationality."

7. *Calvert Cliffs' Coordinating Comm., Inc. v. United States Atomic Energy Comm'n,* 449 F.2d 1109, 1123 (D.C. Cir. 1971).

8. 42 U.S.C. §4332. Compare ibid., §4331(b), which imposes on the federal government the continuing responsibility "to use all practicable means, consistent with other essential considerations of national policy" to achieve stated environmental protection goals.

9. Culhane, "NEPA's Impacts," 693.

10. 40 C.F.R. §§1502.6, 1502.14, 1502.22–23.

11. Frederick R. Anderson, Robert L. Glicksman, Daniel R. Mandelker, and A. Dan Tarlock, *Environmental Protection: Law and Policy* 196 (3d ed., 1999).

12. Michael Ferester, "Revitalizing the National Environmental Policy Act: Substantive Law Adaptations from NEPA's Progeny," 16 *Harvard Environmental Law Review* 207, 210 (1992).

13. *Calvert Cliffs' Coordinating Comm., Inc. v. United States Atomic Energy Comm'n,* 449 F.2d 1109, 1115 (D.C. Cir. 1971). The court quoted another decision in which a federal district court had opined that "[it] is hard to imagine a clearer or

stronger mandate to the Courts" than the one reflected in §102 of NEPA. Ibid., (quoting *Texas Comm. on Natural Resources v. United States,* 1 Env't. Rep. Cas. [BNA] 1303, 1304 [W.D. Tex. 1970]). See also Frederick R. Anderson, *NEPA in the Courts: A Legal Analysis of the National Environmental Policy Act* 16 (1973).

14. The Administrative Procedure Act affords the basis for private litigants to seek judicial review of alleged agency noncompliance with NEPA. Dinah Bear, "The National Environmental Policy Act: Its Origins and Evolutions," 10 *Natural Resources and Environment* 3, 69 (fall 1995).

15. See George Cameron Coggins and Robert L. Glicksman, *Public Natural Resources Law* §10G.01[1] (1990, as updated) for a list of some important examples.

16. *Calvert Cliffs',* 449 F.2d at 1115.

17. *Strycker's Bay Neighborhood Council, Inc. v. Karlen,* 444 U.S. 223, 227–28 (1980); *Kleppe v. Sierra Club,* 427 U.S. 390, 410 n. 21 (1976). See also *Robertson v. Methow Valley Citizens Council,* 490 U.S. 332 (1989).

18. See, e.g., *Sierra Club v. Espy,* 38 F.3d 792, 802 (5th Cir. 1994). In that case the court remarked that NEPA "does not command the agency to favor an environmentally preferable course of action, only that it make its decision to proceed with the action after taking a 'hard look at environmental consequences.'"

19. William H. Rodgers Jr., *Environmental Law* 811–12 (2d ed., 1994).

20. Culhane, "NEPA's Impacts," 693.

21. See, e.g., *City of Alexandria v. Slater,* 198 F.3d 862 (D.C. Cir. 1999); *Northwest Coalition for Alternatives to Pesticides v. Lyng,* 844 F.2d 588 (9th Cir. 1988); *American Lands Alliance v. Kenops,* 1999 WL 672213, at *11 (D. Or. Aug. 24, 1999); *Western Land Exchange Project v. Dombeck,* 47 F. Supp. 2d 1196, 1212 (D. Or. 1999).

22. 40 C.F.R. §1502.14.

23. See Coggins and Glicksman, *Public Natural Resources Law,* §10G.05[6].

24. For an extreme case, see *Baltimore Gas and Elec. Co. v. NRDC,* 462 U.S. 87 (1983).

25. See, e.g., *Oregon Natural Resources Council v. Lowe,* 109 F.3d 521, 529 (9th Cir. 1997); *Salmon River Concerned Citizens v. Robertson,* 32 F.3d 1346, 1356 (9th Cir. 1994); *County of Suffolk v. Secretary of the Interior,* 562 F.2d 1368, 1372 (2d Cir. 1977); *Sierra Club v. Stamm,* 507 F.2d 788, 793 (10th Cir. 1974); *Citizens for Envtl. Quality v. United States,* 731 F. Supp. 970, 995 (D. Colo. 1989).

26. See, e.g., *Northwest Resource Info. Ctr., Inc. v. National Marine Fisheries Serv.,* 56 F.3d 1060, 1967 (9th Cir. 1995); *Oregon Natural Resources Council v. Marsh,* 52 F.3d 1485, 1490 (9th Cir. 1995).

27. See, e.g., *Kerr-McGee Corp. v. United States,* 32 Fed. Cl. 43 (1994).

28. See, e.g., *Northwest Coalition for Alternatives to Pesticides v. Lyng,* 844 F.2d 588 (9th Cir. 1988); *County of Del Norte v. United States,* 732 F.2d 1462 (9th Cir. 1984); *Alaska v. Carter,* 462 F. Supp. 1155 (D. Alaska 1978).

29. As Professor Michael Herz has written, "Requiring consideration of environmental harms, ... even if it does not seem adequately protective in particular cases, will inescapably produce more environmentally protective decisions than would occur absent such a requirement." Herz, "Parallel Universes," 1702.

30. Lynton Caldwell, "Beyond NEPA: Future Significance of the National Environmental Policy Act," 22 *Harvard Environmental Law Review* 203, 207 (1998).

31. Culhane, "NEPA's Impacts," 690. According to at least one observer, the U.S. Forest Service has successfully integrated NEPA into its decision-making processes. Stark Ackerman, "Observations on the Transformation of the Forest Service: The Effects of the National Environmental Policy Act on U.S. Forest Service Decision Making," 20 *Environmental Law* 703 (1990).

32. See, generally, Daniel R. Mandelker, *NEPA Law and Litigation* §11.04[4] (1992).

33. 42 U.S.C. §4332(2)(A).

34. See Mandelker, *NEPA Law and Litigation*, §11.03. Mandelker summarizes Richard Liroff, "NEPA—Where Have We Been and Where Are We Going?" 46 *Journal of American Planning Association* 154 (1980).

35. Campbell-Mohn and Applegate, "Learning from NEPA," 134.

36. Culhane, "NEPA's Impacts," 692.

37. Michael C. Blumm, "The National Environmental Policy Act at Twenty: A Preface," 20 *Environmental Law* 447, 452 (1990). Richard E. Levy and Robert L. Glicksman, "Judicial Activism and Restraint in the Supreme Court's Environmental Law Decisions," 42 *Vanderbilt Law Review* 343, 372 (1989), assert that "[t]he absence of any meaningful substantive review by the courts allows affected agencies to 'jump through the hoops' of NEPA's procedural requirements without giving any real weight to environmental consequences." See also Joseph Sax, "The (Unhappy) Truth about NEPA," 26 *Oklahoma Law Review* 239 (1973); Philip Weinberg, "It's Time to Put NEPA Back on Course," 3 *New York University Environmental Law Journal* 99 (1994).

38. Ackerman, "Transformation of the Forest Service," 729. See also Eugene Bardach and Lucian Pugliaresi, "The Environmental-Impact Statement vs. the Real World," 49 *Public Interest* 22 (1979). William Funk, "NEPA at Energy: An Exercise in Legal Narrative," 20 *Environmental Law* 759, 765–70 (1990), relates how a party dissatisfied with the outcome of an agency rulemaking used NEPA to challenge the validity of a rule, even though it did not really care about the agency's environmental analysis.

39. Anderson et al., *Environmental Protection*, 311.

40. Mark Seidenfeld, "A Table of Requirements for Federal Administrative Rulemaking," 27 Florida State University Law Review 533, 536 (2000).

41. The utilitarian bent reflected in the Reagan Executive Order was anticipated by Executive Orders issued by his three immediate predecessors. President Nixon re-

quired EPA and OSHA to prepare a summary of the costs of proposed regulations and their alternatives. President Ford required all executive agencies to prepare an "Inflation Impact Statement" for proposed rules, including a quantitative assessment of the benefits and costs of regulation. President Carter required a regulatory analysis for proposed "major" rules, and created an interagency task force, the Regulatory Analysis Review Group, to monitor agency compliance. See William F. Funk, Sidney A. Shapiro, and Russell L. Weaver, *Administrative Procedure and Practice* 123 (1997).

42. Exec. Order No. 12,866, 58 Fed. Reg. 51,735 (1993), reprinted in 5 U.S.C. §601 note.

43. Federal mandates include any regulatory provision that would impose an enforceable duty upon state, local, or tribal governments other than a condition of federal assistance.

44. 2 U.S.C. §§1532, §1535(a).

45. See Table 7.1.

46. Regulatory Flexibility Act, 5 U.S.C. §§601–12.

47. Paperwork Reduction Act, 44 U.S.C. §§3501–20.

48. See Table 7.1.

49. Federalism Accountability Act, S. 1214, 106th Cong., 1st Sess. (1999); see also Federalism Act of 1999, H.R. 2245, 106th Cong. 1st Sess. (1999).

50. H.R. 9, 104th Cong., 1st Sess. (1995).

51. S. 343, 104th Cong., 1st Sess. (1995).

52. S. 746, 106th Cong., 1st Sess. (1999).

53. Although these adverse effects may be the unintended consequences of the rationality project, some observers have postulated that restricting the output of risk regulatory agencies, not rationalizing the process, is the principal objective of at least some of the critics of risk regulation. See, e.g., Robert L. Glicksman and Stephen B. Chapman, "Regulatory Reform and (Breach of) the Contract with America: Improving Environmental Policy or Destroying Environmental Protection?" 5 *Kansas Journal of Law and Public Policy* 9, 10 (winter 1996), in which the authors assert that "many proponents of the Contract With America seek deregulation of the activities currently subject to environmental regulation."

54. McGarity, *Reinventing Rationality*, 112–23.

55. Compare *Idaho Mining Ass'n, Inc. v. Browner*, 90 F. Supp. 2d 1078, 1101–2 (D. Idaho 2000), a case in which the court described the manner in which EPA engaged in cost-benefit analysis to meet the requirements of Executive Order 12,866 in establishing water quality standards, even though the Clean Water Act did not require that it do so.

56. Thomas O. McGarity, "A Cost-Benefit State," 50 *Administrative Law Review* 7, 77 (1998).

57. 42 U.S.C. §4332(2)(C).

58. Matthew D. Adler and Eric A. Posner, "Rethinking Cost-Benefit Analysis," 109 *Yale Law Journal* 165, 167 (1999).

59. Richard J. Pierce Jr., "Judicial Review of Agency Actions in a Period of Diminishing Agency Resources," 49 *Administrative Law Review* 61, 64, 66, 69 (1997).

60. Insufficient funding has hampered EPA's ability to oversee the states' compliance with their responsibilities to adopt and enforce water quality standards under the Clean Water Act. See Victor B. Flatt, "A Dirty River Runs through It (The Failure of Enforcement in the Clean Water Act)," 25 *Boston College Environmental Affairs Law Review* 1, 4–5 (1997). OSHA was adversely affected by budget cuts during the 1980s and 1990s. See Thomas O. McGarity and Sidney A. Shapiro, *Workers at Risk: The Failed Promise of the Occupational Safety and Health Administration* 186–87 (1993); Thomas O. McGarity and Sidney A. Shapiro, "OSHA's Critics and Regulatory Reform," 31 *Wake Forest Law Review* 587, 633–42 (1996). According to the National Forest Service, that agency has had available to it only about 20 percent of the funds necessary to fully maintain Forest Service roads in compliance with environmental and safety standards. National Forest System Road Management, 65 Fed. Reg. 11,676, 11,678 (2000). Limited personnel and funding have hampered the process for issuing permits for the taking of migratory birds or to enforce statutory prohibitions on such takings. *Response of the United States of America to the Submission Made by the Alliance for the Wild Rockies, et al. Under Article 14 of the North American Agreement on Environmental Cooperation*, SEM 99–002 (2000). The National Park Service developed a backlog of maintenance problems, as the health of the parks deteriorated because of a lack of funds during the 1980s and 1990s. George Cameron Coggins and Robert L. Glicksman, "Concessions Law and Policy in the National Park System," 74 *Denver University Law Review* 729, 734 (1997). Finally, Jeffrey J. Rachlinski, "Noah by the Numbers: An Empirical Evaluation of the Endangered Species Act," 82 *Cornell Law Review* 356, 386–87 (1997), claims that "[s]pecies are paying a price for the lack of resources needed to fully implement the Act," that "the lack of resources prevents the Act from being all that it can be," and that "lack of funding may make it impossible for the recovery plans to buffer species from economic activity."

61. See, generally, Nathaniel O. Keohane, Richard L. Revesz, and Robert N. Stavins, "The Choice of Regulatory Instruments in Environmental Policy," 22 *Harvard Environmental Law Review* 313, 314 (1998). The authors posit that, "[at] least in theory, market-based instruments minimize the aggregate cost of achieving a given level of environmental protection, and provide incentives for the adoption and diffusion of cheaper and better control technologies." See also Jonathan Baert Wiener, "Global Environmental Regulation: Instrument Choice in Legal Context," 108 *Yale Law Journal* 677 (1999). Market-based instruments are not inevitably more efficient than com-

mand-and-control regulation, however. See, e.g., Kenneth Richards, "Framing Environmental Policy Instrument Choice," 10 *Duke Environmental Law and Policy Forum* 221 (2000); Sidney A. Shapiro and Robert L. Glicksman, "Goals, Instruments, and Environmental Policy Choice," 10 *Duke Environmental Law and Policy Forum* 297 (2000).

62. Lisa Heinzerling, "Reductionist Regulatory Reform," 8 *Fordham Environmental Law Journal* 459, 473–74 (1997).

63. *Corrosion Proof Fittings v. EPA,* 947 F.2d 1201 (5th Cir. 1991).

64. 15 U.S.C. §2605(a).

65. Thomas O. McGarity, "The Courts and the Ossification of Rulemaking: A Response to Professor Seidenfeld," 75 *Texas Law Review* 525, 541–49 (1997).

66. Lynn E. Blais, "Beyond Cost/Benefit: The Maturation of Economic Analysis of the Law and Its Consequences for Environmental Policymaking," 2000 *Illinois Law Review* 237, 247.

67. McGarity, "The Courts," 548.

68. 5 U.S.C. §611(a)(4).

69. *Dithiocarbamate Task Force v. EPA,* 98 F.3d 1394, 1405 (D.C. Cir. 1996).

70. See, e.g., Exec. Order No. 12,866, §10, 58 Fed. Reg. 51,735 (1993), reprinted in 5 U.S.C. §601 note.

71. 2 U.S.C. §1571(a)(3), (b), pursuant to which neither the failure to prepare a regulatory impact statement nor preparation of an inadequate statement provides a basis for judicial invalidation of agency regulations.

72. A statutory mandate to consider costs in relation to benefits would appear to provide a stronger normative tilt toward efficiency as the determinative policy-making criterion than an obligation to consider the cost of regulation.

73. *Corrosion Proof Fittings v. EPA,* 947 F.2d 1201 (5th Cir. 1991).

74. *American Trucking Ass'ns, Inc. v. EPA,* 175 F.3d 1027 (D.C. Cir.), modified on rehearing, 195 F.3d 4 (D.C. Cir. 1999), aff'd in part, rev'd in part, and remanded, 531 U.S. 457 (2001).

75. See Craig N. Oren, "Run over by *American Trucking* Part I: Can EPA Revive Its Air Quality Standards?" 29 *Environmental Law Reporter (Environmental Law Institute)* 10653, 10660–61 (1999).

76. U.S. EPA, *Review of National Ambient Air Quality Standards for Ozone: Assessment of Scientific and Technical Information: OAQPS Staff Paper,* at app. G (1996), quoted in ibid., 10661. For an analogous example of judicial imposition of unrealistic demands on agency decision-makers, see *Gulf South Insulation v. United States Consumer Product Safety Comm'n,* 701 F.2d 1137 (5th Cir. 1983), in which the court, in invalidating a CPSC order banning the use of urea-formaldehyde foam insulation in residences and schools, chastised the agency for its reliance on an animal study in which the levels of exposure to formaldehyde varied considerably. The court con-

cluded its criticism by stating that "[to] make precise estimates, precise data are required." Ibid., 1146. The court neglected to explain what constitutes a "precise estimate" in an endeavor fraught with uncertainty, such as risk assessments of human carcinogenicity resulting from chemical exposures.

77. See *Motor Vehicle Mfrs. Ass'n v. State Farm Mut. Auto. Ins. Co.,* 463 U.S. 29, 43 (1983), which indicates that an agency acts in an arbitrary and capricious manner for purposes of §706(2)(A) of the APA if it "entirely failed to consider an important aspect of the problem."

78. See, e.g., Robert V. Percival, "Regulatory Evolution and the Future of Environmental Policy," 1 *University of Chicago Legal Forum* 159, 192 (1997), which indicates that §6(a)(3) of Executive Order 12,866 requires risk assessment only for "the most significant regulatory initiatives."

79. Two examples of statutes that leave the details to the agencies are 29 U.S.C. §655(g), which requires that OSHA engage in comparative risk assessment by determining priorities for standard-setting, and 42 U.S.C. §300g-1(b)(1)(C), which requires that EPA engage in comparative risk assessment by selecting for regulation the drinking water contaminants "that present the greatest public health concern."

80. See Glicksman and Chapman, "Regulatory Reform," 24.

81. See McGarity, *Reinventing Rationality,* 127. Professor McGarity asserts that the net result of agency regulatory analysis "is an analysis that is laced with guesswork and plagued by large uncertainties."

82. Ibid., 5.

83. Ibid., 5–6.

CHAPTER 8

1. Daniel A. Farber, *Eco-Pragmatism: Making Sensible Environmental Decisions in an Uncertain World* 179 (1999). Farber endorses decentralization and streamlining of the regulatory process as ways to improve environmental learning.

2. Nathaniel O. Keohane, Richard L. Revesz, and Robert N. Stavins, "The Choice of Regulatory Instruments in Environmental Policy," 22 *Harvard Environmental Law Review* 313 (1998).

3. For one description of the taxonomy of regulatory instruments, see Jonathan Baert Wiener, "Global Environmental Regulation: Instrument Choice in Legal Context," 108 *Yale Law Journal* 677, 704 (1999). See also David M. Driesen, "Choosing Environmental Instruments in a Transnational Context," 27 *Ecology Law Quarterly* 1, 7–8 (2000).

4. See, e.g., "Senate Bill would Require EPA to Assess Risks, Benefits before Setting Air Standards," 31 *BNA Environment Reporter* 573 (Mar. 31, 2000).

5. Some critics of command-and-control regulation have asserted that controls based on best available technology do not provide strong incentives to develop new, environmentally superior technologies, and may even discourage their development. See, e.g., Bruce Ackerman and Richard Stewart, "Reforming Environmental Law," 37 *Stanford Law Review* 1333, 1334 (1985).

6. Cass R. Sunstein, "Using Common Law Principles in Regulatory Schemes (with a Note on Victimology)," 19 *Harvard Journal of Law and Public Policy* 651, 653 (1996). Sometimes the critics do more than imply that command-and-control regulation necessarily entails design standards. Professor Sunstein, for example, has charged that "[r]ules that specify end-states are common in modern regulation, in the form of 'command and control' regulation that says exactly what people must do and how they must do it." Cass R. Sunstein, "Problems with Rules," 83 *California Law Review* 953, 1017 (1995).

7. E.g., 33 U.S.C. §1311(b)(1)–(2), which deals with effluent limitations for existing point sources; ibid., §1316(a)(1), (e), which deals with effluent limitations for new point sources; ibid., §1317(b)(1), (d), which deals with pretreatment standards for indirect point sources.

8. E.g., 42 U.S.C. §7411(a)(1), (e), which deals with national emission standards for new stationary sources; ibid., §7412(d), which deals with national emission standards for hazardous air pollutants. Indeed, the statute was amended in 1990 to eliminate provisions that effectively limited the discretion of certain coal-burning sources to choose between scrubber installation and switching to fuels with lower sulfur concentrations as means of compliance with the new source standards. Compare 42 U.S.C. §7411(a)(1) (1988). The act authorizes EPA to promulgate design or work practice standards for new stationary sources, but only if it is not feasible to prescribe or enforce a performance standard. 42 U.S.C. §7411(h). This authority has rarely been invoked.

9. E.g., 42 U.S.C. §7423(c). That provision states that "[in] no event may [EPA] prohibit any increase in any stack height or restrict in any manner the stack height of any source."

10. *CPC Int'l Inc. v. Train,* 515 F.2d 1032, 1045 n. 25 (8th Cir. 1975) (citing U.S. Congress, Senate Committee on Public Works, *Federal Water Pollution Control Act Amendments of 1971,* 92nd Cong., 1st Sess., 1971, S. Rpt. No. 92–414, 1477; U.S. Congress, Conference Committee, 92nd Cong., 2d Sess., 1971, S. Rep. No. 92–1236, reprinted in *A Legislative History of the Water Pollution Control Act Amendments of 1972,* 311). See also David M. Driesen, "Is Emissions Trading an Economic Incentive Program?: Replacing the Command and Control/Economic Incentive Dichotomy," 55 *Washington and Lee Law Review* 289, 297–99 (1998). Professor Driesen asserts that the federal environmental statutes typically authorize the adoption of performance, not design standards, and criticizes attacks on "command-and-control regulation" that

fail to distinguish between criteria for making stringency determinations and decisions about the form of regulatory standards. But according to Robert V. Percival, Alan S. Miller, Christopher H. Schroeder, and James P. Leape, *Environmental Regulation: Law, Science, and Policy* 155 (2d ed., 1996), performance standards "routinely devolve into de facto design standards."

11. EPA issued an Emission Trading Policy Statement in 1986, 51 Fed. Reg. 43,814 (1986), to endorse various forms of both intrafirm and interfirm trading. The "bubble concept" endorsed in *Chevron U.S.A., Inc. v. Natural Resources Defense Council, Inc.,* 467 U.S. 837 (1984), is an example of intrafirm trading. The 1994 Economic Incentive Program was designed to encourage economically efficient reduction of pollutants in areas of the country that have not yet achieved the national standards by allowing sources that have relatively high control costs to purchase allowances to pollute from sources with lower control costs. 59 Fed. Reg. 16,690, 16,696 (1994).

12. 42 U.S.C. §§7651c(a)(1), 7651b(b). See also *Indianapolis Power and Light Co. v. EPA,* 58 F.3d 643, 644 (D.C. Cir. 1995).

13. If a regulated unit could limit its emissions more cheaply by controlling its own emissions instead of buying another unit's excess allowances, it would presumably do so.

14. For further discussion of the use of incentive-based policy instruments under the Clean Air Act, see Frederick R. Anderson, Robert L. Glicksman, Daniel R. Mandelker, and A. Dan Tarlock, *Environmental Protection: Law and Policy* 487–96 (3d ed., 1999).

15. See, e.g., *Citizens Against the Refinery's Effects, Inc. v. EPA,* 643 F.2d 183 (4th Cir. 1981), a case in which the court placed its stamp of approval on a refinery's attempt to satisfy the offset requirement of the Clean Air Act's nonattainment program by relying on decreased emissions of hydrocarbons from Virginia's highways, which the state had apparently already decided to achieve.

16. Robert W. Hahn, "Regulatory Reform at EPA: Separating Fact from Illusion," 4 *Yale Journal on Regulation* 173, 179–80 (1986).

17. Cass R. Sunstein, "Is the Clean Air Act Unconstitutional?" 98 *Michigan Law Review* 303, 363 (1999). Sunstein made the same recommendation earlier. See Cass R. Sunstein, *Free Markets and Social Justice* 354 (1997). Similarly, Jonathan Wiener has endorsed the application of a presumption in favor of allowance trading and pollution taxes over traditional regulation in the international context. See Wiener, "Global Environmental Regulation," 798. Professor Driesen argues against such a presumption. Driesen, "Choosing Environmental Instruments," 11.

18. Sunstein, "Clean Air Act," 377. Among other things, Professor Sunstein's formulation would reverse the burden of proof on the issue of the propriety of the use of incentive-based instruments.

19. Ibid.

20. See, e.g., Farber, *Eco-Pragmatism*, 184 (quoting Robert Hahn and Gordon Hester, "Where Did All the Markets Go? An Analysis of EPA's Emissions Trading Program," 6 *Yale Journal on Regulation* 109 (1989)), which discusses the difficulty of determining the cost-effectiveness of emissions trading schemes because of the absence of effort devoted to evaluating the impact of such schemes. Driesen, "Economic Incentive Program," 313–16, asserts that no evidence supports the claim that emissions trading schemes like the bubble concept have stimulated adequate environmental performance at a cheaper price.

21. Daniel H. Cole and Peter Z. Grossman, "When Is Command-and-Control Efficient? Institutions, Technology, and the Comparative Efficiency of Alternative Regulatory Regimes for Environmental Protection," 1999 *Wisconsin Law Review* 887, 888, 892 (1999). See also Sidney A. Shapiro and Robert L. Glicksman, "Goals, Instruments, and Environmental Policy Choice," 10 *Duke Environmental Law and Policy Forum* 297, 310 (2000).

22. Farber, *Eco-Pragmatism*, 180–81.

23. Kenneth R. Richards, "Framing Environmental Policy Instrument Choice," 10 *Duke Environmental Law and Policy Forum* 221, 225–26 (2000). See also Driesen, "Choosing Environmental Instruments," which asserts that "[m]ost knowledgeable scholars recognize that appropriate instrument choice depends upon context."

24. Cole and Grossman, "When Is Command-and-Control Efficient?" 889, 895 (quoting Martin L. Weitzman, "Prices vs. Quantities," 41 *Review of Economic Studies* 477, 479 [1974]). See also ibid., 894, which postulates that "the comparative efficiencies of alternative regulatory regimes change over time, as the demand for pollution control and the marginal costs of pollution control change."

25. Richards, "Framing Environmental Policy Instrument Choice," 256. Compare Driesen, "Economic Incentive Program," 307, arguing that because nonuniform standards may prove more expensive to design or enforce than traditional, uniform standards, judgments about the relative efficiency of the two kinds of standards should consider not only industry costs of compliance but also enforceability and ease of administration. For purposes of simplicity, we have ignored public finance costs in this scenario. If the combination of increased implementation costs and public finance costs of pursuing incentive-based regulation exceeds the production cost savings attributable to that method of regulation in a particular case, the incentive-based approach is inferior from an efficiency vantage point, even if the increased implementation costs of incentive-based regulation alone would not exceed the production cost savings yielded by that approach. In fact, Professor Richards asserts that "[g]enerally command-and-control regulation should be preferred to the enterprise mode

instruments on the basis of public finance considerations." Richards, "Framing Environmental Policy Instrument Choice," 279.

26. The use of market-based instruments has been justified not only on the basis of their potential to achieve environmental goals more efficiently than traditional regulatory techniques but also on the basis of their ability to do so more democratically by encouraging broad public participation and debate over issues such as the appropriate levels of pollution to permit. See, e.g., Bruce Ackerman and Richard Stewart, "Reforming Environmental Law: The Democratic Case for Market Incentives," 13 *Columbia Journal of Environmental Law* 171 (1988). If incentive-based techniques are not preferable to traditional regulation from a democratic perspective, then the equity and efficacy-based objections to those techniques discussed below take on greater weight, for in such a case it is harder to argue that adverse distributional consequences and higher levels of environmental degradation are an appropriate tradeoff for more democratic decision-making. Lisa Heinzerling has argued that there is good reason to be suspicious about claims that incentive-based techniques will promote democratic values such as deliberation, decentralization, and freedom from faction to a greater extent than traditional regulation does. See, generally, Lisa Heinzerling, "Selling Pollution, Forcing Democracy," 14 *Stanford Environmental Law Journal* 300 (1995). If she is right, then the use of incentive-based techniques may conflict with pragmatism's preference for methods of accountability that promote public participation.

27. Office of Technology Assessment, Congress of the United States, *Environmental Policy Tools: A User's Guide* 146–47 (1995).

28. See, e.g., Bradley C. Karkkainen, "Information as Environmental Regulation: TRI and Performance Benchmarking, Precursor to a New Paradigm?" 89 *Georgetown Law Journal* 257 (2001), which heralds the Toxic Release Inventory as a "watershed" development in the systematic use of performance monitoring as a regulatory tool. Similarly, Clifford Rechtschaffen, "How to Reduce Lead Exposures with One Simple Statute: The Experience of Proposition 65," 29 *Environmental Law Reporter (Environmental Law Institute)* 10581 (1999), describes how California's reliance on information disclosure has contributed to reformulation of products to include less lead.

29. See, e.g., Sidney A. Shapiro and Randy Rabinowitz, "Voluntary Regulatory Compliance in Theory and Practice: The Case of OSHA," 52 *Administrative Law Review* 97, 140–46 (2000). See also Mary L. Lyndon, "Information Economics and Chemical Toxicity: Designing Laws to Produce and Use Data," 87 *Michigan Law Review* 1795 (1989).

30. Office of Technology Assessment, *Environmental Policy Tools*, 145, 147–48, 160, 162.

31. See, e.g., Anderson et al., *Environmental Protection*, 546.

32. Such a scheme may create different kinds of inequities, however. Developing nations have objected to a broad-based international emissions trading regime as part of the Kyoto Protocol for controlling global warming, for example, because of their fear that the industrialized nations will buy their way out of commitments to emissions reductions, forcing developing nations to bear the brunt of those obligations. See ibid., 563.

33. Office of Technology Assessment, *Environmental Policy Tools*, 164.

34. Robert V. Percival, "Regulatory Evolution and the Future of Environmental Policy," 1 *University of Chicago Legal Forum* 159, 179 (1997).

35. 42 U.S.C. §7410(a)(2)(A) (1976).

36. 42 U.S.C. §7502(a) (1982).

37. 42 U.S.C. §7511(a)(1) (requiring marginal ozone nonattainment areas to come into compliance by 1993, but extending the deadline for extreme areas until 2010).

38. In the examples described below, Congress extended statutory deadlines in the context of periodic program reauthorizations. It has also on occasion extended deadlines on a more piecemeal basis in appropriations bills. See, e.g., Pub. L. No. 105–277, §101(a), 112 Stat. 2681 (1998) (codified at 42 U.S.C. §7671c[h]). That law, the fiscal 1999 omnibus appropriations bill, extended the deadline under the CAA for the phaseout of methyl bromide, an ozone-depleting substance, from 2001 to 2005.

39. Anderson et al., 411–12, 180–81, Figures 3–2 and 3–3.

40. 33 U.S.C. §1311(b)(2) (1976).

41. 33 U.S.C. §1311(b)(2) (1982).

42. 33 U.S.C. §1311(b)(2).

43. 33 U.S.C. §1311(i).

44. 33 U.S.C. §1311(k). See also 33 U.S.C. §1317(e) (making deadline extensions available for indirect dischargers subject to pretreatment requirements). A similar Clean Air Act provision applies to new stationary sources of air pollution. 42 U.S.C. §7411(j).

45. 42 U.S.C. §6924(h)(2).

46. Marshall J. Breger, "Regulatory Flexibility and the Administrative State," 32 *Tulsa Law Journal* 325, 331 (1996).

47. Alfred C. Aman Jr., "Administrative Equity: An Analysis of Exceptions to Administrative Rules," 1982 *Duke Law Journal* 277, 278–79. See also ibid., 281, in which the author explains that "administrative equity is concerned with 'a rectification of law where law falls short by reason of its universality'—however equitable the overall purpose of the universal or general rules involved."

48. Sometimes Congress builds differential treatment for individual regulated entities or classes of entities into a regulatory program right from the start by "grandfathering" these entities from regulatory obligations that would otherwise apply. See,

e.g., Valerie P. Mahoney, note, "Environmental Justice: From Partial Victories to Complete Solutions," 21 *Cardozo Law Review* 361, 382 (1999). The rationale is that it would be unfair to subject activities that predate adoption of regulatory obligations to those obligations. Further, the imposition of lenient treatment on certain existing sources may preclude the need to adopt watered down standards for a larger class of risk-creating activities. Grandfathered sources may gain a competitive advantage over regulated entities, however, and the longer the special treatment exists, the more troublesome that advantage can become. These sources can also impose disproportionately heavy burdens on those located in close proximity to them, thereby giving rise to environmental justice concerns. Alice Kaswan, "Environmental Justice: Bridging the Gap between Environmental Laws and 'Justice,'" 47 *American University Law Review* 221, 270–71 (1997). Over time, therefore, it may be advisable to phase out this kind of preferential treatment.

49. See *Chemical Mfrs. Ass'n v. Natural Resources Defense Council, Inc.,* 470 U.S. 116, 130–31 (1985).

50. Executive Order No. 12,875, 58 Fed. Reg. 58,093 (1993), requires that agencies review their waiver application process "and take appropriate steps to streamline that process."

51. Aman, "Administrative Equity," 293–94, 302–3.

52. See, e.g., 15 U.S.C. §2605(e)(3)(B), which authorizes exemptions from restrictions on manufacture and distribution of polychlorinated biphenyls under the Toxic Substances Control Act based on the unavailability of substitutes; 33 U.S.C. §1311(c), which authorizes the issuance of individual modifications from technology-based effluent limitations for point sources of water pollution that extract from the point source "the maximum use of technology within [its] economic capability"; 42 U.S.C. §6924(h)(2), which authorizes the issuance of variances from restrictions on the land disposal of hazardous waste based on the unavailability of adequate treatment capacity.

53. See Daniel A. Farber, "Taking Slippage Seriously: Noncompliance and Creative Compliance in Environmental Law," 23 *Harvard Environmental Law Review* 297, 306 (1999), in which the author discusses *International Harvester Co. v. Ruckelshaus,* 478 F.2d 615 (D.C. Cir. 1973). According to Professor Farber, "at the [*International Harvester*] court's prompting, EPA . . . revamped the statutory scheme to make national variances available." Ibid., 307.

54. See, generally, George Hays and Nadia Wetzler, "Federal Recognition of Variances: A Window into the Turbulent Relationship between Science and Law under the Clean Air Act," 13 *Journal of Environmental Law and Litigation* 115 (1998), which describes 42 U.S.C. §§7410(a)(2)(E), (a)(3)(C), (f)–(g), (l), 7419.

55. 33 U.S.C. §1311(g). See also ibid., §§1311(h), which authorizes similar modifica-

tions for publicly owned sewage treatment plants subject to different technology-based controls; ibid., §1326(a), which authorizes the issuance of individualized efflu-ent limitations for dischargers of thermal pollution based on the extent of impact on receiving water quality.

56. 29 U.S.C. §655(d).

57. 42 U.S.C. §7545(m)(3)(B).

58. 42 U.S.C. §6921(f).

59. Aman, "Administrative Equity," 293, 306–7.

60. *E.I. du Pont de Nemours and Co. v. Train,* 430 U.S. 112, 128 (1977).

61. *Chemical Mfrs. Ass'n v. Natural Resources Defense Council, Inc.,* 470 U.S. 116 (1985).

62. 33 U.S.C. §1311(n).

63. E.g., 42 U.S.C. §7412(i)(4), a provision that authorizes presidential exemptions from national emission standards for hazardous air pollutants based on unavailabil-ity of technology and national security interests; ibid., §7418(b), which authorizes presidential exemptions from Clean Air Act requirements at federal facilities based on "paramount interests of the United States"; ibid., §7671c(f), which authorizes EPA to allow production of CFCs to protect national security interests. See, generally, Ste-phen Dycus, *National Defense and the Environment* (1996).

64. 42 U.S.C. §7410(f).

65. 42 U.S.C. §7671c(d), (g).

66. According to Richard Pierce, "Every regulatory system includes a variety of features that confer favorable treatment on small firms." Richard J. Pierce Jr., "Small Is Not Beautiful: The Case against Special Regulatory Treatment of Small Firms," 50 *Administrative Law Review* 537 (1998). For example, 42 U.S.C. §300g-4(e)(3)(A) pro-vides variances to small public water systems unable to comply with national drink-ing water regulations, while 42 U.S.C. §6921(d) authorizes exceptions for small quan-tity hazardous waste generators. See also 63 Fed. Reg. 17,706 (1998), which affords more lenient treatment to small landfills. For a time, Congress afforded relief to small refiners from the obligations imposed on their larger competitors to phase out the use of lead in gasoline. 42 U.S.C. §7545(g) (1976); *Small Refiner Lead Phasedown Task Force v. EPA,* 705 F.2d 506 (D.C. Cir. 1983).

67. Pierce counts almost fifty examples of EPA regulations alone in which the stringency of regulation varies with the size of the firm or the amount of pollutant emitted. Pierce, "Small Is Not Beautiful," 542 and n. 25.

68. In August 1994, for example, EPA issued a policy under the Clean Air Act that authorizes states to give small businesses that seek assistance a "corrections period" to correct violations. "EPA and the States will eliminate or reduce civil penalties against the small business as a result of this voluntary compliance." EPA, *Office of Enforce-*

ment and Compliance Assurance Fact Sheet Series, Encouraging Voluntary Compliance (Apr. 1996), 1. Basically, the policy allows small businesses that receive compliance assistance from the states up to six extra months to comply with regulatory obligations. See also 65 Fed. Reg. 19,630 (2000). That final policy statement revised EPA's Small Business Compliance Policy to promote environmental compliance among small businesses by providing incentives for voluntary discovery, disclosure, and correction.

69. According to Professor Pierce, "Every study of the relationship between firm size and social bads produces the same finding—small firms account for a disproportionate quantity of the social bads that we attempt to reduce through regulation." Pierce, "Small Is Not Beautiful," 559. Among the reasons he identifies for this phenomenon are "(1) economies of scale in reducing externalities; (2) differential effects of reputational factors on internalization of externalities; (3) differential effects of tort law on internalization of externalities; and (4) differential effects of actuarial science on internalization of externalities." Ibid., 563.

70. Pierce, "Small Is Not Beautiful," 65–91.

71. Farber, "Taking Slippage Seriously," 315–16.

72. Jody Freeman, "Collaborative Governance in the Administrative State," 45 *UCLA Law Review* 1, 6, 34 (1997). See the Negotiated Rulemaking Act, 5 U.S.C. §§561–70.

73. The ESA prohibits the taking—that is, destruction—of endangered fish or wildlife species. 16 U.S.C. §1538(a)(1)(B). In *Babbitt v. Sweet Home Chapter of Communities for a Great Oregon,* 515 U.S. 687 (1995), the Supreme Court found reasonable the Interior Department's view that, in certain circumstances, activity that causes habitat modification can amount to a taking. But the ESA authorizes the Secretary of the Interior to issue permits for a taking that "is incidental to, and not the purpose of, the carrying out of an otherwise lawful activity." The Secretary may issue a permit only if the applicant submits a habitat conservation plan (HCP) in which it commits to taking steps to minimize and mitigate adverse effects on listed species. Any permit issued by the agency must include whatever terms and conditions it deems necessary or appropriate. 16 U.S.C. §1539(a)(1)–(2). The formulation of HCPs and their incorporation in incidental take permits has induced "intense negotiation" between regulated entities and the agency as the former seek to achieve permission to develop without running afoul of the statute's species protection goals. Farber, "Taking Slippage Seriously," 315–16.

74. See, generally, J. B. Ruhl, "While the Cat's Asleep: The Making of the 'New' ESA," 12 *Natural Resources and Environment* 187 (winter 1998). The "No Surprises Policy," for example, assures landowners who agree to comply with the provisions of an HCP that they will not be subject to additional land use restrictions, even if un-

foreseen circumstances arise after issuance of the HCP that require additional mitigation. 63 Fed. Reg. 8,859 (1998).

75. Ruhl, "While the Cat's Asleep," 225.

76. See, generally, Lawrence E. Susskind and Joshua Secunda, "'Improving' Project XL: Helping Adaptive Management to Work within EPA," 17 *UCLA Journal of Environmental Law and Policy* 155 (1998/99).

77. Farber, "Taking Slippage Seriously," 309; Rena I. Steinzor, "Reinventing Environmental Regulation: The Dangerous Journey from Command to Self-Control," 22 *Harvard Environmental Law Review* 103, 122–23 (1998).

78. Freeman, "Collaborative Governance," 55. See also Bradford C. Mank, "The Environmental Protection Agency's Project XL and Other Reform Initiatives: The Need for Legislative Authorization," 25 *Ecology Law Quarterly* 1, 20 (1998). Mank predicts that "Project XL would likely replace limits on emissions to a specific medium with facility-wide 'caps' or 'bubbles' that authorize a firm to trade emissions among pollutants or media."

79. Freeman, "Collaborative Governance," 55.

80. Breger, "Regulatory Flexibility," 333.

81. For a listing of other components of EPA's efforts to rely on voluntary compliance programs and agency-stakeholder "partnerships," see Elizabeth Glass-Geltman and Andrew Skroback, "Reinventing the EPA to Conform with the New American Environmentality," 23 *Columbia Journal of Environmental Law* 1, 18–20 (1998).

82. Breger, "Regulatory Flexibility," 335.

83. See, e.g., Stephen Breyer, *Breaking the Vicious Circle: Toward Effective Risk Regulation* 39–40 (1993).

84. Steven A. Herman, "A Fundamentally Different Superfund Program," 12 *Natural Resources and Environment* 196–99 (winter 1998). See also Guidance on Agreements with Prospective Purchasers of Contaminated Property and Model Prospective Purchaser Agreement, 60 Fed. Reg. 34,792 (1995), which describes the circumstances in which EPA will agree not to sue prospective purchasers of contaminated property who intend to clean it up or redevelop it.

85. See Final Policy toward Owners of Property Containing Contaminated Aquifers, 60 Fed. Reg. 34,790 (1995).

86. *Adaptive Environmental Assessment and Management* (C. Holling, ed., 1978).

87. Kai N. Lee and Jody Lawrence, "Adaptive Management: Learning from the Columbia River Basin Fish and Wildlife Program," 16 *Environmental Law* 431, 442 (1986).

88. Ibid., 450.

89. John M. Volkman, "How Do You Learn from a River? Managing Uncertainty

in Species Conservation Policy," 74 *Washington Law Review* 719, 738 (1999). Adaptive management thus "requires skepticism about existing programs, an active search for the assumptions underlying those programs, and a commitment to test them." Ibid., 739. See also A. Dan Tarlock, "The Future of Environmental 'Rule of Law' Litigation," 17 *Pace Environmental Law Review* 237, 262 (2000) (quoting National Research Council, *Restoration of Aquatic Ecosystems* 357 [1992]): "[A]daptive management recognizes the imperfect knowledge of interdependencies existing within and among natural and social systems, which requires plans to be modified as technical knowledge improves."

90. Lawrence E. Susskind and Joshua Secunda, "The Risks and Advantages of Agency Discretion: Evidence from EPA's Project XL," 17 *UCLA Journal of Environmental Law* 67, 83–84 (1998/99). See also Susskind and Secunda, "'Improving' Project XL," 155. The authors describe adaptive management as "a continuous process of institutional transformation" involving evolution of regulatory philosophies and strategies through "continuous assessment and improvement. Change is driven by a constant flow of information gathered via purposeful experimentation." Ibid., 157.

91. See, e.g., J. B. Ruhl, "Working Both (Positivist) Ends toward a New (Pragmatist) Middle in Environmental Law," 68 *George Washington Law Review* 522 (2000). Ruhl's piece reviews Farber, *Eco-Pragmatism*.

92. See, e.g., Sharon R. Siegel, Comment, "Applying the Habitat Conservation Model to Fisheries Management: A Proposal for a Modified Fisheries Planning Requirement," 25 *Columbia Journal of Environmental Law* 141, 168 (2000), which discusses the role of adaptive management in habitat conservation planning under the Endangered Species Act.

93. Karkkainen, "Information as Environmental Regulation," 277 n. 77.

94. See J. B. Ruhl, "Thinking of Environmental Law as a Complex Adaptive System: How to Clean Up the Environment by Making a Mess of Environmental Law," 34 *Houston Law Review* 933, 996 (1997).

95. Compare Jim Rossi, "Making Policy through the Waiver of Regulations at the Federal Energy Regulatory Commission," 47 *Administrative Law Review* 255, 277 n. 10 (1995). According to the author, "In addition to formal requests for waivers or exceptions, administrative equity might also be provided through agency interpretations of regulations or statutes, rulings, or no-action letters."

96. Farber, "Taking Slippage Seriously," 309–10.

97. Breger, "Regulatory Flexibility," 337.

98. 5 U.S.C. §610.

99. Exec. Order No. 12,044, 3 C.F.R. 152 (1979), reprinted in 5 U.S.C. §553 (Supp. II 1978).

100. See Neil R. Eisner and Judith S. Kaleta, "Federal Agency Reviews of Existing Regulations," 48 *Administrative Law Review* 139, 142 (1996).

101. Exec. Order No. 12,866, 3 C.F.R. 638 (1994), reprinted in 5 U.S.C. §601 (Supp. V 1993).

102. Eisner and Kaleta, "Federal Agency Reviews," 148. "We know what needs to be changed, but we don't have the time or the resources to do it," was the essence of the agency reaction to periodic regulation review. Ibid.

103. Compare Richard J. Pierce Jr., "Judicial Review of Agency Actions in a Period of Diminishing Agency Resources," 49 *Administrative Law Review* 61, 67 (1997), in which Professor Pierce asserts that "[t]he Republican Congress seems much less interested in attempting to craft and enact major amendments to regulatory statutes, than in reducing the level of funding for agencies."

104. See, e.g., ibid.: "For the foreseeable future, agencies will have access to constantly diminishing agency resources to implement their statutory mandates." See also ibid., 87–88.

105. See Eisner and Kaleta, "Federal Agency Reviews," 155–56.

106. Mark Seidenfeld, "Bending the Rules: Flexible Regulation and Constraints on Agency Discretion," 51 *Administrative Law Review* 429, 438 (1999).

107. Cf. Farber, *Eco-Pragmatism*, 173. According to Professor Farber, "burden-shifting can function usefully as a kind of tiebraker." Farber also urges placement of the burden of proof on the polluter in the face of bounded rationality by "taking reasonable safeguards against serious, but unquantifiable risks." Ibid., 198.

108. Colin Diver, "Policymaking Paradigms in Administrative Law," 95 *Harvard Law Review* 393, 430 (1981).

109. Peter H. Schuck, "When the Exception Becomes the Rule: Regulatory Equity and the Formulation of Energy Policy through an Exceptions Process," 1984 *Duke Law Journal* 163, 196.

110. See Seidenfeld, "Bending the Rules," 447, in which the author urges Congress to allow agencies to exempt entities from regulatory provisions "if the agency can persuasively demonstrate that applying these provisions would not serve the announced public purposes of the statute."

111. See Farber, *Eco-Pragmatism*, 197. Professor Farber claims that "[t]he existence of an escape valve might even strengthen support for the environmental baseline by making it clear that later adjustments would be available."

112. Aman, "Administrative Equity," 325.

113. Rossi, "Making Policy," 277.

114. See Schuck, "Regulatory Equity," 283, in which the author argues that "[by] reducing the hardships and the sense of injustice suffered by those to whom a rule applies, exceptions diminish the pressure to challenge the rule itself."

115. Eisner and Kaleta, "Federal Agency Reviews," 145.

116. Rossi, "Making Policy," 295.

117. Farber, "Taking Slippage Seriously," 299. See also Karin P. Sheldon, "Habitat Conservation Planning: Addressing the Achilles Heels of the Endangered Species Act," 6 *New York University Environmental Law Journal* 279, 283–84 (1998).

118. Steinzor, "Reinventing Environmental Regulation," 138–39. Compare Lisa Heinzerling, "Reductionist Regulatory Reform," 8 *Fordham Environmental Law Journal* 459, 474–75 (1997). Professor Heinzerling argues that cross-pollutant and cross-media emissions trades authorized by Project XL "make it hard to figure out whether the new regime provides the same degree of environmental protection as the old."

119. Freeman, "Collaborative Governance," 98.

120. See Diver, "Policymaking Paradigms," 430–31.

121. Farber, "Taking Slippage Seriously," 319. See also Daniel A. Farber, "Triangulating the Future of Reinvention: Three Emerging Models of Environmental Protection," 2000 *Illinois Law Review* 61, 78. In that article, Professor Farber relates criticisms of reinvention efforts based on lack of procedural regularity and public accountability.

122. See Steinzor, "Reinventing Environmental Regulation," 142; Freeman, "Collaborative Governance," 56.

123. Mank, "Environmental Protection Agency's Project XL," 4, reports that environmentalists generally prefer the participation of national advocacy groups in traditional informal rulemaking proceedings to individualized or local proceedings as a way to set environmental policy. They fear that local advocacy groups may incur higher transaction costs in organizing, raising money, and educating decision-makers and that such groups may lack the time and resources to "participate effectively in complex negotiations to develop alternative compliance strategies." See also David A. Dana, "The New 'Contractarian' Paradigm in Environmental Regulation," 2000 *Illinois Law Review* 35, 56–57. Professor Dana asserts that seeking to secure meaningful participation in contract-based regulation will be costly because of its decentralized, site-specific nature.

124. Professor Dana charges, for example, that regulatory contracts "make the private contracting parties to those contracts co-equal partners with the government in the creation, interpretation, and maintenance of public law. The legal regime promised in the contract may be created by the contract itself, which means that the private contracting party's acquiescence determines the law's content." David A. Dana, "Bargaining in the Shadow of Democracy," 148 *University of Pennsylvania Law Review* 473, 541 (1999).

125. Alterations in "contractarian regulation," for example, may require the payment of compensation to affected regulated entities. As a result, "financially strapped governments may forego revisions or supplementation of contractarian regulation even where it has come to be understood as inadequate, or, alternatively, they may

forego research that would reveal whether existing regulatory requirements still are adequate." Dana, "The New 'Contractarian' Paradigm," 57.

126. See Steinzor, "Reinventing Environmental Regulation," 185–86.

127. Breger, "Regulatory Flexibility," 336.

128. Recommendations of the Administrative Conference, 48 Fed. Reg. 57,461, 57,465 (1983).

129. See Rossi, "Making Policy," 296. Cf. Jody Freeman, "Private Parties, Public Functions and the New Administrative Law," 52 *Administrative Law Review* 813, 851 (2000), in which the author recommends reliance by agencies and regulated firms on independent third parties to set standards and oversee enforcement.

130. 42 U.S.C. §9621(d)(4). See also 40 C.F.R. §300.430(f)(1)(ii)(C).

131. See Mank, "Environmental Protection Agency's Project XL," 54. The author favors legislative oversight.

132. Breger, "Regulatory Flexibility," 336. Professor Breger cites Kenneth Culp Davis, *Discretionary Justice: A Preliminary Inquiry* 97 (1996).

133. The Administrative Conference of the United States recommended that when an exceptions tribunal decides a case with broad policy significance, the agency should conduct the proceeding in a manner akin to a rulemaking, with "broadened participation" and "an opportunity for public comments on all significant policy, factual, and remedial issues in the case." Recommendations of the Administrative Conference, 48 Fed. Reg. 57,461, 57,466 (1983).

134. Compare 5 U.S.C. §553. See also Recommendations of the Administrative Conference, 48 Fed. Reg. 57,461, 57,465 (1983). The Conference urged that, to the extent feasible, adequate notice of applications for exceptions be provided to all interested members of the public and that decisions should be made "only after an opportunity for full development of the relevant factual and policy issues."

135. See Farber, "Taking Slippage Seriously," 319. Professor Farber predicts that "efforts to provide more accountability and transparency are likely to hamper the collaborative process that is at the heart of reinvention."

136. See Mank, "Environmental Protection Agency's Project XL," 86. Professor Mank endorses citizen suits at the behest of any person injured in fact to challenge individual Project XL agreements.

CHAPTER 9

1. See, e.g., *American Trucking Ass'ns, Inc. v. Browner,* 175 F.3d 1027 (D.C. Cir.), modified on rehearing, 195 F.3d 4 (D.C. Cir. 1999). The appellate court struck down EPA's national ambient air quality standards for ozone on the grounds that EPA failed to supply an intelligible principle that satisfied the nondelegation doctrine.

That portion of the decision was reversed by the Supreme Court in *Whitman v. American Trucking Ass'ns, Inc.,* 531 U.S. 457 (2001).

2. Sidney A. Shapiro and Joseph P. Tomain, *Regulatory Law and Policy* 30 (1993). The authors cite W. Nelson, *The Roots of American Bureaucracy (1830–1900)* 111 (1982).

3. The third branch of the government is the judiciary. The courts are not composed of elected officials, so vesting in them the authority to make regulatory choices would not represent an improvement over delegations to agencies from the perspective of democratic accountability. Moreover, the courts function basically as a reactive branch, as cases are filed before them and they typically lack the authority or the means to engage in the kinds of information-gathering efforts that the implementation of risk regulation necessarily entails.

4. The courts sometimes ignore accommodations in risk regulation statutes of bounded rationality attributable to factors such as scientific uncertainty. When they do so, they may construe those statutes in a manner inconsistent with congressional intent. See, e.g., Howard A. Latin, "The 'Significance' of Toxic Health Risks: An Essay on Legal Decisionmaking under Uncertainty," 10 *Ecology Law Quarterly* 339 (1982); Howard A. Latin, "The Feasibility of Occupational Health Standards: An Essay on Legal Decisionmaking under Uncertainty," 78 *Northwestern University Law Review* 583, 589–91 (1983). In both articles, Professor Latin criticizes the plurality opinion in *Industrial Union Dep't, AFL-CIO v. American Petroleum Inst.,* 448 U.S. 607 (1980), on these grounds. Other examples of cases in which the courts improperly ignored congressional efforts to fashion statutory standards that refrained from requiring agencies to perform tasks for which the requisite information was not likely to be available to them are discussed in the section of this chapter pertaining to judicial oversight.

5. According to Professor McGarity, agency rules must be circulated to OMB economists, "many of whom are well-known and persistent critics of existing regulatory regimes." Thomas O. McGarity, "The Courts and the Ossification of Rulemaking: A Response to Professor Seidenfeld," 75 *Texas Law Review* 525, 534 (1997). Alan B. Morrison, "OMB Interference with Agency Rulemaking: The Wrong Way to Write a Regulation," 99 *Harvard Law Review* 1059, 1066 (1986), asserts that "virtually all of [OMB's] reviewing staff are economists, lawyers, or public policy analysts, not scientists, pharmacologists, or doctors."

6. Robert V. Percival, "Checks without Balance: Executive Oversight of the Environmental Protection Agency," 54 *Law and Contemporary Problems* 127, 181 (autumn 1991).

7. Morrison, "OMB Interference," 1065. See also Percival, "Checks without Balance," 187. Professor Percival asserts that the Reagan Administration's regulatory review process lacked balance because "[f]rom its inception, the program focused almost exclusively on reducing costs to industry" and that the program's focus on

regulatory relief prevented executive oversight from assessing whether regulatory decisions would maximize net benefits to society.

8. Several courts held that OMB lacks the power to delay issuance of agency rules beyond statutory deadlines. See, e.g., *NRDC v. EPA,* 797 F. Supp. 194 (D. Ariz. 1994); *EDF v. Thomas,* 627 F. Supp. 566 (D.D.C. 1986).

9. Sidney A. Shapiro, "Political Oversight and the Deterioration of Regulatory Policy," 46 *Administrative Law Review* 1, 11 (1994).

10. Thomas O. McGarity, *Reinventing Rationality: The Role of Regulatory Analysis in the Federal Bureaucracy* 282 (1991).

11. Erik D. Olson, "The Quiet Shift of Power: Office of Management and Budget Supervision of Environmental Protection Agency Rulemaking under Executive Order 12,291," 4 *Virginia Journal of Natural Resources* 1, 43 (1984).

12. One observer described the pattern as one in which agencies add additional layers of analysis to the rulemaking process, creating significant delays, as they "become increasingly defensive about their rules" because of "fear of negative OMB reaction." Morrison, "OMB Interference," 1065.

13. Percival, "Checks without Balance," 151 (citing Clean Air Act provision, 42 U.S.C. §7607[d][4][B][ii]).

14. Richard H. Pildes and Cass R. Sunstein, "Reinventing the Regulatory State," 62 *University of Chicago Law Review* 1, 17 (1995).

15. McGarity, *Reinventing Rationality,* 285. See also Olson, "Quiet Shift," 57.

16. Olson, "Quiet Shift," 4.

17. Morrison, "OMB Interference," 1064.

18. Exec. Order No. 12,866, 58 Fed. Reg. 51,735 (1993), reprinted in 5 U.S.C. §601 note.

19. OMB itself took halting steps in that direction as early as 1986 to avoid the loss of funding for its oversight functions. See Shapiro, "Political Oversight," 21–22.

20. Pildes and Sunstein, "Reinventing the Regulatory State," 22–23. For further discussion of these aspects of Executive Order 12,866, see Shapiro, "Political Oversight," 36–38.

21. Shapiro, "Political Oversight," 27.

22. Unless otherwise indicated, the description of the formaldehyde rule provided below is based on Thomas O. McGarity and Sidney A. Shapiro, *Workers at Risk: The Failed Promise of the Occupational Safety and Health Administration* 87–89, 108–11 (1993).

23. *International Union, UAW v. Pendergrass,* 878 F.2d 389 (D.C. Cir. 1989).

24. Department of Labor, Occupational Safety and Health Administration, Occupational Exposure to Formaldehyde, 57 Fed. Reg. 22,290 (1992).

25. See Office of Management and Budget, *Comments on OSHA's Proposed Rulemaking: Occupational Exposure to Formaldehyde*, Mar. 1986, 57.

26. Shapiro, "Political Oversight," at 30–31.

27. See Mark Seidenfeld, "A Big Picture Approach to Presidential Influence on Agency Policy-making," 80 *Iowa Law Review* 1, 19–25, 38 (1994). Professor Seidenfeld recognizes that "the President must not only define overarching policy themes, but also that he must have a mechanism for monitoring agency compliance with those themes."

28. Shapiro, "Political Oversight," 32; Percival, "Checks without Balance," 201.

29. See Thomas O. Sargentich, "Normative Tensions in the Theory of Presidential Oversight of Agency Rulemaking," 7 *Administrative Law Journal of American University* 325, 326–27 (1993).

30. Ibid., 29. The same kind of explanation should also be required for changes resulting from legislative oversight. For an example of a case in which a court remanded a regulation to an agency on the grounds that the agency responded to improper pressure from individual legislators, see *Hazardous Waste Treatment Council v. EPA*, 886 F.2d 355 (D.C. Cir. 1989).

31. Shapiro, "Political Oversight," 30.

32. Richard Lazarus has stated that "[t]he number of times EPA officials testify before Congress is staggering." Richard J. Lazarus, "The Tragedy of Distrust in the Implementation of Federal Environmental Law," 54 *Law and Contemporary Problems* 311, 340 (autumn 1991).

33. See, generally, Joel D. Auerbach, *Keeping a Watchful Eye: The Politics of Congressional Oversight* (1990); Richard J. Lazarus, "The Neglected Question of Congressional Oversight of EPA: *Quis Custodiet Ipsos Custodes* (Who Shall Watch the Watchers Themselves)?" 54 *Law and Contemporary Problems* 205 (autumn 1991). See also Frederick R. Anderson, Robert L. Glicksman, Daniel R. Mandelker, and A. Dan Tarlock, *Environmental Protection: Law and Policy* 171–78 (3d ed., 1999).

34. 42 U.S.C. §§9604(a), 9607(a).

35. E.g., Stephen Breyer, *Breaking the Vicious Circle: Toward Effective Risk Regulation* 12 (1993); James A. Rogers and P. Kathleen Wells, "Superfund Reform Act of 1994," C948 ALI-ABA 773, 777 (1994).

36. U.S. Congress, Senate Committee on Environment and Public Works, S. Hrg. No. 103–559, *Hearings before the Subcommittee on Superfund, Recycling, and Solid Waste Management of the Senate Committee on Environment and Public Works on S. 1384*, 103d Cong., 2d Sess. 34 (Feb. 10, 1994) (testimony of Carol Browner, EPA Administrator); see Rogers and Wells, "Superfund Reform Act of 1994," 799–804; Walter L. Sutton Jr., "The Impact of Environmental Law on Real Estate and Other Commercial Transactions: The View from EPA," C945 ALI-ABA 351 (1994).

37. See "House Democratic Leaders Abandon Superfund Reauthorization Effort," *Inside EPA* 1, Oct. 7, 1994.

38. "Time Restraint, Wrangling Kill Reform Bill; New Effort to Change CERCLA Promised Next Year," 25 *BNA Environment Reporter* 1172–73 (Oct. 14, 1994).

39. "Elimination of Retroactive Liability Seen as Gaining Approval of President," 25 *BNA Environment Reporter* 1912 (Feb. 10, 1995).

40. "House Republican Conference Leader Sees Superfund Floor Action in Summer," 25 *BNA Environment Reporter* 2450 (Apr. 14, 1995).

41. "An Overview of Possible Impacts of 1994 Elections on Environmental Issues," 25 *BNA Environment Reporter* 1392, 1394 (Nov. 18, 1994).

42. As indicated in Chapter 7, however, EPA has since adopted administrative reforms to CERCLA.

43. House Republicans sponsored a bill that would have subjected Superfund cleanups costing more than $5 million to a rigorous new cost-benefit analysis and risk assessment processes that, according to EPA Administrator Carol Browner, would have precluded EPA from placing a contaminated facility on the statute's National Priorities List "without being subjected to more than 60 different points of judicial review." "House Risk Proposal Called Threat to Program; Senate Debate Focuses on Retroactive Liability," 25 *BNA Environment Reporter* 2293 (Mar. 17, 1995).

44. See, generally, Robert L. Glicksman and Stephen B. Chapman, "Regulatory Reform and (Breach of) the Contract with America: Improving Environmental Policy or Destroying Environmental Protection?" 5 *Kansas Journal of Law and Public Policy* 9 (winter 1996).

45. See "House Majority Whip Introduces Legislation to Repeal Several Portions of Clean Air Act," 25 *BNA Environment Reporter* 1787 (Jan. 20, 1995).

46. Pub. L. No. 104–4, 109 Stat. 48 (1995).

47. According to one observer, however, "abuse of the appropriations process has been taken to new and more extreme heights in recent decades, and has been especially prevalent in the environmental area." Sandra Beth Zellmer, "Sacrificing Legislative Integrity at the Altar of Appropriations Riders: A Constitutional Crisis," 21 *Harvard Environmental Law Review* 457, 486 (1997).

48. Pub. L. No. 101–121, §318, 103 Stat. 701, 745–50 (1989).

49. The Supreme Court sustained the constitutionality of the rider. *Robertson v. Seattle Audubon Soc'y,* 503 U.S. 429 (1992).

50. See *Seattle Audubon Soc'y v. Espy,* 998 F.2d 699 (9th Cir. 1993).

51. Pub. L. No. 104–19, §2001(i), 109 Stat. 194, 240 (1995). Constitutional attacks on the rider once again failed. E.g., *Northwest Forest Resource Council v. Pilchuck Audubon Soc'y,* 97 F.3d 1161, 1165 (9th Cir. 1996).

52. See Anderson et al., *Environmental Protection,* 174.

53. *Bragg v. Robertson,* 72 F. Supp. 2d 642 (S.D. W. Va.), stayed pending appeal, 190 F.R.D. 194 (S.D. W. Va. 1999), judgment vacated, 248 F.3d 275 (4th Cir. 2001).

54. "Mining: Byrd Will Seek Again to Attach Rider on Mountain Coal Mining to Supplemental," 31 *BNA Environment Reporter* (Feb. 25, 2000); "Budget: White House Cites Environmental Gains in Omnibus Funding Bill Ok'd by Congress," 30 *BNA Environment Reporter* 1377 (Nov. 26, 1999).

55. Pub. L. No. 103–322, §§112–113, 108 Stat. 2499, 2519 (1994).

56. E.g., Omnibus Appropriations Act of 1997, Pub. L. No. 104–208, §314(a)–(b), 110 Stat. 3009. For a list of some of the other appropriations acts extending the moratorium, see Sam Kalen, "An 1872 Mining Law for the New Millennium," 71 *University of Colorado Law Review* 343, 355 n. 50 (2000).

57. Pub. L. No. 104–19, 109 Stat. 194.

58. "Former EPA Chief Criticizes Congress' Methods for Changing Agency," *Inside EPA* 2 (Sept. 15, 1995).

59. See, generally, Zellmer, "Sacrificing Legislative Integrity," 500. See also Jacques B. LeBoeuf, "Limitations on the Use of Appropriations Riders by Congress to Effectuate Substantive Policy Changes," 19 *Hastings Constitutional Law Quarterly* 457 (1992), which explores constitutional limits on the use of appropriations riders to effectuate substantive policy changes and recommending that Congress avoid using them to adopt substantive legislation.

60. See Seidenfeld, "A Big Picture Approach," 6–7.

61. 33 U.S.C. §1317(a) (1976); 42 U.S.C. §7412 (1976).

62. According to Richard Lazarus, the pre-1990 version of the Clean Air Act, by precluding significant consideration of economic costs and mandating what was often infeasible, "prompted EPA to do very little" by way of regulating hazardous air pollutants. Lazarus, "The Tragedy of Distrust," 359.

63. See Anderson et al., *Environmental Protection,* 715–16.

64. 42 U.S.C. §7412(d). Congress retained health-based standards as a backup mechanism. Ibid., §7412(f).

65. U.S. Congress, Senate Committee on Environment and Public Works, *Safe Drinking Water Act Amendments Act of 1995,* 104th Cong., 1st Sess., 1995, S. Rpt. 104–169, 1.

66. Pub. L. No. 104–182, 110 Stat. 1613.

67. The statute now mandates that the agency regulate each contaminant that may have an adverse effect on health and which is known or substantially likely to occur in public water systems "with a frequency and at levels of public health concern," provided, in EPA's sole judgment, regulation "presents a meaningful opportunity for health risk reductions for persons served by public water systems." 42 U.S.C. §300g-1(B)(1)(A).

68. In addition, the required treatment methodologies were capable of increasing certain kinds of risk more than they reduced others. Chlorine used to kill pathogenic organisms, for example, created increased risks of cancer from exposure to disinfection by-products. See *Safe Drinking Water Amendments Act of 1995*, S. Rpt. 104–169, 14.

69. 42 U.S.C. §300g-1(b)(4)(D), (5)(B).

70. 42 U.S.C. §7651b(b)–(d).

71. Pub. L. No. 104–208, 110 Stat. 3009 (1996) (codified at 42 U.S.C. §9601[20][E]–[G]).

72. Pub. L. No. 106–113, 113 Stat. 1501, 1537 (1999) (codified at 42 U.S.C. §9627).

73. The possibility exists, of course, that Congress will respond "with the wrong medicine." Shapiro, "Political Oversight," 26.

74. Seidenfeld, "A Big Picture Approach," 9, 11. Professor Seidenfeld adds that, "[m]ore pragmatically, members of Congress can communicate their views about the meaning of a statute and how it should be implemented in formal congressional hearings and informal contacts." Ibid., 9. See also Shapiro, "Political Oversight," 23, which explains that "legislators also conduct private conversations with regulators."

75. See *Ethyl Corp. v. EPA,* 541 F.2d 1, 68 (D.C. Cir. 1976), in which the court stated that Congress agreed to make broad delegations only because judicial review could "assure that the agency exercises the delegated power within statutory limits."

76. Richard E. Levy and Robert L. Glicksman, "Judicial Activism and Restraint in the Supreme Court's Environmental Law Decisions," 42 *Vanderbilt Law Review* 343, 344–45, 355–56 (1989).

77. James L. Oakes, "Substantive Judicial Review in Environmental Law," 7 *Environmental Law Reporter (Environmental Law Institute)* 50029, 50030 (1977).

78. *Calvert Cliffs' Coordinating Comm., Inc. v. Atomic Energy Comm'n,* 449 F.2d 1109, 1111 (D.C. Cir. 1971).

79. Levy and Glicksman, "Judicial Activism and Restraint," 345.

80. Richard J. Pierce Jr., "The Inherent Limits on Judicial Control of Agency Discretion: The D.C. Circuit and the Nondelegation Doctrine," 52 *Administrative Law Review* 63, 92 (2000).

81. *International Harvester Co. v. Ruckelshaus,* 478 F.2d 615, 635 (D.C. Cir. 1973).

82. *Kennecott Copper Corp. v. EPA,* 462 F.2d 846, 848 (D.C. Cir. 1972).

83. *Environmental Defense Fund v. Ruckelshaus,* 439 F.2d 584, 597 (D.C. Cir. 1971).

84. Patricia M. Wald, "Judicial Review in Midpassage: The Uneasy Partnership between Courts and Agencies Plays On," 32 *Tulsa Law Journal* 221, 229–30, 258 (1996).

85. Earlier, Judge Wald likened the courts' task to one of legislative "nursemaid" and insisted that "[o]nly a review searching enough to force experts to justify their decisions in an intelligible form can lend legitimacy" to bureaucratic government.

Patricia M. Wald, "Making 'Informed Decisions' on the District of Columbia Circuit," 50 *George Washington Law Review* 135, 138, 154 (1982).

86. Mark Seidenfeld, "Demystifying Deossification: Rethinking Recent Proposals to Modify Judicial Review of Notice and Comment Rulemaking," 75 *Texas Law Review* 483, 524 (1997).

87. Thomas O. McGarity, "Some Thoughts on 'Deossifying' the Rulemaking Process," 41 *Duke Law Journal* 1385, 1400–2, 1452–53 (1992). McGarity credited former EPA General Counsel E. Donald Elliott with coining the term "ossification." Ibid., 1385–86.

88. Frank B. Cross, "Pragmatic Pathologies of Judicial Review of Administrative Rulemaking," 78 *North Carolina Law Review* 1012, 1014, 1019–20 (2000).

89. Alfred C. Aman and William T. Mayton, 16 *Administrative Law* 67 (1993) (citing *Yick Wo v. Hopkins*, 118 U.S. 356, 369–70 [1885]).

90. See McGarity, "Some Thoughts on 'Deossifying,'" 1412, 1419. See also Cross, "Pragmatic Pathologies," 1014, asserting that "[t]he threat of judicial review ossifies the rulemaking process, making administrators slow and timid to address their responsibilities." Professor Cross also argues that "[j]udicial review inevitably increases the transaction costs of regulation, which, axiomatically, means less regulation." Ibid., 1022.

91. Cass R. Sunstein, "Is the Clean Air Act Unconstitutional?" 98 *Michigan Law Review* 303, 371 (1999).

92. Adrian Vermeule, "Interpretive Choice," 75 *New York University Law Review* 74, 77 (2000).

93. *Corrosion Proof Fittings v. EPA*, 947 F.2d 849 (5th Cir. 1991).

94. *American Trucking Ass'ns, Inc. v. EPA*, 175 F.3d 1027 (D.C. Cir.), modified on rehearing, 195 F.3d 4 (D.C. Cir. 1999), aff'd in part, rev'd in part, and remanded, 531 U.S. 457 (2001).

95. U.S. General Accounting Office, *Toxic Substances Control Act—Legislative Changes Could Make the Act More Effective*, GAO/RCED 94–103, 1994 WL 840961 (1994).

96. Sunstein, "Is the Clean Air Act Unconstitutional?" 371. EPA may be willing to try again, however. It published an advance notice of proposed rulemaking in which it indicated its intention to use its authority under TSCA to eliminate the use of methyl tertiary butyl ether as a fuel additive. Methyl Tertiary Butyl Ether (MTBE); Advance Notice of Intent to Initiate Rulemaking under the Toxic Substances Control Act to Eliminate or Limit the Use of MTBE as a Fuel Additive in Gasoline, 65 Fed. Reg. 16,094 (2000).

97. For analysis of the D.C. Circuit's decision in the case, see Sunstein, "Is the Clean Air Act Unconstitutional?"; Pierce, "Inherent Limits"; Craig Oren, "Run Over by *American Trucking* Part I: Can EPA Revive Its Air Quality Standards?" 29 *Environ-*

mental Law Reporter (Environmental Law Institute) 10653 (1999); Craig Oren, "Run Over by *American Trucking* Part II: Can EPA Implement Revised Air Quality Standards?" 30 *Environmental Law Reporter (Environmental Law Institute)* 10034 (2000); Robert W. Adler, "*American Trucking* and the Revival (?) of the Nondelegation Doctrine," 30 *Environmental Law Reporter (Environmental Law Institute)* 10233 (2000).

98. 42 U.S.C. §7409(b)(1).

99. 175 F.3d at 1034, 1037.

100. Pierce, "Inherent Limits," 91. The term "science charade" was coined by Wendy Wagner. See Wendy E. Wagner, "The Science Charade in Toxic Risk Regulation," 95 *Columbia Law Review* 1613 (1995).

101. *Whitman v. American Trucking Ass'ns, Inc.,* 531 U.S. 457 (2001).

102. *Natural Resources Defense Council, Inc. v. Fox,* 93 F. Supp. 2d 531, 554 (S.D.N.Y. 2000) (quoting *Natural Resources Defense Council, Inc. v. EPA,* 902 F.2d 962, 972 [D.C. Cir. 1972]).

103. Cross, "Pragmatic Pathologies," 1039–40.

104. *Farmworker Justice Fund, Inc. v. Brock,* 811 F.2d 613 (D.C. Cir. 1986). The case is described in more detail in McGarity and Shapiro, *Workers at Risk,* 309.

105. 811 F.2d at 614.

106. See, generally, Oliver A. Houck, "TMDLs: Are We There Yet? The Long Road toward Water Quality–Based Regulation under the Clean Water Act," 27 *Environmental Law Reporter (Environmental Law Institute)* 10391 (1997); Oliver A. Houck, "TMDLs III: A New Framework for the Clean Water Act's Ambient Standards Program," 28 *Environmental Law Reporter (Environmental Law Institute)* 10415 (1998).

107. *Alaska Ctr. for the Env't v. Browner,* 20 F.3d 981, 987 (9th Cir. 1994).

108. *Sierra Club v. Hankinson,* 939 F. Supp. 865 (N.D. Ga. 1996).

109. See, e.g., Sidney A. Shapiro and Robert L. Glicksman, "Congress, the Supreme Court, and the Quiet Revolution in Administrative Law," 1988 *Duke Law Journal* 819, 834–35.

110. U.S. Const. art. II, §3. See, e.g., *Lujan v. Defenders of Wildlife,* 504 U.S. 555, 577 (1992).

111. It avoided the question, for example, in *Vermont Agency of Natural Resources v. United States ex rel. Stevens,* 529 U.S. 765, 778 n. 8 (2000), a case involving a qui tam action under the False Claims Act. For arguments that neither qui tam actions nor citizen suits for civil penalties violate Article II, see, generally, Peter M. Shane, "Returning Separation-of-Powers Analysis to Its Normative Roots: The Constitutionality of Qui Tam Actions and Other Private Suits to Enforce Civil Fines," 30 *Environmental Law Reporter (Environmental Law Institute)* 11081 (2000).

112. E.g., 33 U.S.C. §1365(b); 42 U.S.C. §7604(b).

113. 42 U.S.C. §4332(2)(C).

114. 40 C.F.R. §1502.19(c).

115. E.g., *Steel Co. v. Citizens for a Better Env't,* 523 U.S. 83 (1998); *Lujan v. Defenders of Wildlife,* 504 U.S. 555 (1992).

116. E.g., *Lujan v. National Wildlife Fed'n,* 497 U.S. 871 (1990).

117. E.g., *Bennett v. Spear,* 520 U.S. 154 (1997).

118. E.g., *Friends of the Earth v. Laidlaw,* 528 U.S. 167 (2000); *Federal Election Comm'n v. Akins,* 524 U.S. 11 (1998).

Index

The authorized representative in the EU for product safety and compliance is:
Mare Nostrum Group
B.V Doelen 72
4831 GR Breda
The Netherlands

www.ingramcontent.com/pod-product-compliance
Lightning Source LLC
Chambersburg PA
CBHW021552210326
41599CB00010B/412